AS YOUR ACKNOWLEDGED LEADER

AS YOUR ACKNOWLEDGED LEADER

The Best of Lynn Ashby

TexasMonthlyPress

Texas Monthly Press, Inc.
P.O. Box 1569
Austin, Texas 78767

A B C D E F G H

Text Design by Janet Brooks

Library of Congress Cataloging in Publication Data

Ashby, Lynn, 1938-
    As your acknowledged leader.

    1.   Houston (Tex.) — Addresses, essays, lectures.
I. Title.
F394.H845A83   1983   976.4'235   83-493
ISBN   0-932012-64-7

To my mother

CONTENTS

PREFACE

It has often been said that the three greatest misstatements of fact in the English language are:

"The check is in the mail."

"Of course I'll respect you in the morning."

"I'm from the government and here to help you."

To this should be added one more:

"Why don't you put out a book of your columns? It won't take a minute—you've already done all the work."

I shall not tell you all the details of how this book came about, mainly because I know you don't care. Suffice it to say that I have written about 3,000 columns for *The Houston Post* since I first began in 1968. Of that number, 2,825 are not here.

The pruning down was done nightly at my dining room table as I tossed out old friends, angry tirades, brilliant opinions. It was a terrible ordeal, and slow going. That is when I came upon Ashby's Axiom of Success: If you want something done right, get out of your wife's way. Her hours and hours of help—along with dunning letters from MasterCard—inspired me onward.

What went in and what stayed out depended upon many points. For example, the monthly awards and the TV listings were often too topical, and therefore dated. Other columns, however, while dated, still ring with immortal truths for all mankind. I mean, owls will always be owls. The same goes for Aggies.

Eventually, we got the number down to about 450 and sent copies to Barbara Rodriguez Reavis of Texas Monthly Press, who began her own selections. In a remarkable example of independent geniuses at work, our final choices were largely the same. Still, the columns in this book were my decision and mine alone. I dare not trust my life's work to anyone else.

If you have been a reader of that part of *The Houston Post* over the years, you will recognize some old friends and mutual enemies. (If, on the other hand, you have not, you will never know what you missed.)

You will also notice that some of your favorites are not here. That makes us even. Right now I am looking at a large stack of columns on my desk which didn't make the cut.

"Don't worry," I was told. "If this one takes off, we'll just put the others in a second book. It won't take a minute—you've already done all the work."

Finally, my thanks to the many people who daily make me realize that I've got the best job in Texas.

AS YOUR ACKNOWLEDGED LEADER

HE'S A REAL PRO

He's a Real Pro

THE PHONE – Ring, Ring.

"Hello?"

"Hi, this is Wallace down at Wombat Motors. Your wife brought in her car for new windshield wipers."

"Right, although I really couldn't see that she needed to leave the car there. Why was that?"

"We've got a lot of work backed up and wanted to make sure we did a good job. Anyway, Jerry, the windshield wiper technician, noticed while he was taking off the windshield that you've got some pockmarks."

"Taking off the windshield? To change the wipers?"

"Jerry likes to change them from the inside. He's a real pro. Anyway, since we've already got the front windshield off, would you like us to go ahead and put in a new one?"

"What'll it cost?"

"With parts and labor, $133."

"No, thanks."

"Look at it this way. You're already paying $111. That's $2 for the wipers and $109 for the labor. So the new windshield will only cost you $22."

"Oh, OK."

"Thanks. I always like to check with a customer before authorizing anything else."

"Goodbye."

Ring, ring.

"Hello?"

"Wallace again, down at Wombat Motors. Say, while Johnston was changing the right wiper . . ."

"Johnston? What happened to Jerry?"

"Jerry only handles left wipers. Besides, he's gone for the summer, to his condo in Aspen. Anyway, Johnston noticed your air filter is dirty. You can get better mileage with a clean filter."

"Hold it right there. How did Johnston notice my air filter was dirty while changing my windshield wiper?"

"You have to take off the air filter to remove the dash. Johnston likes to work from the bottom. He's . . ."

". . . a real pro. I know. How much?"

"Just $43."

"OK. Do it."

"Plus parts and labor. Total $195."

"Plus parts and labor? Then what's the $43 for?"

"Estimate. Oh, did you know your left rear tire wobbles? Now I don't know about you, but I wouldn't want my wife and kids driving around with that sort of potentially dangerous situation. I couldn't stand the guilt if, well, you know, something were to happen."

"I'll think on it."

"God would never forgive you. And the police might get to wondering. I'd have to tell them if they ask. We're sworn to."

"All right! Change the tire! Goodbye."

Ring, ring.

"Hi, this is LeRoy down at Wombat Motors."

"What happened to Wallace?"

"Oh, he always goes to Kenya this time of year. You ought to see his den. It was in *Sports Illustrated*. Anyway, your car is almost ready."

"Great."

"But I just wanted to tell you, while it's up on the rack. The axle squad spotted some leakage in your oil pan. Want us to put a new gasket there?"

"No."

"Only $4.35 more."

"More than what?"

"More than the $387.32 for the driveshaft replacement."

"Wait a bloody minute! I didn't authorize any driveshaft replacement."

"It says here that you authorized a new A-777."

"I did, but we were talking about piston rings. I was assured they'd never make it around the block."

"Yeah, well, an A-777 is the driveshaft. You needed a new one. I'm surprised you made it this far. It was in terrible shape. Almost as bad as the brakes. OK, I'll tell . . ."

"Go back a minute. Brakes? What's the matter with the brakes?"

"Well, I don't know about you, Mister, but I wouldn't let my wife and kids . . ."

"OK, OK. Fix the brakes."

"We already did. Wallace said you'd understand, being the good father and husband that you are."

"Thanks."

"You know, if the brakes fail, the crash can cause contusions on the medulla, the optic nerves can be severely bruised and, of course, the cerebellum is the tricky part."

"You sound like a neurosurgeon, LeRoy."

"I used to be, but with kids going to college and the bills coming in,

I had to get into something else to make ends meet."

"I get the picture."

Ring, ring.

"Hi, this is Marston over at Wombat Motors."

"What happened to LeRoy?"

"Oh, he's in service. I'm in sales. Do you know that for just $320 more, you can own . . ."

Texas law dead

Sigh. Raise a glass and remember the good old days, when Texas had the Paramour Statute. You recall it, don't you? It was that uniquely Texas law saying that if a man found another man in bed with his wife, he could kill the scoundrel, then and there. Not only would the husband go scot-free, but he could usually get a bounty from the neighbors.

Alas, the law was tossed out in 1974 when the new Penal Code went into effect. "It was a vestige of the old frontier days," says Assistant DA Allen Stilley. "You ought to take such a case to the divorce court, or sue in civil court. But you shouldn't be allowed to murder the guy." Others disagree, however, claiming that the Paramour Statute kept more wandering husbands at home than any amount of hot chicken soup. One would think twice about grazing in other pastures if the price was instant erasure.

The law was legally called Article 1220 of the Texas Penal Code. It seems to have been enacted in 1911, although there are court cases based on it going back into the 19th century. "I'm reasonably sure we had some such law ever since there was a Texas," says Stilley. It came under the laws dealing with justifiable homicide, and had several appealing points. First, the license to kill was limited to men. Wives could not plug their husbands' sweeties under the same conditions, which seems only right and proper.

Also, the husband could not kill his wife, nor could the wife kill the husband. The State of Texas is very big on the sanctity of marriage. Five years ago we had the case of a Mr. Morris, who found his wife and her boyfriend in flagrante delicto (look it up). Bang-bang. Morris explained that he was only trying to kill the lover, and hit his wife by mistake. The jury refused to believe that anyone could miss from three inches away, and Morris lost.

Also, the law said the husband had to come upon the cozy scene "before the parties to the act have separated." But as Stilley notes, "Juries would kind of extend that." Later decisions said the cuckold was justified in the killing if, "with reasonable certainty to a rational mind," he thought the fellow was about to commit adultery with his wife, or had just finished. That pretty well covered the waterfront.

The Texas Court of Criminal Appeals, for instance, has ordered a new trial for James Dillard Shaw of Houston, who fatally stabbed his wife's alleged lover in the kitchen. (Fortunately for Shaw, he did it before New Year's.) Although the slaying was not in the alleged love nest, the court ruled that the jury should have considered the Paramour Statute. Besides, who keeps a butcher knife on his night table?

"One guy shot down his wife's lover on the street," Stilley recalls. "He beat the rap by using the Paramour Statute. In addition, he was an assistant Harris County DA." But even that law wouldn't cover everything. Mr. Holman saw his wife and a friend heading for a hotel, and Mr. McFarland's wife and her friend went to a movie. Both evoked the statute, and both lost.

The old law also prohibited any killing if the husband set up the tryst. "We had a case of the husband obviously setting up his wife with another guy," Stilley says. "Then the husband killed him and got off because of the Paramour Statute." It's known as Murder, Texas Style.

Meetings in brothels didn't count, and the husband did not get immunity if he only inflicted serious bodily injury on the interloper. In other words, shoot to kill. Yet, to be fair, the law liked to give everyone a sporting chance, so "the paramour does not forfeit his privilege of escape, nor does he wholly forfeit the right to defend his life." As you can see, lovers have lobbyists, too.

And the courts realized that extracurricular activities did not always lead to bloodshed. It ruled that death is not "the usual or expected result" of adultery in Texas, and thus ordered a $5,000 life insurance policy to be paid. The insurance company had argued that the fellow had, in effect, committed suicide.

But perhaps the best argument against keeping the Paramour Statute occurred right here in Houston in 1973, when a husband came home unexpectedly to find his wife and her lover in bed. He fired, killing both, just as his unclothed wife was yelling: "Wait! Wait! I can explain!" Thus legal history was denied hearing what had to be the greatest defense case ever concocted. And that's a crime.

Ahoy, podnuh!

GALVESTON—Avast and ahoy! For we are off once again on a nautical adventure starring those beloved misfits of the seven seas, the Texas Navy.

Now, you and I have followed their exploits before, as they fought assorted foes, including the Mexican Navy (in the world's first battle between sailing and steamships—we had the outdated sails, and won), the shore patrol (the Texas Marines mutinied in New Orleans, and won), politicians (Sam Houston once officially declared the entire navy to be pirates, and lost) and low budgets (President Lamar needed funds so badly that he rented out our navy for $8,000 a month to some Mexican rebels, who lost).

Then there was the little problem of seamanship. Here in Galveston, we beached two ships in one day. Another vessel, the San Antonio, went out and never came back, and one ship could never get out of the harbor. Still, the seagoing cowboys tried mightily, and many were killed in the endeavor.

Anyway, let's get back to why we are in Galveston, mucking through the mosquitoes. In researching for this exhibit, Carol Jean Carefoot of the archives came across a letter, from one Richard Pearse in Galveston, to "His Excellency Sam Houston, President Rep. Texas, Houston." The postage is marked "Free."

The four sheets of paper, written on both sides in dark brown ink, tell a great non-story which is indicative of how the Texas Navy operated. But let's take it step by stumbling step, as reported to His Excellency by Richard Pearse, whoever he was.

It is midnight of April 23, 1838, at the Texas Navy Yard in Galveston. The situation is its usual drum-tight efficiency. The C.O., Captain Thomas Thompson, is in bed recovering from a recent wound. This is the well-known "Mexico" Thompson, a nickname he picked up while fighting for the other side. Thompson was born in England, became a U.S. citizen while sailing out of New Orleans, ran a bar on a levee, became a Mexican naval officer but was twice captured by the Texans. The first time he beat a piracy trial. The second time he suddenly saw the error of his ways and became a devout Texas naval officer. *That* Mexico Thompson.

His wife is sick in bed. Taylor is also ill. Here's a brief rundown of the rest of the command, as described by Pearse, who seems to have a bit of a spelling problem:

"Some of the marines had been on the sick lists for some time past, two or three other had deserted, and the duties of those who remained on service had been so severe as to induce the extention of what lenity could be allowed. But one sentry was planed, and but one officer on the alert. One officer with two marines, were about in pursuit of deserters. One of our civil magistrates had gone over to Point Boliver to arrest some counterfiters, and the other resigned his commission yesterday."

So, you can see that the Navy Yard is in good hands. One officer and one sentry on guard. No doubt lots of atmosphere—thick fog, rats scurrying down decks, foghorns and bells, laughter from a waterfront tavern down the street. It is midnight, but all is not well.

For sneaking up on the Navy Yard is a bad bunch of black hats:

Giles—the leader, was once a pirate with Lafitte, and "has been tryed for murder," currently he is "late of the navy."

Hews—"a Boatswain of the Potomac, and a deserter."

Lewis—"late an armorer in the Navy Yard, and discharged for disorderly conduct, was a chief instigator." In addition, Lewis' son-in-law, Reed, is one of the magistrates. Reed also hates Thompson. It seems just an awful lot of people hate Thompson.

All told, 13 men, bent on vengeance. OK, the mutiny begins. A man approaches the sentry at the gate, feigning intoxication. As the pretend-drunk is talking to the sentry, Giles, the leader, creeps up behind him, knocks him down and grabs his musket.

Meanwhile, the deserter, Hews, is approaching the other side of the Yard, in the rear of the guard room, where the lone officer is on duty. Now Hews is a gutsy fellow. He saunters up to the officer and salutes. The officer recognizes Hews and they begin talking. It is known that Hews likes to drink, so when he asks the officer for a bit of liquor, the officer is not surprised.

The two men go into the guard room—Hews first, followed by the officer, who closes the door behind them. At this point, Hews throws himself between the officer and the door, pushes open the door and yells, "Enter, guard! Take possession of these arms!"

This must be the signal, for at this point, a swarm of swarthy swashbucklers rushes into the guard room and grabs the officer and his weapons.

"And at the same instant, Hews informed the officer he was a prisoner," Pearse reports, "and upon the pain of instant death, commanded him to be silent. The battery was immediately taken in charge; and in an instant, without awakening a soul, the whole Yard was in the power of the mob."

Giles, who hates Thompson with a fury, and two others, enter the Thompsons' house and approach the captain's bedside. All three men "thrust their swords thro' the mosquito bar, before he or his wife awoke."

Mrs. Thompson sits up, and almost impales herself on a sword. Thompson is repeatedly hit by Giles, who keeps telling the captain to give no alarm. Giles then tells Thompson about the takeover, and orders him to come along.

Now for the heavy dramatics. Mrs. Thompson has an idea what's about to happen to her husband, so she falls on her knees in the bedroom and "implored the miscreants to spair his—Thompson's—life." Thompson tries to comfort his wife and the whole scene is so tear-jerking that the mutineers grow soft. Mrs. Thompson wrings a promise from the gang that they will not kill her husband, and this—strangely enough—seems to make him mad. We now have the captain's speech:

"Giles, you know, I fear not death. I have found it too often, and in too many shapes, to tremble at it now. It is for my wife and children I feel. You have pledged your self for the safety of my life. I claim the redemption of your pledge. You command me to follow you. I will do it, believing that that Power, which has protected me in all extremities, will do it, in this. Lead on."

Heavy stuff. Pearse writes to President Houston: "They were taken by surprise, and attacked by an enemy, of whom, they had not even dreamed. Their own consciences."

The mutineers take Thompson outside, and they immediately fall into an argument among themselves as to their next action. Shoot him? Hang him? No, they promised his wife. OK, just a good tar-and-feathers. Well, one thing leads to another, what with the arguing and all, the 13 swashbucklers have a terrible row right in the midst of their victory. They almost come to blows.

Captain Thompson is no dummy. He steps in with authority, and demands to know their grievances. Speak up, I say!

"All quailed before his scrutinizing interrogations, and ultimately agreed, that if Thompson would promise them impunity from the guard, they would conduct him back to his house. Thus inded this disgraceful transaction. No blood was spilled, and no other injury done, than the loss of some of the arms, which the miscreants carried off with them."

And that's all there is to the circus. No mass mutiny. No swinging from the yardarms. No firing squads. Not even 20 lashes, Mister Christian. It's really a sorry bunch of sailors. Here they are, with split-second timing they take over the entire base. They have their archenemy at their mercy. They should at least shoot up Galveston and sail away to history. But no, they crater. The Texas Navy simply did not turn out good mutineers.

As for Captain Thompson, he ends up in the clover. The last third of Pearse's report is a glowing defense of this great and fine man: "He is coarse, it is true, and so must every man be, who plays his part, on the theater assigned to Thompson." He pulls out every stop: "Mexico lost an officer she could not appreciate, and Texas, has gained a prise . . ." Like I said, Pearse had a spelling problem.

But we might well ask ourselves, what's in it for one Richard Pearse? Why this long and detailed report about a rebellion which wasn't? He gets to that in the very last paragraph:

"I have been here, with my family, since the first of this month, and shall fix my residence here, if I find sufficient encouragement. I want an appointment, if there are any to be disposed of."

It's not armed rebellion you have to watch for, it's sneaky bureaucrats.

Semper fidelis!

The army has put beer in the barracks and broads in the barroom. The New Navy has beards aboard the battlewagons. And the Air Force—always among the more flamboyant—will probably paint its jets Braniff Hot Pink and put its pilots in parachutes by Pucci.

This, of course, is part of a massive effort to make the military more attractive and eventually do away with the draft. As such, it has certain merits, but perhaps they are selling American youth a bit short. There are still those who do not want the soft life of civilians.

For them, there is still a niche—the same one that has been around since November 10, 1775—the U.S. Marine Corps. Now the Corps has grudgingly made one slight concession to the 20th century—to ease up on recruits the first few days. This is so drill instructors can spot the oddballs and misfits, and does not reflect on any softening of their government-issue hearts. After the screening process is over— gangbusters.

My own formal introduction to the Marine Corps came just after my arrival at San Diego's Lindbergh Field when I dialed the number given by my friendly recruiter.

The voice on the other end said something about "Sergeant-JonesspeakingSir" to which I replied, "There's a bunch of us down here and . . ." "How many's in a bunch, idiot?" Sergeant Jones said. Right then I knew I was in trouble.

The Corps sent for us and about 2 a.m. I was tossed to the tender mercy of my drill instructor, Daddy Webb. Now Webb did not need five days to sort out the misfits. It took him about three seconds of study, whereupon he declared the entire platoon was incapable of existing on the same earth with him. We were not worth shooting, but if he had a rifle handy he would give it serious consideration.

Alas, Daddy Webb was right. As a matter of fact, he was never wrong. We tried his monumental patience. We all had left feet. Iwo Jima was a lark compared to the disaster of Platoon 351.

Beer in the barracks? For three months we never saw a movie or a woman, never chewed gum or drank a Coke. The only music we heard was reveille, taps and The Marine Corps Hymn. Of course, Daddy Webb did sing to us in his own melodious voice, although the lyrics were unusual.

Through the days he marched us and ran us, he put us to sleep and woke us up. We were told how to shoot a rifle and an azimuth, how to kill an enemy and save a friend. There was also a heavy dose of history and tradition of the U.S. Marine Corps—a group we might join some day if hell freezes over.

We were particularly struck by a tradition following a bloody battle in Samar in the Philippines. For years following, whenever any of the handful of survivors would enter a room, the order was given: "Rise, gentlemen, for he was at Samar." Daddy Webb tried everything.

But it did no good. Our archenemy, Platoon 350, which had an Oriental drill instructor, bested us at every turn. At inspection the People's Volunteers trounced us. In hand-to-hand combat the Yellow Peril left us in the dust. Daddy Webb was growing testy. "You people," he declared during our 300 pushups, "couldn't lick a wound."

We were banned to the battalion head—bathhouse—with orders to clean and mop it until we decided we were ready to be Marines. And so from dawn till dusk we polished the brass, we swabbed the floors, we buffed the porcelain—70 sets of calloused hands shining toilet seats and bitterly nursing a grudge against the god of drill instructors and particularly against those goody two-shoes in Platoon 350.

Finally, however, the head was clean—so clean in fact that we made it off limits to all. Then as we were just finishing up, the double doors sprang open and in poured Platoon 350, ready to shower. Gad! Our mortal foe. Poised to hang our head.

To a man we charged. No prisoners! Bugles blew, fists flew. Oh, 'twas a donnybrook. We fought in the showers, we fought in the urinals, we fought with mops and malice, brooms and buckets. We pushed them back through the double doors and onto the company streets, we had a ball.

But poor private McLaughlin got it the worst. Somehow he fell to the floor whereupon he was kicked senseless by those martinets from 350, although come to think of it, they were all in step. Suddenly we were all aware of a volcano standing in the doorway, then it erupted. "Gadzooks and Odsbodkins," said Daddy Webb. This is not a literal translation but you get the picture.

He proceeded to untangle 350 from 351 with his usual tact and deference to our feelings, then he packed poor Private McLaughlin off to the sick bay. Finally, Daddy Webb reported to the captain, who wanted a word with him. Something about damaging government property.

That night, amid great fear and trepidation, we reported to Daddy Webb's presence, hoping that we would be let off with a mass mercy killing. But, most strange, Daddy Webb spoke quietly, telling us that when Marines fight, they fight as a team. And remember one thing more. They win.

Just then the door swung open. Was it 350 back for a rematch? No, just Private McLaughlin, looking like the Spirit of '76, swathed in bandages. Daddy Webb surveyed the situation for a moment, then said, "Rise, gentlemen, for he was at the head."

We had finally made the team.

House ghost

THE HALL—There seems to be a drip on my head. A steady drip. Coming down from the ceiling. That's odd. Usually, drips in my house are from the ends of faucets, like the one in the children's bathroom which never stops.

That kind of drip I can understand. But this drip is coming down on my head. Drip. Drip. Drip. A broken pipe? A leaky valve? A raccoon which has taken up habitation in my attic? It is probably all of the above, but—more importantly—it is the work of Lawrence. My house's ghost. Lawrence of Suburbia.

You do not have to live in a Scottish castle or a New England mansion to have a ghost. You do not have to be Lady Macbeth. You need not dwell in a 17th century windmill or a medieval fortress to have a spirit stalking about. You can live right in the heart of a large American city, as I do, and have a ghost. Because I've got one.

Lawrence is not what you'd call a really evil ghost. He does not curse my descendants for generations yet unborn, branding them with the plague or halitosis or terminal acne. No, Lawrence just makes things go drip in the night. He wanders around, generally behaving himself, until he gets bored. Then he causes things to rust, peel, burn out, boil over.

My first clue that he was in action again, having returned from his summer vacation, was a few weeks ago when I got the window washer on my wife's car fixed. Took it up to the Chevy place and got it fixed for something over $100, which hit me as astronomical. Anyway, the little nozzles spurted out just fine, until we drove up the driveway. Now they don't work.

Drip. Drip. Drip. Maybe the little Dutch boy in my attic is on strike. Maybe it's raining outside and leaking down through the roof. No. There is no rain. It is only the reign of Lawrence.

24

He wanders through the room now, burning out lightbulbs and causing varicose veins to appear in my walls.

"Stop that," I say. "You've caused enough mischief. Why are you doing this?"

Lawrence looks at me blankly. "Why, because it's there," he says, laying his hand on the stereo, which sputters, then goes out.

"You're an anti-Oral Roberts. You ought to be ashamed of yourself," I say angrily. "Everything was doing just fine. I had finally got the gutters unstopped and the garbage disposal working again, and you come back to haunt my happy home. Now the only thing which works around here is me."

"And the lawnmower," he says.

"It's early in the day," I reply. "You really have it in for me. You're making this house the Murphy's Law of Memorial."

Lawrence looks hurt. He sits down on the sofa, which gives out with a "ping," followed by a ripping sound. "Don't take it personal."

"How else can I take it?" I reply. "You got a beer from the refrigerator, and the compressor went out. You flushed the john and I had to call Roto-Rooter. You lost my garage key and burned out my oven."

"It's my duty," he says, airily waving a hand. "I'm doomed to walk these halls, causing plaster to crack and roofs to leak for the rest of time."

Lawrence gets up and trudges down the hall, as a picture falls to the floor. Drip. Drip. Drip. Water is coming down on my head. It is obviously from the air conditioning runover pan, which is now running over. Lawrence did it to me once before when we were gone for the weekend. By the time we returned, my back hall looked like the Brownwood subdivision at high tide.

He's really much worse during a full moon. Once in the spring of '75 he managed to make all the clocks stop and broke the belt on the clothes dryer during a commercial in the 10 o'clock news.

It's not that I take this curse lying down. Not long ago I decided to exorcise him. I burned unpaid bills from Kennedy & Cohen in the front yard, then—holding aloft a picture of Mr. Goodwrench roasting on a pile of Firestone radials—I walked around the garage three times and chanted slowly: "Thanks for coming by."

Next, I went in the house and assumed the lotus position on the Formica, and slowly intoned:

> Prince of darkness,
>   My own devil,
>   You who made my
>   Home split-level,

You who squelched
My pilot light,
Caused my garden
Plants to blight,

You who've mildewed,
Leaked and rusted,
Misfired, misplaced
Battered, busted.

You who've taken
My last dollar,
Grab the ring
Around the collar,

And to prove
You have a heart,
Stomp my roaches
And depart.

Not only did the exorcise fail, but this afternoon the lawnmower broke.

Among Redmen

THE WILDERNESS—The drums are beating among the septic tanks. Mice and moose flee to places never seen by white men. The grass grows down and the leaves curl up in fear, for once again the mighty Indian Guides are taking to the outback to wrestle with nature on her own terms, and possibly win two out of three.

We are the Apaches, the outcasts of Freeway Flat, fathers and sons ("Pals Forever") determined to enjoy a weekend communing with flora and fauna if it doesn't rain and if the room service is acceptable. Our start thus far has not been too auspicious. On the way to our happy hunting ground we received two separate warnings from the Highway Patrol—obviously the Long Knives heard the drums, too—and my own charge, Little Brave, is complaining of a headache.

And there were other problems. Our Noble Leader, Sleeping Turtle, got caught up in some ridiculous argument over whether to drill in the North Sea or South Yemen—as though anybody but the Lapps and the Bedouins cared—and was late. Then we got separated before we left Houston, some didn't show at all, others came late, and all in all, it was a typical start for the Apaches.

But now we are here, running barefooted through the cow paddies and trying to keep the little Indians from placing fishing hooks in one another's eyeballs. From the kitchen we can hear the tribal chef, Greasy Spoon, booming forth in song as he prepares Eggs Benedict a la Arnold. ("It tastes like something the troops had at Valley Forge.")

The small Indians are on the pier, swimming and fishing and crabbing. I am out here papoose-sitting. Cute little fellows, all smiling and laughing and . . . odd, one of them seems to be staring at me. "Are you all right, He-Who-Steals-Hubcaps?" I ask.

"Scratching Bull," he says (that's me), "I seem to be drowning."

"Eh?" I say.

"I'm going under," he says, and, indeed, he does.

Quick as an oil-company profit increase, I leap up and prepare for action. Off with the shoes. Off with the shirt. Take off watch, put in pocket, and leap into the water. Splash-splash. Ah, here he is. I stand up and the water laps at my kneecaps. "I was sinking into the mud," he explains. And so do I. The mud is waist deep.

Back on the pier now, the small Indian scampers off to play while I lie down in total exhaustion. They just don't make big Indians like they used to. I am poking at the bubbles under my watch crystal when a small voice says, "Scratching Bull, blub-blub." Here we go again. Same song, different papoose. This mud is treacherous.

Speaking of which, it is time for the big braves' nippy-poo. "A little firewater warms the wigwam," is the old Indian saying we learned from an old Indian. Now it is night. The small braves are asleep and the big braves sit around the screened-in campfire reciting tribal tales of yore, most of which seem to be set in Nuevo Laredo.

But two of our number strike out for the ocean. The tribal doctor, Running Sores, and the tribal veterinarian, Foaming Mouth, are to spear fish for our breakfast. Man against nature, walking unarmed into danger.

Comes the dawn, and promptly at 10:30 I leap from the rack and head for the kitchen, visions of eggs and trout dancing in my head. "We got eggs and sausage," sings Greasy Spoon.

"I didn't know you caught sausage at low tide," I say. Greasy Spoon swats a fly with his spatula.

"You don't. They didn't bring back enough fish for the tribe."

"We caught one," says Foaming Mouth brightly. "That's enough."

"You ought to see what he can do with loaves of bread," says Bottoms Up.

The rest of our stay is relatively uneventful. My own papoose, Little Brave, runs enough fever to fry an egg on his stomach, and spends the entire time in bed. So does our Noble Leader, Sleeping Turtle, who spends hours on end meditating with the Great Spirit. Their mode of communication rather reminds one of snoring.

The others have a fine old time of it, lounging around and doing what comes naturally. For the small Indians, this means keeping wet at all times. Gradually soggy clothes build up around the tepee like leaves in the great forest. For the big braves, it consists of munching on whatever Greasy Spoon is passing out, then washing it down with Running Sores' homemade wine. ("Wednesday was a vintage year," he says proudly.)

But all good things must come to an end. And as the sun slowly sinks in the west, we pack to return to our urban warfare. Then our little caravan turns northward along the trail of beers, and all is quiet once more in the wilderness, except for the flora and fauna, which collectively heave a huge sigh of relief.

Greatest gift – 1975

Miss Ima is gone. After 93 years, one month and nine days, she has gone on to a place where there are no music critics, only music; no politicians, only statesmen; no questions, only answers.

She had arrived in 1882 – a time when Great Britain had Victoria, the United States had Chester A. Arthur and the Russians had the newly-crowned Czar Alexander III. Houston had 17,000 souls, Texas had six congressmen and the U.S. had 38 states.

She was the only person I knew who could recall those splendid days in Berlin before the war – World War I. "The Kaiser used to ride his horse in the park on Sundays and I used to go down with my friends to wave at him. He was a large man, and he loved music."

A few weeks ago she had a dinner party at Bayou Bend for a young Mexican couple and told how she and her father had once taken a train to Mexico, where the president himself had given them a ball.

"Which president was that?" asked the young man.

"Why, Porfirio Diaz," said Miss Ima.

The young man was speechless.

But it would be a terrible injustice to think of Miss Ima as one who lived in the past. No, she was infinitely interested in the present and the future. "I worry about Houston," she once said. "I worry where it's going. Where do you think it's going? What do you think about young Hofheinz? What we need is a city ethics code."

In the background I was saying, "Yes, ma'am. No, ma'am. I dunno, Miss Ima." I could never quite keep up with her train of thought. Once I was under the added handicap of several Old Fashioneds mixed up by Lucius, her long-time chauffeur and helper. He would serve them up in a silver cup big enough to bathe in, and they would clean your fillings, they would. Somehow I had expected sassafras tea.

Then again, Miss Ima did not always do the expected. (The night before she left for London she was at a teen-age birthday party, eating hot dogs and chili.) For instance, she was deep into ESP or "hunches," as she put it. "It ran in the family," she once explained. "My aunt was once on a stage going to Dallas when she ordered the driver to turn around because she had a hunch. She got back just in time to pull her younger brother out of a well." The governor also had a hunch and bought some land which turned out to be the West Columbia oil patch.

When she was a small girl, the family was in Hawaii. They were boarding a ship headed back to northern California—the baggage and a maid were already aboard—when suddenly Ima started crying for no reason, and yelling: "Something awful is going to happen!"

Her father, showing patience few men can muster, ordered all the bags and the maid off the ship, which sailed without them. The ship was never heard from again.

If her father was patient, Miss Ima was certainly one of the most devoted daughters around. The only time I ever heard her get mad was when an out-of-state author wrote a book on the Sharpstown scandal, *Shadow on the Alamo*. It included a blistering indictment of Gov. James Hogg.

"Who does he think he is?" she said over the phone. "How could he write such things? Doesn't he know anything about Texas history?"

"No, ma'am. Yes, ma'am. I dunno, Miss Ima."

She was first introduced to Texas politics by her father, and never lost interest in the political process or in Texas. "This is special," she said a week before she died, as she gave a small package to a friend. It was a Texas flag.

The Sharpstown scandal upset her, and she held little sympathy for those who had let Texas down. "How could they do this?" she snapped. "My father was so honest, when his term was over he had to borrow money to move out of the governor's mansion."

Otherwise, the matter of money was rarely discussed by Miss Ima. She often referred to herself as "poor," but thought that inherited wealth was a public trust. More than once she would confront someone of inherited wealth and ask what he or she intended to do with all that money. The answer was usually lacking, at least in Miss Ima's eyes.

"When I was little, my father would give me a quarter allowance each week," she said once, explaining her views. "I lost it but needed some money to go skating, so I borrowed a quarter from one of the servants. My father found out about it and asked, 'Missy, how did you get the money to go skating?' I told him and he lectured me severely. He paid back the quarter and took five cents out of my allowances for the next

29

five weeks. He wanted me to be more careful in the future."

Still, she could be a soft touch. Not too long ago a young man here in Houston—in bad trouble with his family due to a series of misdeeds—asked Miss Ima for a substantial sum to get back on his feet. He got it, eventually came back into the fold, and Miss Ima killed the fatted calf by calling off the IOU.

Such was Miss Ima Hogg. She loved antiques, butterflies, fish, mother-of-pearl, music and Bayou Bend. And she hated to impose on anyone. On her last day in the London hospital, she began to feel a little bit better and was aware that those gathered around her bed were worried that she was so sick, so far from home.

"Whatever happens," she told them, "remember that it is the way it was meant to be. I'm doing what I want to do. I'm where I want to be. I have no regrets."

And now she is gone, leaving behind a long list of achievements, from civic to music, which have substantially changed our lives for the better.

But her greatest gift didn't cost a cent—it was her outlook on life, inquisitive, optimistic, peripatetic. She worried, but she hoped, as well.

"I have no answers," she once wrote me, "only a burning desire to see something encouraging happen."

Drying time

Every now and then it is time to count our blessings. It is hard to know where to start. We are not locked up. We are not starving or naked or trying to sneak into this country so that we can gripe about how rotten things are here. We can be thankful for the air and the water and the Oilers and the peaceful transfer of power. Yes, it is, indeed, hard to know where to start in counting our blessings. But I have tried and, after a great deal of contemplation, braced with interviews and research, I have easily come to the conclusion that, above all, we should be thankful for towels.

Yes, towels. Ah, I can see that you are not quite on my wavelength. You look puzzled, some of you are even laughing out loud at my stupidity, but you are only exposing your own crassness and ignorance. For towels are the greatest boon to mankind ever. Without them, we'd all walk around wet. If you give this some thought, I am sure you will concur.

I shall start on common ground: We might all agree that towels are nice and fluffy and clean and feel good after stepping from a hot shower or bath. There is no argument there. But you might be hesitant to go on the record, as I have, and flatly state that towels, above all, should be the chief recipient of thanks on Thanksgiving Day. If that is the case with you, then just ask yourself one very simple question: Where would we be without towels?

We would be miserable.

Let me set the stage. You come in after a long, hard day. You desperately need a drink and a hot bath. The drink is mixed and consumed. Then the bath. Ahhhh. How fine it is. It soothes the senses, relaxes the nerves, cleans the body. But then you step from your hot bath into the cold air and, suddenly, there is no towel. There are no towels, anywhere. They have not been invented, manufactured, distributed, sold and bought. You are alone and wet, with no towel.

See? Now, clearly, if we had no towels, we would still come in after a hard day and have a drink and a hot bath. But we would have to stand there in the bathroom, naked and chilled for 15 or 30 minutes, drip drying. There would be pools on the floor, which means every bathroom would have to have drains, which would stop up.

Obviously, if there were no such things as towels, Western ingenuity would come up with an alternative. We might have massive sponges to roll in. Big blotters, perhaps. The more luxurious hotels would have machines like you find in public restrooms, so we could be blown dry. Poor people would simply call in thirsty dogs.

We tend to think of towels in such an everyday way that we overlook the historic fact that towels were not invented until 1932. The first towel was patented a year later by E. J. Cannon, a fabrics manufacturer who had tried, and failed, to market a fuzzy sheet that would allow one to dry off while sleeping.

Before that, there were untold cases of pneumonia, although history tells us of many private efforts to find a towel. As far back as the Romans, slaves armed with large palm leaves would rub their masters dry. Augustus Caesar declared, "The Roman baths are sadly lacking something, although I can't quite figure out what." The First Crusades failed because of the lack of drying apparel: The knights refused to bathe unless there was a way to dry off. Then, cooped up in their armor on hot afternoons with the visor down, fully half of them fainted, leading to their defeat at Damascus in 1099.

It was the Duke of Wellington who observed, "Waterloo was won in the shower stalls of Eton." And we all know the motto of the Order of the Bath, *Lava et scrumptious.* The French, who once used the grape press as an alternative, like to say, "Better to be flat and dry than up and around."

Even if some of us in America have overlooked the multitude of benefits inherent in drying off, others have not. In literature, we have "The Towel and the Pussycat," in music there is Dvorak's "Concerto to

Dry By in Nap Time" and it is a rare Las Vegas nightclub comedian who can go through his act without: "The towels in this hotel are so fluffy I could hardly close my suitcase."

So when you think about it, you will agree with me that we should give thanks for that much overlooked boon to mankind, the towel. Thank you.

A platterful of platitudes

THE FRONT DOOR – Here I am at home, snug and contented, and there is a knock on the door. Now who could that be? I open the door and there stands a wizened old codger with a slight smile on his face.

"Hi," I say. "What can I do for you?"

"Experience are the mistakes we like to remember," he says

"I beg your pardon?"

"Husbands are like fires. They go out when unattended."

"I'm afraid I don't understand the drift of this conversation, Sir," I say. "Did you want something?"

"There's no money saved by turning out the lights and going to bed early if the result is twins."

"Uh, Mister, we don't seem to be on the same wavelength. Just who are you?"

He cackles a wry cackle. "Why, son, I'm the Old Philosopher. With dry and witty observations about the comedy of life."

"No, thanks. I heard at the office."

"How's that?" he asks.

"Every office has its in-house philosopher. All the time I have to hear that guy's dry and witty observations on the comedy of life. I'm up to my earlobes in that drivel."

He smiles a knowing smile. " 'Nowadays, the average person respects old age only when it's bottled,' the Old Philosopher sez."

"Why is it that Old Philosophers always 'sez'? Everyone else 'says'."

"We Old Philosophers always sez. And seems."

"Huh?"

"You know. 'Seems like today when a girl finds out she's not the only pebble on the beach, she gets a little boulder.' "

"That's another thing that annoys me about you Old Philosophers. You are always putting down everything we do today. You keep making acidic comments about the way things are going as though the Great Depression was the bloody Garden of Eden."

"Seems like today's. . . ."

"Oh, shut up," I say, slamming the door. "These supercilious, pompous self-styled wisemen give me a pain," I mutter. Suddenly the door opens again.

"You rang?" the Old Philosopher asks.

It's him again. "I thought I told you to take your sob and shove it," I say.

"Sound-Off loves me," he cackles.

"Then go pester Sound-Off. I really don't have any time for spectators in the game of life."

"Very good," he cackles. "But it would be better, 'any time for arm-chair quarterbacks in the game of life.' A little more countrified, you know."

"Why does it have to be countrified?"

"We Old Philosophers are all rural hicks. That's a most important point. The more backwoods we are, the better it contrasts with our subtle and sophisticated wisdom."

"I won't stand here at my front door swapping cracker barrel philosophy with a Descartes in denim."

"Actually, I lean more towards Hegelianism with just a tad of Platonism as interpreted by Spinoza. Show me a milkman in high heels and I'll show you a dairy queen."

"That's not Hegel. That's Henny. Henny Youngman."

"We Old Philosophers are getting old. Sometimes we can't remember the details, but it's our age and experience that saves us. It's our wiser-than-thou piercing yet down-to-earth outlook that people like."

"Not me, buster. Now go away."

I shut the door and stomp back to the den just in time to hear a knock at the back door. It's him again.

"Show me an Old Philosopher who keeps bothering decent folk and I'll show you a toothless old man," I shout as I fling open the back door.

"Here are your Girl Scout cookies," says a neighbor's daughter.

"Oh, sorry," I say apologetically. "I thought you were a dirty old man."

"If God had wanted dirty old men, he wouldn't have invented soap or strokes," she says, thrusting four boxes of cookies into my hands and skipping off.

Bang-bang-bang. Now it's the front door again. I rush there. "You forgot about 'If God had wanted!'" I shout to the smiling codger at the door. "What kind of Old Philosopher are you, when you don't even have a couple of 'If God had wanted's'? You are a fake and a phony."

"Seems to me that a retired husband is a wife's full-time job," he replies lamely.

"Not good enough."

"If God had wanted grown men to answer the door holding an armload of Girl Scout cookies, he'd have given them a merit badge. Or five to 10 years in Huntsville," he cackles.

"When I want your opinion, I'll give it to you," I say.

He nods in appreciation. "You're getting better. Try it with, 'My cousin Elmer always sez. . . .' "

"I told you before. It's not *sez*. It's *says*."

"Ain't that the truth."

"OK, there you go again. You Old Philosophers keep saying 'ain't.' "

"A lot of people who ain't saying ain't, ain't eating," he cackles.

"You stole that from Dizzy Dean."

"That's *Dissy* Dean," he sez.

'Ah! Finalmente'

JONES HALL— The lights dim, the music starts and the curtain rises. "Tosca" is airborne once more for the umpteenth time since its debut at Rome's Teatro Constanzi on Jan. 14, 1900.

Angelotti staggers on stage, having just escaped prison. He has a remarkably strong voice for one who has been subsisting on gruel and black bread. "Ah! Finalmente! Nel terror mio stolto," he sings. For those who do not know Italian, Angelotti is singing: "Ah! I can breathe now . . ." or words to that effect.

He hides as an ancient monk comes by, and a bit later an artist named Cavaradossi enters. He's the hero, all hot and bothered over Tosca, his love. The old monk bugs out with a basket of fruit, but an orange drops out and rolls around on the floor. Cavaradossi is going to step on that orange and flip head over floodlight if he's not careful.

At this point I notice that four people are sitting next to me on the aisle. Sitting there in the dark. On the aisle. Strange. Ah, Tosca enters and lets loose with an operatic: "Mario." He fires back with a catchy: "Here I am." The opera is fraught with this kind of zippy dialogue.

A bit later, amidst a minor riot by some choirboys, a band of blackrobed baddies enters, headed by Scarpia. He is an evil chief of police, a totally fictional character, to be sure. I am a little worried about Scarpia, all dressed in black and waving a handkerchief, surrounded by blackbooted buddies. He almost steps on the errant orange as the choir sings: "Te aeternum Patrem omnis terra veneratur!" which means Te aeternum Patrem omnis terra veneratur!

The lights go on and the action switches to the row in front. The quartet waiting out the first act sitting in the aisle now approach the four on the aisle. They compare tickets. The four sitting in the seats refuse to move, explaining that while their tickets are actually for someplace down on Row E, they are here because of some reason I can-not fathom.

Enter the usher, who asks the musical question: "What are you doing in these people's seats?" The obvious leader of the four squatters is a bleached blonde swathed in furs, clutching opera glasses like Jack Nicklaus holds a nine-iron.

She explains that she is sitting there and that is that. The usher looks at the squatters' tickets. "These are for February," says the usher. More explaining. Row E. Etc. The four standers stand around, apologizing for the trouble but they do have tickets to those four seats on this night.

I leave the fight at this point to retreat to the bar where, earlier, I had noticed a big juicy sign: Champagne $1.10. A long wait later I am at the bar. "Champagne," I order. "Sorry, Sir, but we're all out. We'll have more in time for the next intermission." Yeah. "Somebody gets stabbed in the second act," one opera goer says to another. "Who?" asks the second o.g. "I dunno, I don't speak Italian."

"Get the ticket manager," says the blonde. "I'm not leaving until you get the manager." Obviously, nothing of consequence has transpired since I left. The four sitters are still sitting, the four standers are still standing.

"I've got some other tickets for you," the harried usher says. "Where are they?" asks the blonde. She is out for blood. "Back there," the usher says, gesturing a few rows back. The blonde shakes her bleached bubble. "No. I'll stay here till the management comes."

"I'm sorry for the inconvenience," says one of the four poor souls who went to the opera with the ridiculous notion that tickets for four meant four seats. They quietly scatter and take other positions around the hall as the blonde looks on triumphantly.

Meanwhile, back in Rome, Scarpia turns out not to be gay after all, but actually only a charming old lecher, hot after Tosca. He arrests Cavaradossi, the artist, and tosses him to the torture chamber to tell where the escaped prisoner, Angelotti, is hiding. Cops can get a bit testy at times. Cavaradossi is taking it all rather well, singing from the rack: "No, it's nothing. Courage, courage, I laugh at pain." They don't make artists like they used to.

Scarpia is put out because there is no wine for his meal, and sends a waiter to get some. Tosca picks up a steak knife and carves Scarpia a new buttonhole, whereupon he falls to the floor singing: "I'm dying." Curtain, a quick race back to the bar. "I'm sorry, Sir, but we're all out of champagne." I briefly consider falling to the floor while singing, "I'm dying," but chicken out. Scarpia got his wine, but he had pull. "Kick me when they get to the aria," says one o.g. to another.

Back to my seat. "Hello, reverend," says one of the four squatters.

"Hello, there," the reverend says back. "Say, are these your regular seats?" "Uh, no, they aren't." Music, the curtain goes up. Poor Cavaradossi faces a firing squad made up of crack shots from the Italian Army. He stands a better than even chance of coming out untouched. Bang. He falls. Dead. Tosca sings: "Dead . . . Mario! Mario!" He is, indeed, dead. Even the Italian Army has its good days.

Curtain, applause, a party down at the bar in the basement. Louis Quilico, who sang the part of Scarpia: "Everything went fine except that there was no wine in the bottle. I had to send out for more."

Enter Tosca—Teresa Kubiak—the star. She is accompanied by four people who look vaguely familiar. Good grief, it is the chairless quartet, who spent most of the night fighting fruitlessly for their rights. They should have summoned Scarpia, he would have known what to do with the interlopers. And I would have loved the hear the blonde singing: "Courage, courage, I laugh at pain."

You're on, pal

THE RADIO— Hi there, gang. It's Time to Tell Bell. Just call in and talk to me, your old radio buddy. You'll feel a lot better getting your gripes off your chest. I'm Bell, and I'm here to listen.

Ah, our first caller. You're on, Howie.

Am I on?

Yes. You're on.

Am I really on?

Yep, Howie, you're on the radio. What's on your mind?

Gee, I never thought I'd be on the radio. I've been calling in for weeks now. Am I really on?

Bye, Howie. Hi, there, Maud.

Bell, I want to discuss the Iranian situation. I think . . .

Maud, let me tell you about the Iranian situation. Now I think we should have gone in there with paratroopers and nukes long ago. No more Mister Nice Guy. I know these Nervous Nellies think we should negotiate but I. . . .

Bell, it seems to me. . . .

Quit interrupting, Maud. We should cut 'em off at the pass, that's what I say. John Wayne wouldn't stand for . . .

. . . but Bell, if we . . .

I say, John Wayne wouldn't stand for it. And another thing I think is that too many Americans don't appreciate America. For 200 years . . .

. . . but, Bell, I feel we should . . .

I said to shut up, Maud. I'm still talking. Didn't your mother ever teach you any manners? We should go in and show those pinkos and perverts what we're made of. And I also think too many Americans are talking and no one is listening. Right, Maud? Maud? Maud, you there? OK, Charlie, you're on. Time to Tell Bell.

Bell, I want to gripe about Congress. Those ding-dongs are ruining this country. I think . . .

Wait a minute there, Charlie. I'm tired of everybody putting down Congress all the time. Those guys aren't perfect, but they're trying. And dummies like you are always criticizing 'em. I don't have to listen to any more of that garbage.

OK, Alice, it's time to Tell Bell.

Hi, Bell. I just want to say that I love my mother.

Alice, that's ridiculous. Why should you love your mother? I mean, everybody loves her mother. You want to be just like everybody else? Alice, you average people make me gag.

Thomas, you're on.

Bell, I think you're an overbearing pompous ass. Your program is one long ego trip, and you never give anybody a chance to express . . .

Drop dead, Thomas. OK, Conrad, we're listening. Time to Tell Bell.

Bell, I want to say a good word for Congress. Those guys got a tough job up there and I think . . .

What are you, some kind of PR flack for politicos? Congressmen are a bunch of free-loading turkeys who ought to be kicked out next election. Every one of them. I'm tired of people calling in here to say nice things about Congress. You make me sick, all you Pollyannas. Griff, you're on. Tell Bell what's bugging you.

I'm sorry I'm not in right now. When you hear the chime you have 30 seconds. Please leave your . . .

Go ahead, Constance, let's hear what's on your mind.

Bell, the inflation situation is . . .

I'll tell you about inflation, Constance. I was down at the grocery store yesterday and the . . .

. . . Bell, I want . . .

Who cares what you want? Anyway, I was down at the grocery store yesterday and eggs were more than a buck a dozen. Can you imagine? A buck a dozen. Meat was just out of sight. The canned corn . . .

I went to the store, too, Bell. You want to hear about it?

Not particularly. OK, Marty, your time to Tell Bell.

Bell, this crime rate.has really got me bugged.

You're bugged? What about me? I was walking through a parking lot yesterday . . . That's a dumb thing to do . . . So I was approached by this guy . . . it's not really very interesting . . . I think it's real interesting.

This guy ... oh, shut up ... he ... I ... that's stupid and you're a disgrace. But he ...

Bell, you're arguing with yourself. I haven't said a word.

Who asked you? Go ahead, Mildred, time to Tell Bell.

Bell, I just want to say what a terrific job you're doing.

Oh, really? Tell me all about it.

Left out in cold

How could 260 million people, including Gerald Ford, be a persecuted minority? Easy. They're all left handed. They are misfits in a right-handed world, and are reminded of this everytime they button their shirts, drive a car, shoot a rifle or shake hands.

But no one seems to care. There are no frenzied demonstrations in front of General Motors demanding that the driving machinery on the car—not to mention the radio knobs, cigarette lighter and gas tank top—be redesigned for lefties. No one screams at the makers of cameras, pencil sharpeners, guitars and door knobs. No one even publishes books that can be read from back to front.

So the southpaws suffer in silence, and usually pay for it. Experts say that while only one person in 10 is a lefty, the percentage of left handers among male alcoholics is about three times that of the general population. Left handers are often poor spellers and bad readers, and make up nearly half of all remedial reading classes. An unusually high number of lefties is found among victims of cerebral palsy, epilepsy and mental retardation.

Casey Stengel, who finally got out of dentistry because he couldn't learn to use right-handed dental equipment, once said: "Left-handers have much more enthusiasm for life. They sleep on the wrong side of the bed, and their heads become stagnant on that side." Casey wasn't as stagnant as one might think.

It is now believed by many researchers that the right lobe of the brain—which apparently controls the left hand—is nonverbal, musical and artistic. The left lobe—which controls the right hand—seems to be verbal, rational and analytical. Therefore, southpaws should not bother with becoming mathematicians, lawyers, computer programmers and the like since they, themselves, are not programmed for this line of work. They should concentrate on becoming jazz musicians, abstract expressionists and baseball players (the latter because a lefty batter is one or two paces closer to first base).

This is not to say that being a left-hander is some kind of overriding handicap. Gerald Ford made it. So did Harry Truman and James Garfield. Alexander the Great seems to have muddled through; so did Charlemagne, Picasso, Benjamin Franklin and Leonardo de Vinci. (Before you lefties get too uppity, let us note here and now that Jack the Ripper was definitely left-handed, as was the Boston Strangler.)

Two of the Beatles—Ringo Starr and Paul McCartney—were southpaw strummers. Rock Hudson acts left-handed, so did Judy Garland and Charlie Chaplin. Lewis Carroll wrote "Alice in Wonderland" left-handed, but there is no indication how she wrote back.

It wasn't always such a problem. The writings of the ancient Greeks and Egyptians may be read from top to bottom, left to right or even back and forth. Then things went downhill.

The Israelites were defeated by a Benjaminite army of "700 men left-handed." The Romans, never forgetting this tale of military trickery, kept a wary eye out for lefties—they were obviously an untrustworthy bunch.

'Tis said that the Romans introduced the custom of grasping one another's right hand to ensure that neither could draw his sword, and to this day, we shake right hands.

Remember Judges 20:16.

Thus it is that the Latin word for "right" is "dexter" but for "left" it's "sinister." (The French word for "left" is "gauche," but that's another story.)

We've come a long way from watching out for errant swords, but today's lefty is still no better off. Telephone booths, scissors, fishing reels. There was the fellow who asked for a left-handed can opener and the clerk wondered if he would like a left-handed can to go with it. Remember in school when the desk had that flat arm to write on? It was almost always for right-handers.

They now make golf clubs for lefties, but one of them, Ben Hogan, learned how to hit right-handed when he realized that the courses were laid out for the northpaws. Playing cards are made for the 90 per cent majority; so are surgeons' knives, wrist watches and even slot machines.

A left-handed compliment is a put-down, a leftist is a troublemaker and a left-handed marriage is when a male of the nobility marries beneath his station. And no one ever says he'd rather be left than president, even if he's a left-handed president.

Joyful noise

Let us now consider a question long debated by theologians, but as yet still undecided: Is God a Christian? First, of course, we must decide whether there is a God. Some say there is, some say there is not. I, personally, opt for the former, particularly in times of great danger, fear and outright threats against my safety. At other times, when all is well and fat and rich, as with most people, I really don't give it much thought.

But let us assume for the sake of this debate today that there is, indeed, a God. This, however, lands us squarely in the midst of another argument. To illustrate, one of my brothers—the one who mucks about Asia—was once sitting with a Harvard lawyer who had flown out there and a Chinese businessman. They were going over a contract about 32 pages long, including seven pages which dealt with "Acts of God."

"I hope the contract is in order," says the Harvard lawyer.

"Indeed, it is," says the Chinese businessman. "Except for one small point. Whose God?"

It did not stop the business deal, but it did stop the lawyer in his tracks. Harvard had failed to cover that point. It was no small matter as many religions believe that fires, floods, pestilence and famine are not quirks of nature but retribution ordered from on high for not tossing the needed number of virgins into the volcano or whatever.

Doubtless both the lawyer and the businessman felt God was on his side of the table. This is not unusual. Never has an army marched off to war without the solemn understanding that God is on its side. Indeed, my own church, the Presbyterians, split down the middle over the Civil War, arguing over whether God wore blue or gray. The split lasted for years and may even still be around. I have not bothered to find out lately and, in all probability, neither has God.

Okay, if there are various Gods, then are there various heavens? Is there one for the Buddhists and one for the Jews and one for the Protestants and so on? There might very well be, for obviously my idea of heaven is not the same as yours, and certainly the shepherd in Pakistan has yet another idea. Who is right? No one has written home to say, but I feel we must figure that there just can't be millions of heavens, so there is probably just one, set up so that we would all like it. Like Lyndon B. Johnson, heaven has something for everyone and is all things to all people.

If there is one heaven, does it stand to reason that there is one hell? If so, I personally would imagine that hell is one large front yard which I am forced to mow. And by the time I finish it all, I look back where I started. It has grown up again and I need to go back and do it all over once more. So on into eternity, I am doing yard work to pay for my sinful life on earth. My neighbors in hell will probably be German generals, French politicians, English rock groups and American corporate lawyers. Some sins are more original than others.

40

But must the occupants stay there forever? Oh, I know all about the permanence of such things, but maybe it's all relative. Maybe hell is like a jail sentence.

This brings up another point. Is someone keeping tabs on our every move? Is there an angel walking around behind us with a clipboard, very officiously jotting down our every deed? No, I don't think so. As a matter of fact, I have it on very good authority that nothing of the sort goes on. God does not farm out such projects to helpers. He just drops by every now and again to see how you are doing. Maybe as a waiter or a car parking attendant or a voice on the phone wanting to know if Martha is home. Last week He was driving 55 on IH 10 and took down all sorts of names.

There is one school of thought among theologians that God is dead. God will neither confirm nor deny this rumor, but a lot of dead theologians are finding out first-hand if they are correct. There is another school of thought that God is an atheist. I have not yet made up my mind, but several eminent theologians are debating the matter. Until they have a definitive opinion, I plan to be courteous to car parking attendants.

The Greek "fix"

THE DEN—Ah, peace and quiet. An evening at home. A little soft music, a bit of brandy, and . . . eh? The phone is ringing.

"Hello?" I say.

"Get over here," says this vaguely familiar voice.

"Who is this?" I ask.

"It's the Idi Amin School of Charm. We need you. Now."

"Calpakis, you sound alarmed. What's the matter?"

"Come over. Right now. Only you in the western world are capable of this task. Seconds count."

I drop the phone and race over to the house of my friend and neighbor, Calpakis the Wily Greek. It is obvious that he is in dire need. I come upon him in the dark, sitting in the driveway surrounded by parts of our jointly owned lawnmower.

"Here," he says, handing me a flashlight. "Hold this."

"What?" I yell. "You got me all the way over here from my den to hold a flashlight?"

"Well, now," he says, "you wouldn't do me much good holding the flashlight over there in your den, now would you?"

"But why is holding this flashlight so important?" I ask, getting down by the lawnmower.

41

"Because," he explains patiently, "if you don't hold the flashlight, it'll fall down."

C-the-W-G takes off some strange pieces of metal. "Also," he says, "I'm doing you a favor, fixing your lawnmower for you. My price is less than you would pay at the shop."

"Wait a minute. We went into this lawnmower 50-50. Why is it that everytime it breaks, it's suddenly *my* lawnmower?"

"I've been wondering about that myself," he says. "You ought to be more careful. Here, hand me that wrench."

"Wrench," I say.

"Pliers," he says.

"Pliers," I say.

"Bourbon and water," he says.

"What bourbon and water?"

C-the-W-G scowls. "You mean you came alone?"

"But you never said anything about bringing you a bourbon and water," I say.

"You obviously forgot to look at the note nailed to the liquor cabinet," he says as he pokes into the innards of the machine. "Yes, just as I thought."

"What?" I ask.

"It's broken," he says.

"What's broken?"

"The *lawnmower*, of course," he says.

"But I know that," I say. "It's been broken for a week, and I keep saying we need to take it to the shop."

C-the-W-G pulls out some more machinery. "There is no point in paying someone to do something when you can do it yourself."

"That's what you said last week when we chopped down the tree."

"What tree?"

"The one that fell onto the garage."

"Oh," he says. "*That* tree."

He unscrews three bolts and lifts up a disc. "I was right all along. The gimcrack is lodged against the wheedle." He screws in some bolts. "Start it up," he says.

I try. And try again. And again. And again.

"It won't start," Calpakis announces.

"Puff-puff-wheeze," I say.

He takes it apart again, and holds up the sparkplug for closer examination.

"Obviously it won't work," I say.

"Why not?"

"Because the sparkplug is unscrewed."

42

"It is difficult for you to hold the flashlight and talk at the same time," says C-the-W-G. "And of your two talents, I prefer that of flashlight holder."

"Maybe it needs gas," I offer, ignoring his advice.

"It's got gas."

"Ah," I say, holding up a bent piece of metal. "No wonder it won't work. This is bent like an L."

"It's supposed to be bent like an L," says C-the-W-G. "It's a socket wrench."

"Maybe we should just invest in a couple of sheep," I suggest.

"I don't know how to repair a broken sheep," says Calpakis, thumbing through the repair manual. "Which one is the A-34 rotating flacid?"

"We've got all these parts and none of them fit," I say. "I feel like it's late Christmas Eve."

"It looks like the B-34 rotating flacid," says C-the-W-G.

"Maybe we should take it to the shop," I say.

"That's throwing away money. Now start it up."

I grab the rope and yank. Nothing. Again. And again, nothing. Once more with feeling, and we hear a slight wheeze. Again, and a cough. I yank again. Two coughs, a wheeze and a slight shake. Five yanks later and the lawnmower is chugging along like a tubercular jogger. My right hand is worn through by rope burns. The mower dies and I am contemplating a similar state.

In my last act on this earth, I yank the rope again and again, but the engine refuses to start.

"Your lawnmower won't run," says Calpakis, putting up his tools. "I suggest you take it to the shop."

"Good idea," I say. "Wish I'd thought of that."

Driven batty

THE CHURCH YARD—Driving along this street, with the first pollen of spring coming down, I spot a strange scene: children playing baseball. Could it be that winter has flown away and baseball is upon us? Already? Yes, indeed, the athletic seasons seem to span the calendar. The Super Bowl is hardly over before the first fall exhibition game. And the World Series has been gone these few days yet already we have the first Astro exhibitions.

Yet the scene here is not major league stuff. I would put hard money that not a single one of these small children will ever be paid a dime to play baseball, but their fathers don't know that, won't hear that. And neither will their coaches. Little League is a big league, and don't ever beat a different drum around the diamond.

Much has been said and written – probably too much – about parents' aggression on behalf of their offspring on the athletic fields. We have all heard, seen, read about the over-eager mothers, screaming, "Kill the ump!" while mouthing platitudes about how it's only a game. We have seen television shows and *The Bad News Bears* and all the rest, warning about frustrated jocks, disguised as fathers, pushing their sons into uniforms.

It is standard Americana, this isn't-it-awful? tsk-tsking over parents' behavior in the stands and coaches' tirades on the fields. Yes, like the Ugly American, we all know those types and know that we are not. The only problem is that those types do exist. They flower. For all the nay-saying, they are alive and well on your neighborhood field.

My own brood brought this home to me, as I wandered into the bleachers overlooking a score of playing fields to watch them drop baseballs, footballs, volleyballs, basketballs and anything else that is round. Each time, I heard parents tsk-tsking about the off-field cursings of coaches. Then I watched them yell, "Hang him!" at some 11-year-old.

What is it that makes frothing animals out of bankers? Foul-mouthed fools out of lawyers? Angry, life-is-a-battlefield advocates out of otherwise peaceful pediatricians? I look at those Nazi rally films with greater understanding and fear of cultivated hysteria.

My children were generally fortunate that they came under the wings of coaches who kept their perspectives about them. Most of those fathers fully realized that they were not grooming tomorrow's champions, but were simply trying to teach small children how to play a game. They showed patience – an endangered species on Houston's athletic fields – and tolerance and class, for the most part. And they must have felt terribly alone at times.

I once met a father at a game who cornered me behind home plate and proceeded to talk my ear off the whole game about something else entirely. Later I was told he had been barred from several athletic encounters because of his screamings, so I suppose I served a purpose that day. Mothers whom I know to be peaceful and charming folk have thundered obscenities at umpires which would gladden a drill instructor's heart. And the officials are not without some problems. I was acting as third base coach and, after urging a six-year-old to head for home, was tongue-lashed by an umpire, loud and long, for speaking out of turn. He got his jollies that night but I hope at work the next day his shovel broke.

Showing small children the need for teamwork, staying in shape, learning the rudiments of plays and plans is no doubt a good thing, but I can't help wondering if the negative factors haven't so out-distanced the pluses that athletics should be outlawed for anyone under 12. Are we really doing our children any good teaching them new curse words between home and first? Are we building a better America by putting Earl Campbell's number on an 8-year-old and telling him to get out there and hurt someone?

We are a competitive society. It is the solid base for everything we do. As children we compete for grades in school. Later, we compete to get into the best universities. Unlike some societies where marriages are made by parents, in our society we compete for the heart and affection of potential mates. Then we compete for jobs, and next for promotions and salaries. We compete all our lives, so I am not so sure we need to start this race in kindergarten. Our children will compete until the day they die. Why not give them a few years of non-combative enjoyment? Or, to be blunt about it, just who are these tournaments for, the children or the parents? Honest?

It has been argued that organized, supervised and uniformed sports for tots groom them for future endeavors. Do you really think your son is going to be a linebacker for the Los Angeles Rams? Indeed, do you *want* him to be? If you sincerely feel you should begin early on to prepare your children for their upcoming careers, you might better hand them a stethoscope or a wrench or a Smith & Wesson. Better yet, how about just leaving them alone? Kick-the-Can is competition and is played on many a street on any warm evening without a numbered uniform in sight and without any of those handful of parents who take all the fun out of games.

Despite what everyone wants to quote, the Duke of Wellington never did say that the Battle of Waterloo was won on the playing fields of Eton. It makes a good story, but he denied he ever said it. What he probably said, while driving by in his carriage one day, was, "Good Lord. They'll kill off each other quick enough. Must they start so soon?"

Owls in family tree

THE PATIO—It's not what you would call a terrace overlooking a vast vista of my lands and crops. Rather, it is a small patio surrounded on three sides by my house. The fourth, and open, side gives a view of the back fence 25 feet away. The crops this year consist of St. Augustine decline and vintage mud.

But it is mine, all mine. My patio. And it is time to put it to use, for fall is upon us. I can already feel the first nip of Old Man Winter on my Entex bill. I can already watch thousands of office workers rush out during their lunch hour to partake of the beautiful weather excluded from their place of work by windows which won't open. You can always tell when it's autumn in Houston. You don't have to air-condition your sauna.

So it is out to the patio, unused these many sultry months, to wallow in the autumn afternoon. To watch the leaves turn red and gold and fall merrily to the ground with a silence. So here I am in the great outdoors. Pull out the chair. Push back the table. Have my Scotch and water nearby. A cigar. Something to read. Ah, breathe in that cool, clear Houston smog.

Splat.

Huh? What splat? Something has dropped down upon my table, right near my drink. A bird has announced its presence. Or a squirrel. No, wait a minute. This appears to have once been a bird or a squirrel. Don't tell me. Not again!

I look up into the pine tree, searching through the branches and needles and clusters of cones, searching for the tell-tale sign I don't want to see. But there it is. Or, rather, there they are: two evil eyes peering back from the midst of a round, feathery face. It is a huge, brown-and-white visitor, Owl Capone. He is squinting down at me, no doubt through cross hairs, lining up his next bombing run. He looks sleepy, and probably is, this being the middle of his night, but he cannot pass up a chance to ruin my day.

"Begone!" I shout. Now, to be sure, that is not what one usually shouts, but then one does not usually shout anything at an owl and "Begone!" seems as good as any. He blinks. Owls must be the only birds in the world that can blink. At least, I've never seen any other bird blink, not that I go around looking. When owls meet up with other birds, they probably say, "Bet you can't do this," then blink. Owls are pompous.

They are also nocturnal and are God's pest controllers. They whip around town at night, while most of Houston sleeps, grabbing off foolhardy mice and rats and assorted beasties we don't like. If there were no owls in Houston, we would be overrun with varmints. Owls prevent that, so we should be kind to them, treat them with the respect they think they so richly deserve. I am all for owls, but not over my patio.

I reported earlier that this particularly messy and evil bird, Owl Capone, had come to roost in my tree last spring. Soon he brought along his chippy, clearly to impress her with his accuracy. I screamed and shouted and threw pine cones at them to no avail. Frankly, I think they liked to see me down here, railing and ranting fruitlessly.

Say, that reminds me. Where is the other one? Owlice, we called her. "So, she left you, did she?" I cry happily. "Took the eggs and went back to mother. Or maybe she tossed you out of the nest because you couldn't bring home the rodents. Were her civil rats violated, ha-ha-ha? Owlice doesn't roost here any more!" Owl Capone says nothing, but nods over one wing. Two branches over, there is Owlice. She blinks at me, then lets loose.

Somehow my drink has lost its attraction, sitting there among yesterday's in-flight meal. My cigar no longer has its former charm, snuggling up to mouse fur.

I pick up a pine cone and loft it toward the aerial flophouse. It doesn't come close. So weak is my counterattack that they both close their eyes and go back to sleep. "Go! Leave!" I shout, waving my fist at the heavens. "There are a million branches in the naked city, and I am no longer interested in being showered with snakes and dead rats." The silence is broken only by the audible stare of two neighbors who are looking over the fence at me with totally blank expressions.

Cruising along

ON BOARD—There are several things one should know before taking a trip on a cruise ship. Therefore, pay attention and I shall save you a lot of embarrassment, time, trouble, money and perhaps a keelhauling.

Ship—This is where you are. It is not a "boat." A "boat" is a lifeboat, of which there should be several tied up on each side of the ship. If there are no "boats" on the ship, you might ask about it.

Captain—He is the biggie on any ship. He can be easily spotted by the fact that everyone calls him "captain," a nautical code used on the high seas. It is considered very chi-chi if the captain asks you to sit at his table for dinner. That means you are very In. If, on the other hand, the captain asks to sit at *your* table, you are either *very* In or your ship has a very insecure captain.

The Deck—On land it would be referred to as "the floor." On some ships during long voyages part of the deck may be used to feed the boiler fires, which makes shuffleboard difficult. From this we have the old nautical term, "not playing with a full deck."

Cruises are not so much a trip as a social experience. Oneupmanship is extremely important and ships—like small towns—are very, very catty. Therefore, one must be careful about one's company. Here are some fellow passengers to avoid:

Anyone wearing an albatross around his neck.

Anyone named "Blind Pew."

Anyone accompanied by a friend named "Friday."

Any passenger who wears a life preserver in the ship's swimming pool.

Anyone who does not fully understand the term "poop deck."

Likewise, there are several passengers one should cozy up to, for they are high on the social ladder and should be treated with deference. These include:

Anyone who has the same name as that of the ship.

Any passenger who, when handed the wine list, nods and says, "Yes."

Any woman passenger who, when asked why she is wearing a life preserver to dinner, replies: "But I'm not wearing a life preserver."

Any beautiful woman passenger who, when asked, "Have you come across before?" just smiles.

Any passenger who gets off the ship and walks awhile – and you're still out at sea.

The Crew – Your ship should have a crew. If not, I suggest you find yourself another ship. Members of the crew run the ship, cater to your every need and eat money. Crew members include:

The lookout, who stays up top and watches the horizon constantly to make sure the ship does not fall off the edge;

The engineer, who makes the ship run, either by keeping an eye on the boilers or by slowly and rhythmically beating a large drum;

The purser, who carries a large purse;

The steward, who carries a large stew;

And the bo'sun (pronounced boatswain), who walks around the deck yelling such orders as, "Splice the flyswatter! Stow the frambler! You there, look alive and marinate the nebula!" No one pays him any attention, but it gives local color to the cruise and the passengers think it's quaint. You may ignore his various orders except for two: "Repel boarders!" and "Bail!"

Things to avoid: Scurvy, "Jaws," little Dutch boys, coin-operated lifeboats, lobster-with-chili during rough seas, steerage class, sitting in a deck chair if your cruise ship has a periscope and torpedo tubes, and eggs more than three weeks after your last port of call.

How to spot a bad cruise: You know that you have made a mistake if:

Your cruise ship has disembarkation nets down the sides.

The navigator uses an Exxon road map.

Announcements begin with a whistle and, "Now hear this."

Your vichyssoise is served in a helmet liner.

Your ship's last port is Ellis Island.

Fight song

> *Will you come to the bow'r*
> *I have shaded for you?*

I have decked it with roses
All spangled with dew.

SAN JACINTO—They are reshaping the landscape around here. Because of subsidence, dikes are being built to keep back the waters of the San Jacinto River and Buffalo Bayou, and the air is filled with the bellows and chugs of giant equipment.

It is not too musical, but it is a reminder that this place has changed since 1836, when other sounds filled the air. Including those of the Band of the Republic of Texas Army.

Yes, indeed, we didn't have money, material or muscle, but we had music, including a rather bawdy tune, *Will You Come to the Bower?* And today let us examine what little we know of the army band.

First, let's get situated. Houston's army was camped here, on the banks of Buffalo Bayou near where the USS Texas rests. The army had been chased clear across Texas, with nothing to show for its efforts but defeat. The soldiers had a dozen languages and God knows how much mayhem among them, but they were united that cold morning right here.

The day began at 4 a.m. with music—the drumbeat of Dick, a massive Negro freedman (yes, blacks as well as Chicanos were in our little army—we were too besieged to be bigoted). At least one contemporary account reports that Gen. Sam Houston used a drummer, rather than a bugler, to sound reveille because he didn't want to wake up Santa Anna's much larger army just over the rise.

This tells us two things: 1) There was a drummer. 2) There was a bugler in the Texan Army whom Houston did not want to hear. At 3:30 p.m., Houston lined up his troops, two men deep, along this part of the meadow. Then, at 4 o'clock, he ordered them forward. The cavalry, led by 38-year-old Mirabeau B. Lamar, was over there. The artillery—two cannons called the Twin Sisters—were right here in the center. The infantry was spread out along the line.

The army moved out, walking up through the grass and the mushy mud. In front of everyone was Houston, 42 years old, the only man in history who would be governor of two states, senator of one country and president of another.

And, of course, there was the band and the song.

The number, the makeup, the song selection of the band that afternoon are confusing. "To the cavalry's left was the artillery with the musicians: three fifes and a drum; and four companies of infantry," reports David Nevin in *The Texans.*

A soldier, John S. Menifee, wrote later: "We marched upon the enemy with the stillness of death. No fife, no drum, no voice was heard until, at 200 yards, the Mexicans started shooting at us."

We do know this. There were at least three professional musicians in the Texas Army: Peter Allen, who was not at San Jacinto, Thomas Wesson, who may have been there, and John N. Beebe, who was definitely there. And there was Frederick Lemsky, variously described as a German and a Czech, who was a fifer in the army. It is known that the musical instruments in Texas at the time included the drum, fife, clarion, bugle and cymbals. Clarence Wharton, in *San Jacinto: 16th Decisive Battle*, reports that we had a "four-piece" impromptu affair, including one huge drum brought in from New Orleans as military supplies. Robert Penn Warren, in *How Texas Won*, says we had one fife and one drum. Lota M. Spell, in *Music in Texas*, says we had two drummers and a fife.

And there is William Simpson, a local antique-and-documents dealer and a Texas history buff, who came across a fellow named Ricks some years ago. Ricks reported that his great-great-grandfather, also named Ricks, was one member of the Harrisburg Detail, sent to the rear to guard the baggage during the battle. In the baggage, Ricks found a drum, sent from New Orleans. Now, it seems that Ricks had been a drummer boy in the War of 1812. He took the drum and set off to find the army, which he did, on April 20, 1836. And, as he told his children and grandchildren years later, he beat that drum in the battle.

Houston, in his official report, makes no mention of a band. Neither does Lamar. None of the earliest sources write of an army band, but gradually, the music appears. In *The Raven* by Marquis James, "a fifer" is mentioned; and Frank Tolbert in his *The Day of San Jacinto* writes that the tune was possibly suggested by the German-Czech Lemsky (who later lived in Houston and taught music), or it could have been suggested by Lamar, a great admirer of Thomas Moore, who wrote the words for the song. (Oscar J. Fox edited and arranged the music.) The song was known to the English as "Dilly Dilly Duckling, and Be Killed." It was a racy tune, full of innuendoes, and proper for the parade.

Well, historians can argue, and we may wonder, but it happened right here at 4 p.m., April 21, in 1836.

Houston signals with a sweep of his battered campaign hat. The gunners wheel and fire, shattering the quiet. The cavalry charges. The infantry takes up the cry, "Remember the Alamo!" The drums roll and fifers fife:

Will you come to the bow'r
I have shaded for you?
I have decked it with roses
All spangled with dew.

"The smaller excellencies"

"I think no innocent species of wit or pleasantry should be suppressed; and that a good pun may be admitted among the smaller excellencies of lively conversation"—James Boswell (Samuel Johnson's biographer), 1740–1795

I feel it is my duty to tell you, however, that James Boswell died of a venereal disease.

Scott L. Weeden of Houston reports that during a recent trip to southern Europe, an Englishman was a guest for lunch at a local monastery. He was served a delicious meal of fish and chips. It was so good, in fact, he asked the brothers if he might be allowed to meet the cook to thank him personally for the meal. "Well, I'm the fish friar," one brother replied, "and that's the chip monk over there."

Now an Aggie joke. Well, not exactly. More like a joke *from* an Aggie. It comes from J. R. Eulberg of the department of psychology at A&M, who tells us that a couple in Iran had planned a festive Western-style wedding for several years, as opposed to a more traditional Moslem wedding. However, the new legal code issued by the reigning ayatollah forbade any marriages with Western trappings. So the couple called off the engagement. It was the first situation in which Khomeini's books spoiled the troth.

Did you know that Texas and A&M have played more often than Army-Navy? In view of what happened this fall in Austin, it seems only fair to get even.

So, what's the best three years in an Aggie's life?

The second grade.

And then there was the transvestite sea bird with supernatural powers, known as Drag: the magic puffin. That comes from *Post* assistant news editor Charley Reinken.

"How did the aftershave tycoon manage to be in two places at once?" asks another *Postman*, photographer Joel Draut.

"I give up."

"He cologned himself."

This bit of wisdom comes to us from F. B. Wells of Memphis, as quoted in the *Chemical and Engineering News*. Two poets in England were collaborating on various *morceaux*. A third, slightly unbalanced poet became obsessed with the idea that the collaborators were planning to steal from his work. He laid in a supply of English baked goods and left them in the sun until they were hard as rocks.

Armed with these missiles, he spotted the two poets, who were out for a stroll, and, from behind a bush, let fly with his weapons. His first shot dropped one poet, then ricocheted, leveling the other. Our hero had nailed two bards with one scone.

From Greg Reilly, who contributes an occasional effort, we have a late news bulletin: The Russians are incorporating. It will be called Red, Inc.

He also tells about a fellow from Prague who was floating down the Danube when a huge wave hit his boat, washing him overboard. After much splashing and swimming, he finally pulled himself ashore in Austria. A border patrolman came rushing down, asking, "Do you want political asylum?"

"No," said the fellow, "I'm just a Czech on an out-of-town bank."

John Paul Cook, a UH student, says that in his organic chemistry class one of his classmates asked the professor, Dr. Willcott, if formic acid really did come from ants. Willcott explained that formic acid is commercially synthesized, not extracted from ants. He explained that it's the naturally occurring substance that gives an ant sting its stinging properties. The student wondered what possible commercial value formic acid could have. Willcott replied, "Don't you know? It's ant-acid."

Frederick W. Harbaugh of Houston, who hasn't reported in for several months, returns with this: A health problem developed in the central religious temple in ancient Babylonia when the temple's pyramidal tower, or ziggurat, became so infested with roaches and lice that the faithful began staying away.

The chief priest solicited bids from local exterminators and awarded the extermination contract to the low bidder, who promised to purge the tower with a powerful smoke bomb. The plan succeeded, but no one remembered to alert the tower's custodian, a dwarf, who perished in the smoke. Grief-stricken when he learned of the little janitor's death, the high priest publicly proclaimed that ziggurat smoking is hazardous to your elf.

THERE *IS NOT* A DROOPY

There *Is Not* a Droopy

SOUTH OF MANNHEIM—The train rips through the German night carrying its mysterious passengers on secret and seamy missions. The compartment is empty except for four persons. One is obviously the murderer, the other is the spy, the third is making off with the Swiss bank account of the Shah of Iran. The fourth unquestionably is the true heir to the throne of Portugal, on his way to Lisbon to claim what is rightfully his.

"It must be Droopy," says one.

Silence. Will the lights go out? A shot? A scream?

"No. There is not a Droopy."

"Yes, there is. It's Droopy."

If the conversation is bugged by the Shah's men in the next compartment, they must be madly flipping through their codebooks to ascertain the true identity of the notorious Droopy.

Silence. The train, bound from Heidelberg to Frankfurt, keeps ripping through the German night. These four mysterious strangers are obviously not Germans. Italians, perhaps. Or Norwegian. Their papers show them to be American news reporters, but that is patently false. They are wearing shoes.

"It's not Droopy. It's Sleazy."

"Sleazy? Come on."

A whistle pierces the chill night air as the train, virtually empty in most compartments, winds its way northward along part of the 32,072 kilometers of German rail track.

Behind is the university town of Heidelberg, where students plot the overthrow of a dozen nations. Maybe that is what's going on here now. In code.

"Who've we got?" says the murderer to the prince apparent.

"Grumpy."

"Check."

"Sneezy."

"Check."

"Happy."

"Check on Happy."

"And we've got Dopey and Doc."

"Check and check," says the short fellow in the trench coat who is probably not a spy at all, but the escaping missile scientist from Tashkent.

Silence. We look at one another. Sigh. Not a murderer in the lot, not even a slightly mysterious stranger. Just four very tired American reporters who have been walking through most of West Germany. Now it is the end of a long, long day, and we are heading back to Frankfurt am Main.

Our minds are a morass of medieval manors and modern miscellany. And, amidst all these Old World treasures, with the Alps to the south and the Rhine to the west, with Aldo Moro shot dead, with NATO dissolving, the Warsaw Pact maneuvering, with Brezhnev dying, Carter vacillating, tensions rising and the dollar plunging, we are trying to remember the Seven Dwarfs. Look, we're beat, and even Jesus went to wedding parties.

"Dumpy."

"There was no Dumpy. It was Raunchy."

We are not making any progress. I had led off in a fit of confidence, having earlier known that Charles Darwin and Abraham Lincoln were both born in the same year (1809). Then a minor setback when I missed the third baseman in Tinkers to Evans to Chance (look it up).

But the dwarfs? No sweat. Within seconds, as the train ripped through the German night to the shrill toot of a whistle no doubt to hide the three shots fired into the Ninth Duke of Argyll by his lover's lover, I ticked off five dwarfs.

That was all. Then the sixth, Sleepy, made his appearance just as the border guards closed in on the diamond smuggler from Port Said.

"Filthy," offers a photographer.

"There is no dwarf named Filthy," replies the reporter from Washington. Reporters from Washington know everything.

"Grungy."

"No."

"Blitzen?"

A man comes down the aisle. He is disguised as a porter selling beer, but a mere child can spot Rudolph Hess behind that putty nose, making his getaway to Argentina.

"We are missing the seventh dwarf."

Silence. The Gestapo closes in on the Jewish refugee with the false papers showing he is Pope Pius on spring break.

"I can see him now. Short fellow. Fat nose," says a short newsman with a fat nose. "Turkey."

"Turkey was not one of the dwarfs," I say. "It was Lucky."

Silence, as the last train from Heidelberg rips through the German night, carrying the code breaker to Oslo and the bearer of a last-minute proposal to the U.N. Security Council which may prevent World War III.

"Who do we have so far?"

I check my note pad. "Grumpy, Sneezy, Happy, Dopey, Sleepy and Doc."

Silence, broken only by the dull thud of the lead pipe smashing the skull of the sultan's bodyguard.

"I think NATO wouldn't last three days."

"Switzerland just bought Italy."

"The Red Brigades wear army boots."

The train is due into Frankfurt at 10:55. It arrived in Heidelberg promptly at 9:55, on schedule, and left three minutes later. Again, on schedule. "Bashful."

Silence.

"Bashful?" quizzes a reporter. "Was there a dwarf named Bashful?" Everyone nods affirmatively. It is settled. The western democracies are safe for another day. The train from Heidelberg pulls into Frankfurt am Main at 10:55.

Love for Jessie

It is rather unusual today, but it wasn't then. It was commonplace to be raised by a black mammy. Mine was Jessie, a huge woman who loved baseball, fried chicken, chitlins, hot summer afternoons, iced tea, neighborhood gossip and a swarm of white kids running in and out of the house like Chinese bandits.

She did not like cold weather, small footprints across her freshly mopped floors, ostentation, idle-talk during the bottom of the ninth, recipes ("Just some of this and a pinch of that") and outsiders who had the audacity to scold any of her charges.

Jessie ran a tight ship. Her mere size was weaponry enough to support any edict, and the family small fry knew who was the captain of our happy home.

She was never referred to as "the maid" or "the cook" or "servant." No, she was simply Jessie, which encompassed all things, answered every need, laid down every law, handled every problem before it became a problem.

All of which left my mother free to do the things mothers do today, only without a Jessie to hold down the home front. Thus, when my parents hopped off to a party, or for two weeks in Mexico, there was never any haggling about baby sitters and all that. There was Jessie, who would have tossed any interloping baby sitter out on her lilywhite ear.

She was the major-domo, the top sergeant, the family forager who pushed the shopping cart down the aisles loudly complaining about the skyrocketing price of meat. And Lord help the butcher who tried to tip the scales.

Here she comes, barreling along, squeezing lettuce and thumping watermelons, with a gaggle of us wee ones following in her wake, bouncing in every direction like a handful of B-Bs dropped on the floor.

We-want-this, we-want-that, we-want-some-of-these. "Child," she would say with the serenity of a Princess Grace, "shut yo' mouth!" This command would enforce silence for maybe an aisle and a half, then it was we-want-this, we-want-that once more. We knew way down deep Jessie was a marshmallow.

The only time she really got angry was over a blatant case of unauthorized pie slicing. She could make the dreamiest pies—chocolate, lemon, apple—cooked from the flour up. Pie mix? Are you mad? Mixes are unhealthy, probably a Communist plot (she was a super-American) and in any event contained absolutely no nutrition. We would all come down with scurvy by nightfall. So she would cook these beautiful pies. The smell would rouse us from our Tinker Toys and force us to hang around the kitchen. Just in case.

Also. Her pies were to be seen but not eaten. They were too pretty to cut. Do not touch. Sometimes hours would drag by before she would reluctantly agree to the surgery. But one day, after she had labored for hours in the August heat on a perfectly fantastic lemon pie, she left the kitchen for an instant.

Shortly thereafter, a howl was heard throughout the hemisphere. Someone had sliced and eaten a wedge of her pie. Seconds later, my older brother came flying by with Jessie hot on his heels. Luckily, he escaped and lived to tell about it, but for a few frightening moments it appeared there would be one less for dinner.

As she lived behind us—you would not call it the servants' quarters, not if you wished to be welcomed in our house—she voted each election at the elementary school right down the block, the only non-Caucasian in the precinct.

Jessie never discussed how she voted, but she never missed an election. And long before anyone ever heard of civil rights and sit-ins, she was there in the voting booth, switching those switches and pulling those levers and no one, no one at all, ever dared give it a second glance.

Years later, after the brood had grown up and left home, Jessie got sick and died. My shirt-ironer and nose-wiper, my backyard Plato who taught me about double-plays, flowers and shoe laces along with the difference between right and wrong and why it made a difference, got sick and died.

Perhaps, as usual, Jessie was right—it was a good time to go. She left before the professionals came forth to patiently explain to all of us that we really didn't get along, we only thought we did. She left before anyone thought it odd that she would want to vote, and that I would think it odd that they thought it odd.

She picked up her large sweaty iced tea glass and departed before learned social scientists got rich writing books explaining that she was a miserably put-upon handkerchief head and I was an arrogant racist with a masochistic complex. To see us coming down the grocery store aisle, I would swear it looked just the opposite.

Those days, such a short time ago, are gone and will never return. They have been lost and destroyed, through a simple combination of unrelenting time and overt national effort.

Now, no one in his right mind would consider sitting in the back of the bus as part of the good old days. Denying anyone basic human rights and responsibilities is Neanderthal, to be sure. But not all movement is progress, for our children and their children will probably never know and love a member of any other race but their own, and all of us will be the poorer for it.

Times have changed and we must change with them. Mammies are out. But I loved Jessie and she loved me, and no one can ever change that.

Yankees: You're on war-torn turf

It comes as a slight shock to newcomers from the North that The War is still being fought around here. Or at least they think it is. This is easy enough to understand because The War—the Civil War or the War Between the States or, as my grandmother called it, the War for Southern Independence—is mostly forgotten up there. The North won. It did not suffer as much, and a few years after Appomattox there were few signs in the North that there had ever been a conflict. But in the South, The War and the terrible aftermath stayed on. It stayed on in a proud and bitter people who never quit believing that they were right. They fought for their rights and they fought an invader.

Afterward, there were federal pensions for the victors, partially paid by taxing the vanquished, but there were no U.S. pensions for the losers. The devastated Confederate states had to scrape together their own small pensions for their maimed veterans and penniless widows. That was hard to accomplish. All of that plus Reconstruction didn't do a lot for the Southern standard of living or state of mind. To this day, we tend to grow bitter about it, and—we like to feel—with justification.

None of this took place in the North, so it is that Northerners coming down here are a bit shocked to see the Stars and Bars, to hear *Dixie*, to see parks and streets and high schools named for Lee and Davis, Johnston and Jackson. And, even more so, to feel that down here, although The War was lost, it's not yet over.

Perhaps a bit of background will help them understand. By a vote of 168 to 8, the Texas Secession Convention approved the pullout. That was ratified by the voters, 46,129 to 14,697. Eventually many of those who were initially opposed to secession backed the rebellion. Some Unionists, such as Sam Houston, suggested that Texas simply return to being a republic.

More than 60,000 Texans joined the army and a good many of them never came home. When you visit the Texas Capitol grounds, you might see a man on horseback, a monument to Terry's Texas Rangers. Two-thirds of them were killed in the war. Gen. Albert Sydney Johnston, former adjutant general of the Republic of Texas Army, was killed in a peach orchard at Shiloh along with a goodly chunk of the Texas Infantry. An observer noted that after the battle you could walk clear across the orchard and your feet would never touch the ground. Newcomers don't know that, but we do.

Others came to Texas from the South after the war, nursing their wounds. Some left part of their lives back there, and today if you pass by Winchester, Va., under the trees of Stonewall Cemetery you will see a large crypt sporting crossed Confederate sabers and the words: "The Brothers Ashby." These are not things an outsider should be expected to know, but don't ask us to forget them.

Texas was lucky, in a way. It suffered, but less than other states. Galveston was captured, but it wasn't sacked and burned. Houston was occupied, but it wasn't leveled. Actually, during the war we gained a real estate development: Where the University of Houston Downtown College stands today was the site of a Yankee POW camp. I don't think the tour guides point it out, but it did happen here.

You aren't going to get into a bar fight over the fact that Texas Confederates captured Santa Fe and Albuquerque and claimed Tucson, because gray ghosts do not hover over our society the way they do in some parts of the South where the cost was much greater. In fact, The War really isn't talked about a lot in Texas, certainly not the way it is in, say, Virginia and Georgia. It's no big deal around here, not the way the Alamo and the Oilers are. But don't ridicule it. Don't laugh too much when we mark Jefferson Davis' birthday or scrub up Dick Dowling's statue on St. Patrick's Day. It's part of our history and heritage, just like longnecks and lariats, because one of the stars in the bars was the Lone Star and we paid dearly to join the club.

So to our newcomers from the North we can say only that we don't ask you to like it, or even to understand it. But stop going around continually expressing amazement that it exists. It does. You are in what was for several years the Confederate States of America, and if our forefathers had their way, you'd need a passport to get here. Love it or hate it, that's up to you. But just remember that you're on our turf now.

Night-lights

THE BEDROOM — Study any wall covered with graffiti and somewhere among the "Girl Scouts also wear Green Berets" and "Be Alert — This Country Needs More Lerts," you will find "John Wayne Sleeps With a Night-light."

This somehow is supposed to show that the Duke was really a cowardly, timid soul who was afraid of the dark. Well, let me tell you one very simple fact of life. Anyone who *doesn't* sleep with a night-light on is a dummy. A fool. Or at least foolhardy. When things that go bump in the night turn out to be your nose on the unbending closet door, you'll wish you had a night-light blazing in the background.

For the proper night-light is a necessary item in any 20th century home. Without it, you break faces, stumble over coffee tables, shout obscenities into the swallowing darkness, bend limbs, twist ankles, and refuse to let sleeping dogs lie, which, suddenly awakened, sink deep fangs into the intruder's kneecap. No, a night-light is no sign of cowardice or nervous Nellies. It is the sign of a thoughtful and forward-looking householder who cares for both his family and his furniture.

I have carefully investigated various night-lights on the market and, as your shopper's guide to the best and the brightest, I will now impart my vast knowledge. First you should know that night-lights fall into two basic categories:

1) Those which work.
2) Those which don't.

After due study, I have determined that those which work are preferable. They show the way to the aspirin and Kleenex and soften the blows of bedposts. This brings us to the next breakdown. Of those which work, we have three kinds:

1) Those which are too bright.
2) Those which are too dim.
3) Those which are just right.

Again, I suggest that you choose a night-light which is just right for you. Some people require a bright spotlight which flashes brilliantly across the room. They shield their eyes from its stabbing arc, and savor the pain of dilating pupils. They are sick. Some people require only a slight glow on the horizon, just a candle flickering in the background, more a mental reassurance that all is right, rather than a pathfinder to the john at 4 a.m.

If you are a trend setter, you can get those which automatically go on and off at various times to show burglars lurking in the aspidistra that there are humans—locked and loaded—in this house and that the slightest stir at the door will produce gunfire equal to that of a Houston police officer arresting a curbside flower vendor.

Careful investigation into this matter has left me with but one choice, which I shall now pass on to you, and which—if you've a dash of gray matter—will be burned indelibly on your mind when you go to make your own purchase: Of all on the market, I have found that the best of the lot is the Donald Duck night-light. It is the one above all others and the one which I have chosen to guide me personally through the minefield in my bedroom.

Yes, Donald Duck. He is perfect for the occasion. His little blue hat on top is dark enough to prevent a loud and raucous light from blinding me as I attempt to quelch a ghastly thirst at dawn, the result of a previous debate with two old friends, Haig & Haig. Donald's face glows with a reassuring softness which is just right, not too bright, not too dull. His dark, red base, like the hat on top, hides the unwanted candlepower from my glassy stare. Other night-lights could have done the same, they could have used a sailor suit similar to that on Donald Duck, but they did not. No, when the true test of science came, they turned tail and retreated to the more secure realms of elves, happy faces and Snoopies. But I ask you, is this how the West was won? Certainly not. We must forge forward into the virgin fields of knowledge.

Some, of course, disdain any kind of night-light. They lean more toward the bedside reading lamp. They feel that a night-light is totally unnecessary because, when they get out of bed in the dark, they just reach over and click on the waiting lamp. It sounds simple enough, until, in the blackness, you reach out toward the lamp, knocking over half-filled beer cans, bottles of pills, digital clocks, small radios, large vases and a stack of *TV Guides*. Dogs bark, babies howl and your wife says, "What's wrong?" in that voice which tells you:

1) She knows exactly what's wrong.

2) She is rubbing it in by letting you know that you have awakened her yet another time because you refuse to buy a night-light.

3) When you have cleaned up the mess you have just made, don't come across the king-size bed humming sweet things and nudging elbows, because she'll pretend she's asleep.

After in-depth research, I think I can safely state that bedside lamps have their place, but they are not beside the bed, nor are they to be used as ersatz night-lights. That, however, does not mean that among night stalkers there is unanimity as to what kind of night-light is best. I must tell you straightaway that not everyone agrees with my Donald Duck theory. For instance, I have it on good authority that John Wayne preferred a Davy Crockett night-light, although at his condominium in Acapulco he had a Cantinflas night-light that said "Viva!" across the bottom.

Rumor has it that Larry Flynt of *Hustler* magazine has a night-light which I won't even bother to describe. Henry Kissinger made one out of his Nobel Peace Prize. Idi Amin made one out of a former cabinet minister. And the Food and Drug Administration doesn't even use night-lights as they might cause cancer. Still, after all is said and done, Donald Duck is unquestionably the best, and if you take my advice, you'll get one at first light.

Crime invisible on Main St. beat

MAIN STREET—"Hi," says a seedy looking fellow, approaching me. "Got a light?"

"Yeah," say I, flicking my Bic.

"Thanks. Oh, by the way . . ."

"Yes?"

"Stick 'em up."

"You're going to rob me?"

"No," he says. "I'm going to discuss the overall implications of AT&T's court case involving diversification in light of the Roosevelt-esque approach to trusts."

"Then gimme back my watch."

"Hold it right there!" says a somewhat familiar voice. "One move, alleged perpetrator, and it's Slab City."

Running up to us is a puffing, red-cheeked fellow swathed in a scarf, hat, earmuffs, gloves, overcoat and snow boots. Pinned to his coat is a badge. "Good grief, it's Officer Bovine!" I shout. "Thank goodness you're here."

"Get those hands up," Bovine says to me.

"No, wait. *I'm* the one getting robbed."

"A likely story. You're the one holding the wallet, right? You have the right to remain silent, the right to hire a lawyer of your choice provided you can afford one, which is unlikely if you're innocent. You have the right to sue me for false arrest, to bite, kick and curse me, and gripe about rampant crime in the streets. So help you God."

"Officer Bovine, I was just handing this guy my wallet because he was robbing me. He's got the gun. Look."

"You got witnesses? How do I know he hadn't just wrestled it away from you? I'll bet it isn't even registered to him. Do you have tape or video recording of this alleged stickup?"

"Of course not."

"Then buzz off, J.J."

The gunman wanders down the street, looking for a light.

"What is this 'J.J.'? You *know* him?"

"Sure. I never forget a Saturday night special. That's J.J. Jay. Twenty-one convictions, 12 acquittals when he promised not to do it again and two thrown out for insufficient evidence when all the witnesses were shotgunned in the courthouse lobby."

"Then why is he walking the streets?"

"Can't steal a car, I guess."

"Say, Bovine, what are you doing walking here on Main Street? You live in your patrol car, even get to take it home to Waco every afternoon."

"I am the new Main Street patrol. We're walking beats again to make the city safe for the Guardian Angels."

"Does that make you the Arch Angels?"

"More like Sole Brothers."

"Well, I think it's a good idea, Officer Bovine."

"That's because you don't have to do it. This is not fun, on the coldest day since the Ice Age, walking my beat. The only people not in ski masks are the bank robbers. It's not only freezing, but hard on the feet. And what's more, it's not safe. You know there's a lot of crime on Houston's streets."

"What blocks are you patrolling?"

"Just downtown Houston, plus the Medical Center and Sharpstown."

"What? You mean you alone have all that area, just you? I read the other day that we have the seventh largest police department in the nation. Where are all your colleagues?"

"Most of them work in the Recruiting Division and are in Hawaii right now signing up more cadets. You know we're awfully shorthanded. And the others are guarding trees in Memorial Park."

"How is the foot patrol working out?"

"OK, except that all the criminals are in cars. Makes high-speed chases sort of one-sided."

"How about using horses?"

"I had one when I started this morning. Somebody stole it."

"Yeah, this is a pretty tough part of town."

"You're telling me? Around here, they strip down cars that are still moving. A portable TV is your set on the way to a pawnshop."

"Yeah, I saw a sign down the street, 'Good neighbors make good fences.' "

"And when you want to buy nylon hose, the clerk asks your head size."

"How is your own job going today, Bovine?"

"Not worth a darn. We keep hearing and reading about all the crime on Main Street, but I haven't seen any since I started walking the beat. Just shows you can't believe the press."

"Maybe. But it might show that so long as you're out here on the job, in sight, you are the second greatest deterrent to crime there is."

"Second? Who's first?"

"An outraged public which will demand less legal smokescreens and more swift justice."

"Fat chance," says Bovine, walking off. "See you later."

"Right."

"Hey," says a voice. "Got a light?"

Getting with it

THE CHURCH—Everyone else all around me is sitting. Properly, pensively, quietly listening to the music. Everyone except for a few who are looking at me.

The reason they are looking at me is that I am standing. Right up here on the second row—I always end up on the second row by some universal design. I am standing here for one very simple reason: I don't know what I'm doing, and the reason is that I am a Southern Presbyterian and this is a Roman Catholic church.

Catholics stand and sit and occasionally kneel. They have been doing it this way for some 2,000 years and by now have it down pat. We Presbyterians, on the other hand, are not so athletic. We tend to sit until the pain is such that we stand and sing. We have been in this business only about 400 years so there are still some theological, as well as muscular, kinks to work out.

In any event, here I stand, trying to figure out some inconspicuous way to sit down without causing more grief to my wife and three small children. You see, they are all Catholics. Ours is an ecumenical family and we get along splendidly except when Father makes an idiot of himself by standing when everyone else falls on his knees.

This is one of the few problems that has not worked itself out. For instance there was the Sunday morning in Edinburgh, Scotland, when we went looking for a Catholic church. Have you ever tried to attend mass in Edinburgh? John Knox didn't brook much opposition. I felt both cocky and defensive at the same time. Until the next Sunday. We were in Rome. Have you ever tried to find a Presbyterian church in Rome? These days the only confusion around our happy home is when the half-breeds can't figure out why the old man won't get with the program. "You do it like this," one patiently explained recently at the dinner table, slowly making the sign of the cross.

"I know how to do it, Offspring. It's just that I don't do it."

"Why not?"

"Because of an old injury."

"Who did it to you?"

"Martin Luther."

Outside of standing when everyone else is sitting and vice versa, there are a few other tithes that bind, but they are usually surmountable if I keep off my toes. For instance, Catholics seem to end the Lord's Prayer a few beats before I do. I just continue to mumble "for ever and ever, Amen" and no one seems to mind.

Then there are the songs. It seems to me that Presbyterians used to sing a lot more than Catholics, but today it's about even. Some songs are the same, but the Catholics are going in for folk masses now with young people playing guitars. It might shake John Knox up a bit, but I like it. And I can dig right in to "Amen." (Remember Sidney Poitier singing it in "Lilies of the Field"?)

I miss "The Old Rugged Cross" and "Shall We Gather By the River" although I think those are Baptist songs, anyway. Now that I mention it, the Mormons sing better than anyone. Must have something to do with that dry salt air out on the desert.

Over the past few years, things have changed so drastically that it seems the Catholics have surpassed the Protestants in keeping attuned to the times. Some Sundays I follow my little flock into Pew 2 in some ultra-modern church where they are singing "We Shall Overcome" and I don't know if I'm attending a mass or a protest rally.

As I said, things are going along quite smoothly, and should continue that way if we don't invite Ian Paisley to dinner. Besides, I refuse to get wrought up about it all since I fail to believe there are zoning laws in heaven. My only current complaint is that Catholics still try to make Christmas some kind of religious celebration. They just won't get with the program.

Discipline down

THE CHECK-OUT LINE—This is an odd place for deep thoughts, but I have suddenly been hit with a couple of disturbing events and am pondering the reason why.

Coming to the grocery store, I drove by the entrance which is marked, "No Parking, Fire Zone." So I drove on and parked right down the way. Walking to the front door of the store, I noticed a woman—middle-aged, well-dressed, driving a new Buick—zoom up and park in the empty fire zone spot.

OK, so I do my meager shopping—a six-pack and cigars—and head for the express line, which is plainly marked, "Eight Items or Less." And here in line is another woman, also middle-aged, well-dressed, and so on. She is checking out 14 separate items.

These two events, so close and so minor in themselves, lead me to wonder what is happening to us, when rules are for other people. You know what it is? We have lost our discipline.

Not all our discipline, but our social discipline, and that may prove to be the most important of all. Now, when you bring forth the subject, you are immediately attacked. All together now: "Discipline? The Nazis had discipline. Is that the kind of country you want to live in?"

To which I reply: "If you can't tell the difference in social discipline and blind obedience, butt out of this discussion, because we don't have time for you. This is heavy stuff."

There, now where were we? Oh, yes, social discipline. It is easy, and usual, to begin any discussion about rules and laws by noting that the lower income classes are responsible for X amount of the crime and welfare and so forth due to a lack of social discipline, and indeed, they are, like it or not. The facts are there and are inarguable by the most bleeding of bleeding hearts. So what else is new?

This is what: "Gulf Oil Admits It Paid $4.2 Million to Officials Abroad to Shield Assets." Then there is United Brands Co., which admitted it paid $1.25 million in bribes to a Honduran official. Northrop Corp. paid or committed $30 million in suspicious commissions. The SEC has sued Gulf, Northrop, Phillips Petroleum Co. and Minnesota Mining & Manufacturing Co. for giving money to CREEP and then hiding it in their books. And Braniff, don't forget Braniff.

So before we all start banging away at the easy and most downtrodden of our targets, let us look at the other end of the income spectrum. The biggies, the wealthy and powerful who should know better, have cheated and lied and stolen in ways never dreamt of by the busiest liquor store bandit.

No, there is absolutely no way that Big Business or the country club set can cast the first stone. No way whatsoever. Or government, which gives us Haldeman, Ehrlichman, Nixon, Gray, Mutscher, Agnew—shall I go on?

We have come to the point where the police are testifying behind closed doors about breaking the law. When the best paid lawyers are those who can beat the law, not uphold it. When our school teachers spend more time on the picket lines than in the classroom, then are eligible for unemployment compensation in the summer.

Without a doubt, we have lost our social discipline. Not everyone, of course, but enough of us to tip the scales so that it is now an acceptable way of life. It's even chic. Who goes over 55? Who allows their children to ride motorbikes on public streets, unlicensed and illegal? Who pads their expense accounts? Who tells the girl in the theater box office that Junior is just big for an 11-year-old? Right. A majority.

So now it is acceptable. It became official during Watergate, when the hard-pressed Nixon apologists explained: "They all did it." A mention of Nixon's income taxes was answered by Johnson's TV station. Spiro Agnew equalled Bobby Baker. Breaking and entering equalled search and destroy. They all did it and that makes it OK.

When was the last time you heard a child say "Yes, Ma'am" or "No, Sir"? True, it might not change western civilization; then again, it might. It certainly might. Because social discipline is simply a reflection of our thinking. Tossing a beer can out the window, fixing an election or waging a war are not differences in degree, only in opportunity.

All right, maybe I'm making too much out of all of this. Then again, some day centuries hence, historians may well record the decline and fall of the American Empire as the day an educated, well-groomed, intelligent, upper-middle-class woman consciously weighed right and wrong, then parked in a fire zone. Don't laugh.

Vanishing act

THE CLOSET—There is something very, very strange going on. Just why, eludes me. Perhaps it is part of a larger plan for taking over the Western World. Then again, maybe it's only someone out there who is trying to drive me bonkers. There is even the slight possibility that I'm becoming a raging paranoiac. No, that's not true, because I don't think they're out to get me, I *know* it.

The problem has to do with shirts. Don't snicker. Small items have a way of ballooning. Remember the War of Jenkins' Ear. And Watergate. In a nutshell, someone is stealing my shirts. No, I'm not imagining things. By actual count, my shirts are disappearing. What's more, I can tell you which ones and where. But not why. That's the mysterious part. All I know is that there is a highly organized international plot to steal my used shirts.

The story begins in Chile four years ago. I was staying at the Carrera Hotel in Santiago and discovered one day that two of my dress shirts had simply vanished. I had not worn them, they didn't disappear in the laundry, they just vanished. Why would anyone want two dress shirts with rather frayed collars? It made no sense, but I'd read enough Agatha Christie and seen enough Alfred Hitchcock to know Something Is Afoot. It also worried me because shirts are rather expensive to replace, and I didn't feel right about putting them on my expense account.

OK, there the story rested and over the years I'd pretty well forgotten about it. Then, last fall I went to the Middle East. In Saudi Arabia I checked into the Marriott in Daharan.

One evening after a hard day in the desert, I came back to my hotel room to see my laundry neatly placed on my bed. But the shirt wasn't my shirt. I rang up the laundry room and explained my problem to the Pakistani in charge. He came up and tried to convince me it really was my shirt, since the markings were for my room. But my name was not von Halstonberg or something like that and I didn't weigh 260. A few hours later, the laundry room manager came back with two more shirts. Neither was mine.

"Then it was mistakenly sent to either of these two men," he said. He showed me laundry receipts for two guests at the hotel. One name was something like Tanaka Tushetoto and the other was James Smith or close to it.

"OK," I said, getting more and more suspicious of the situation, "take these shirts to their rooms and see if they have my shirt."

That seemed to make sense, and he disappeared. Thirty minutes later, a knock on my door. All right, I am thinking, let's solve the shirt problem so that I can fix my attention to lesser important matters like the oil crisis.

"Sorry," says the Pakistani, "but both Mr. Tushetoto and Mr. Smith have abruptly checked out."

The hotel knocks $15 off my bill to cover the cost of one slightly used shirt, and some day I'll remember to put it on my expense account, but that's not the problem. The main one is: Who are Tanaka Tushetoto and James Smith, if those are really their names, and why did they steal my shirt? It was thoroughly broken in, and wearing it would hardly make them the *chic* of Araby.

Now it is January, and I am, of all places, back at the Carrera Hotel in Santiago. I sit for hours in the lobby, hiding behind last week's *Manchester Guardian*. As I suspected, the place is full of both Orientals and Occidentals. I page them by name, watching closely as the bellboy wanders through the bars and lobby ringing his little bell and holding up a sign on which is chalked the names: Tushetoto and Smith. No one steps forward. Perhaps, indeed, I have made this whole thing up. It's getting to me. Each morning at the hotel I wake up and count my shirts, which are getting a bit wrinkled between the mattress and the springs. They are all there. I scan the hotel register for clues, even keeping an eye out for a Pakistani laundry manager. Nothing.

I go down to the Straits of Magellan for a few days, then return to Santiago and the Carrera. I am trying to put the entire matter out of my mind, and eventually I do. Nothing more happens in the Case of the Shirt Off My Back. Nothing, that is, until I get home to discover *I am missing a yellow dress shirt. It disappeared while I was gone.* Yes, that's it! The gang didn't strike when and where I suspected—while on the trip—but lured me away so they could sneak into my closet at home and steal my yellow shirt. Of course! How could I have been thrown off such an obvious track!

So here the situation stands. Needless to say, no one in the neighborhood recalls seeing an Oriental-Occidental burglary team cracking my house. They're too smart for that. Yet they came here, all right, and ripped off my yellow shirt. But why? And, of equal importance, how can I put all this on my expense account? "Two shirts missing, Santiago, 1976, $40. One shirt lost, Saudi Arabia, November, $15. One shirt missing from home, January, $20." Mrs. Hobby is not in business to pick up my missing shirt bill.

And who would believe that I am the center of an international, diabolical shirt-stealing plot? That someone is out to get me, that Something Is Afoot? That's why I'm here in the closet with a nine-iron and your disguise doesn't fool me for a minute. You so much as touch a sleeve of my dwindling shirt supply and I'll chip you into eternity, Mr. Tanaka Tushetoto.

What you see . . .

And it came to pass that the angel of the Lord came down and announced: "Fear not, for I bring you good tidings of great joy, which shall be to all people."

The multitudes surged to and fro, across street and sidewalk, pushing and shoving and cursing. They were buried under brightly wrapped packages of gifts, turkeys, bottles, plastic boxes containing Baby-Bobbie who can walk and talk and has 43 drip-dry outfits. They carried obscene Christmas cards and Marshall Dillon fast-draw revolvers. They carried model tanks and bazookas and G.I. Joe Killer Kits.

And the angel of the Lord announced again: "Fear not, for I bring you good tidings of great joy, which shall be to all people."

The multitudes pushed ever forward, walking on the DON'T WALK, double-parking, driving over 55, skidding on ice-covered roads and crashing into one another. They piled into bus, train and plane terminals, lying about their children's ages so they could get on half fare. The airlines, ever alert for no-shows, overbooked and left half the customers sleeping all night at Love Field.

And the angel of the Lord fled the cities with their bright lights and Baby-Bobbies and went into the fields where the shepherds kept watch over their flock by night.

"Fear not," the angel said, "for I bring you good tidings of great joy, which shall be to all people." But the shepherds were too busy plotting how to hold their sheep off the markets to inflate prices and get bigger government subsidies for not raising sheep. They paid no heed to the angel of the Lord.

Next the angel went to the highways and byways of the nation to alert the faithful travelers to the glorious news. "Fear not," he said, "for I bring . . ." but his message was drowned out by the sound of truckers abandoning their rigs in the middle of the road so traffic could back up for 14 miles and thus generate sympathy for the truckers' plight over the rising cost of diesel fuel.

Thus it came to pass that the angel of the Lord went on television to announce his glorious news: "Behold, for unto you is born this day in the city of David a Saviour, which is Christ the Lord." But the multitudes quickly changed channels, for it was fourth and goal.

Then the angel of the Lord went even unto the City of David itself to announce the news. "Fear not," he said, "for I bring you . . ." A SAM missile flew past, followed by an artillery duel that shook the desert sands from Egypt unto Syria. A tank battle and a bayonet charge drowned out the part about, "and on earth peace, good will toward men."

The angel of the Lord tried again in the city where he had begun. And lo, the multitudes frantically marched on the counters in an effort to finish their shopping during their lunch hours so they wouldn't be late for the Christmas office party.

"And this shall be a sign unto you," he shouted above the shopping mall stereo playing "Here Comes Santa Claus." "Ye shall find the babe wrapped in swaddling clothes, lying in a manger."

Suddenly, as if by magic, the multitudes stopped their petty pursuits and surged toward the angel of the Lord. And he rejoiced, until he discovered he was standing beside the last hand calculator on sale in the store. He was lucky to escape unharmed, and at that time he decided to stop saying "Fear not," for it was obvious that the multitudes were afraid of nothing, except, possibly, running out of hand calculators.

The angel of the Lord watched silently as bands played and balloons swirled upwards and the multitudes gathered to watch a fat man in a red suit arrive by helicopter. Finally, he surveyed the land as ITT reported record earnings and filling stations closed. He listened as Gallup reported that no one trusted anyone anymore, least of all their leaders. And the leaders replied that they didn't trust Gallup.

Then the angel of the Lord quietly left, saying to himself, "What you see is what you get."

Sea's sickness

THE NORTH SEA — Thor Heyerdahl is probably the only person to achieve fame by proving that he wasn't original.

He first captured the world's attention in 1947 when he sailed his small raft, Kon Tiki, across 4,300 miles of the South Pacific in 101 days, thus proving that ancient man could have immigrated to Polynesia from South America.

In 1969, he tried to show that South America could have been settled by raft-riding pioneers from North Africa. His craft, a papyrus boat christened Ra I, went from Sofi in Morocco to a waterlogged grave 3,000 miles and 58 days away, near the West Indies. But profiting from that failure, the next year Heyerdahl and his crew — including a monkey and a duck — tried once more, this time in a different sort of papyrus boat, named Ra II.

After 3,200 miles covered in 57 days, the Ra II arrived in the West Indies. Thor Heyerdahl had once again proved his point.

He was lionized and listened to, feated and feted, wined and dined.

"The Modern Viking," journalists liked to call him, likening his Nordic looks and oceanic adventures to those of his Norwegian ancestors.

Without question, everyone likes to hear Thor Heyerdahl tell of his daring projects, yet as he sits here sunning on the deck of the ocean liner, Royal Viking — a far cry from his previous crafts — he is a bit perturbed because no one wants to hear much about a far greater danger than stormy seas and low supplies. He calls it "the invisible enemy" — the rapid pollution of our oceans.

"For 43 of the 57 days we were at sea on Ra II," he explains, "we spotted floating chunks of crude oil. From the size of rice to that of a potato. It also varied in color. The fresh samples looked like tar, the older were browner in color and had barnacles on them. Now, it takes a great many months for barnacles to form, so obviously these bits of pollution had been around for some time.

"We turned our samples over to United Nations experts and they said the oil had come from different geographical sources. In other words, everyone is polluting our seas. You can take it for granted that the oil came from tankers which were cleaning out their tanks at sea. Many ports won't let them even enter with dirty tanks, so they have to be flushed out.

"The tank owners tell me they are sorry, so do the oilmen, but they all say that it costs too much to do it any other way. So, it really boils down to the consumer. Everyone who drives a car must eventually decide whether he wants to pay a little more for his oil and gas so we can save this earth. You can't just blame the oil industry or the tankers.

"I have asked the UN to help because this is not just a national problem—it is an international one. We must build new tankers with special equipment and storage tanks to hold their oil refuse, and ports must have ways to receive and use this refuse.

"The problem is getting rapidly worse. On Kon Tiki in 1947 I kept a lookout for pollution but found none. In 23 years we have done this. I live in Italy now, studying the flora and fauna of the Mediterranean. On the coast you can see where the oil has covered the cliffs—patches of oil, lumps of it, from gray to black, killing all marine life there. But coastal cliffs are essential in the life cycle for most marine life. If we kill it, we eventually kill ourselves.

"Modern man understands the moon better than he does his own planet, at least in some ways. The ocean is much, much smaller than we think. It is a lake, bounded on all sides by land. The ocean has no outlet but evaporation, and that takes only clean water. All our pollutants—even in the air—eventually return to the sea. They are washed into streams, then into rivers and then into the ocean. It is the final sink of everything.

"If you take an average global map of the world—one you can hold in your hands—do you know how deep the ocean would be in relation? Not as deep as one coat of paint. We like to think that it is bottomless, inexhaustible, but it isn't." Thor Heyerdahl ponders his pet problem for a moment. "A dead ocean," he recently wrote, "equals a dead planet."

"Plastics and things of that nature are basically ascetic pollutants," he continues. "And even oil pollution, as bad as it is, is still not the worst. The worst are those chemicals we can't even see. DDT, for instance, is now showing up in the arctic. Insecticides are made simply to kill—that's why they exist—and they can't differentiate between what they are supposed to kill and what they aren't. So they kill everything.

"The UN pollution conference in Stockholm didn't really accomplish a lot, but it did focus world attention on the problem.

"I am really, basically, a planner and organizer, and let me tell you that modern civilization is the worst planned thing there is. We spend so much for armaments, to protect us from enemies we can see, but we are spending practically nothing to fight this invisible enemy.

"I used to be a biologist, then an anthropologist, now I guess that I am a writer. I try to do what I can about his problem . . . but I just don't know. I'm happy with many of the things that I have done in my life, but I'm not particularly proud of them. There is so much to do. I wouldn't be afraid to go to the moon because I've talked to several astronauts and they are people just like the rest of us, but I think I have enough to do right here on this planet."

Thor Heyerdahl peers out at his ocean from the gently swaying deck of a luxury liner. His invisible enemy is gaining on him and his fellow travelers aboard spaceship earth, but no one is doing anything about it. Everyone would much rather hear about big men and small rafts.

Stiff upper lip

It's about the expression, "Not to worry."

It worries me.

The reason is simple. More and more I hear it being bandied about by people who bandy about these sorts of things, I can see it on the horizon, coming my way. But I don't know if I can handle it. I don't know if it is really *me*.

You can't just pick up an expression which doesn't fit. A truck driver, slicing open his hand on a broken beer bottle, wouldn't slip into, "Well, mercy me." By the same token, a nun who trips would hardly let loose with a profane oath. No, some things just won't do. A mincing drill instructor, a direct politician, a cab driver spouting Sartre. Words must fit.

All right, all right. I shall quickly admit that this is not the burning issue before mankind right now. It probably won't come before the U.N. Security Council for at least another month. There are wars and peace and inflation, all of which require our furrowed brow and clicking of tongues.

But that's exactly the point. All of them, in one fell swoop, would disappear if I could simply wave my hand in nonchalance, and deliver a confident, "Not to worry."

Yet, there are problems with this expression. First of all, "Don't worry" would get upset. It has served me well these many moons. Should I abandon "Don't worry" for some sleek new saying? Is that what friendship is all about? Secondly, "Not to worry" sounds slightly put on. You know, like placing your coat so the Neiman's label shows.

To be blunt about it, the expression smacks of Anglophilia if not Anglomania. Yes, that's it. Too British to sit neatly on the offspring's tongue. Stuffy British:

The minister for the colonies is sitting by the fire at his club, polishing off a last bit of sherry. The general lights a cigar and sighs, "And what about the Sepoys? They seem to be getting a bit upset about the hog lard on the bullets."

The minister waves his hand absently. "Not to worry," he says, thus putting an end to the problem. The fact that, three months later, the general has his pancreas yanked out by an ox team as the Sepoys cheer wildly does not dampen the phrase. It still stands there, tall among the "So's your old man" and "Drop back and punt."

Perhaps that's really the nub of the matter. "Not to worry" has class, and I don't. So I don't feel comfortable using it. Too pseudo-British, that is. Like writing "colour" and "programme." (True, some Houstonians are such Anglophiles that they drive on the left-hand side of the street, but that's another matter entirely.)

No, it's just not my style. On the other hand, I hear people I know well letting drop a "Not to worry" with ease, and their fathers had to social climb to get to the criminal class. I hear "Not to worry" used by people who think Tip O'Neill is a filter cigarette. They have mastered their self-consciousness, why can't I?

Maybe I should try it out on the dry cleaners. The bartender. Work my way up to the fellow who takes all my money for allowing me to pump my own gas. It must become a comfortable part of my vocabulary:

"Ah, I'm doing 80 in a 30, officer? Not to worry." It might work. "You think I'm subtracting from the overall quality of this paper? Not to worry."

Like a new pair of shoes, maybe I could break it in a little at a time. That worked back in college with "I can't believe etc. etc." It was a hard one to master, all right. Sorority girls couldn't get through an entire sentence without it, but I had trouble making the *belieeeeve* string out far enough. I was a junior before it really worked properly.

Then there was "Sock it to me." Frankly, it sounded awfully dirty at first. Yet it was on prime time, and everyone was saying it to everyone else, so about the 14th time I used it I didn't feel guilty.

Not to worry. Not to worry. No, it still sounds as though it should emanate from someone far more important than a mere poet. On the other hand, I shy away from "Don't worry," worthy friend though it has been these years. It seems as though I have outgrown "Don't worry," and need to move on, to improve myself.

Not to worry. Like grand opera or treason, it gets easier every time.
"Daddy, the dog is in the dryer."

"Not to worry."

I'm getting the knack of it now.

Wait a minute. Maybe it's not Not-to-worry at all. Maybe it's Not-*too*-worry. The *too* with two o's. I've only heard it spoken, not written. What if it means that you should not be too worried? Not *too* worry. Who would know for sure?

The best way is to find a person who constantly refers to himself or herself as "one." You know, "One must do the best one can for one's career."

Don't get me wrong. "One" is a perfectly good word. I use it myself. "One must wonder . . ." That sort of one. Every now and again, one is fine. But one who uses it all the time is suspect of phony British pretensions, and that's exactly the type of person who would know how many o's belong in the middle of that expression we were discussing.

So, I shall find a person who uses "one" all the time and ask if it's "Not to worry" or "Not too worry." He'll be easy to spot—wearing a tweedy jacket with those leather patches on the elbows, smoking a pipe, riding a bicycle and pointing out that there's nothing worth watching on television.

I'll find him. Don't worry.

Four-Play News

> *Four-Play News!*
> *Sex and booze!*
> *Don't touch that dial,*
> *Don't blow a fuse.*
> *Not much thought,*
> *Lots of ooze:*
> *Turn off your mind,*
> *With Four-Play Neeeeews!*
> *Hahahaha!*

Hello, out there, videolanders, KAKL-TV, your laugh-a-minute station, presents the man with a smile in his style, a spin in his grin, Denny Den-tures!

Thank you and good evening. Our top story tonight is the result of the latest poll from *TV Guide*, which shows that 27 percent of the viewers said they selected a news show because of the people anchoring the newscast. While only 8 percent said that they chose a newscast because of its weather forecaster. Speaking of which, we'll have the weather tonight with Rainer Shine. What's brewing in the heavens, Rainer?

Denny, frankly, I think that poll is fixed. You don't know the number of people who say they can't stand you. They tune into Four-Play News just for me.

The weather, Rainer. Are we going to have any? Hahaha!

You're a dead-weight anchor, man. I'm not even going to give the weather tonight.

Right, Rainer. Speaking of that *TV Guide* poll, only 3 percent—3 percent, ladies and gentlemen—said they watch the news because of the sports coverage. Which brings us to our own foul ball, superfan Homer Fields. What's in sports tonight, Homer?

Suck pigeon droppings, Denny. Ever since that poll came out you you've been a son. . . .

And, of course, we have our consumer affairs reporter, Connie Cleavage. What's new with the counterculture? Hahahaha.

What's that, Denny? No snide comment about the percentage of viewers who tune in to watch the consumer affairs reporter?

I was going to, Connie, but that category didn't even count enough to count. Hahahaha. Anyway, back to our main story, the *TV Guide* survey, a poll of. . . .

Excuse me, Denny.

Yes, Rainer?

Do you really think that's the lead story? I've got a hurricane. . . .

Who cares?

But Galveston is headed toward Tampico and they can't find Corpus. The National Guard is using snorkels to locate Port Arthur and. . . .

Yeah, Denny. In sports I've got the NFL strike and the baseball playoffs and Moses Malone is suing the U.S. Treasury for non-support while. . . .

Big deal. Back to our top story. *TV Guide*'s poll shows that anchormen with lots of teeth and lots of hair are more important than bald old men who wheeze.

Denny, that's ridiculous. Abraham Lincoln had a high, squeaky voice. And George Washington's teeth rattled and. . . .

Connie, it's not content, it's *packaging*. *TV Guide*'s poll proves conclusively that viewers will believe anything if it's uttered in deep, pear-shaped tones by a male with authority. Like me.

Denny, you're a pompous ass.

That's very important, Homer. Surveys show that viewers have such oatmeal minds that they love a pompous ass. Meantime, on the stock market, it was bananas 33 cents a pound, bacon $2.34 and Kleenex was two for a. . . .

Denny, you boob. You're reading your wife's grocery receipt.

Oh? In other news, this same survey appearing in the October 2 issue reports over half—56 percent—said that they depend on TV as their principal source of news.

Oh, come on, Denny. That's ridiculous. All we can give are headlines.

Shut up, Rainer, or it's back to the assembly line for you. Or was it the evangelistic circuit?

Denny, at which paranoia plantation was this survey done?

It was conducted by a reputable survey outfit. It shows that far more people want the nightly network news held to 30 minutes than expanded to an hour.

I don't doubt that, Denny. Those marble minds out there don't have the attention span God gave a coathanger. Hey, are we still on? I thought a commercial. . . .

Elsewhere in the news, a survey reported in *TV Guide* found that less than one-third of TV viewers surveyed thought there was too much violence on the news, while about one-half said TV showed "only what is necessary." This body being pulled from a well is obviously from the other half. Meantime, a bomb in an orphanage in Akron . . . oooh, just look at that. . . .

Not enough violence, Denny?

That's what the survey found, Connie.

Interesting. Three customers in a meat market today—roll the film, boys—were hacked to death when a. . . .

In the weather, a one-time cloud watcher in St. Cloud, Minn., stepped over the edge of a cliff, and, ugh, that's him down there.

In sports, we have film of two would-be racers in Mexico who slammed their busses into. . . .

Uh, Homer, Rainer, Connie, if I might have the spotlight back, seeing how an overwhelming 27 percent said they selected which news to watch because of the anchorman, I would now like to report on how I spent my vacation. Roll the film.

Denny, if brains were sliced bread, you couldn't make a sandwich.

Hey, Homer, I like that. Did I tell you about my fishing trip?

Why should I care about your fishing trip?

Because half of those surveyed said they enjoyed the banter and wisecracks among local newscasters.

Really? Gee, I should have complimented you on your tie.

Here are some pictures of my kids.

Connie, that dress looks fetching.

Oh, thank you, Rainer. How was the picnic?

Denny, tell us how the sheetrocking is going.

Yeah, and anything else about that survey.

Well, it found that almost 70 percent found no ethnic or racial bias in network news.

They must have asked a bunch of honkies.

Yeah. And Polacks.

And Chinamen and. . . .

> *Four-Play News!*
> *WASPs and Jews.*
> *Blacks and whites and lots of blues!*
> *Ethnic jokes for all you folks.*
> *Gringos choose*
> *Our Four-Play News!*
> *Hahahahaha!*

Accent on Independent

HIGHLAND PARK—There she stood, or rather drooped, behind the steam tables at Armstrong Elementary School, a bejeweled spaghetti server.

She had gone to the Super Bowl the preceding Sunday, then flown in her private jet to Austin for some pre-inaugural parties. Early Tuesday her pilot had flown her back to Highland Park in time to serve the children as they passed.

"Why don't you go home and get some rest?" one of the teachers asked.

"Oh, no," said the jet set waitress. "It's my time to serve the spaghetti." The other dowagers up and down the serving line nodded in agreement.

One does one's duty in Highland Park. It is the proper thing to do, and nothing less is tolerated. For Highland Park, a suburb gift wrapped by Neiman's and set down on the rolling plains of Dallas County, deals only in the basics—duty, money, God, football and the Republican Party.

Dallas is a nice place to visit but you wouldn't want to marry one. River Oaks is nouveau riche and Hyannis Port simply doesn't exist. There is Highland Park and heaven, although occasionally the locals get the two mixed up.

This is not to say they are stuffy or ostentatious. Far from it. Their lifestyle would make a Trappist monk feel right at home. Frills are for those who need them to feel secure.

Take, for instance, their pride-and-joy: The Highland Park Independent School District, with the emphasis on Independent. It seems that

Washington discovered there are no Negroes in the HPISD—which includes neighboring University Park—and threatened to cut off federal funds.

The district explained that no Negroes lived in Highland Park, so it was a bit difficult to integrate. Besides, they did not accept federal funds—creeping socialism, you know.

"That's ridiculous," the reply came back. "Everyone accepts federal aid."

Highland Park finally convinced them otherwise, and added ominously that any further bureaucratic meddling and HP might cut Washington off without a cent.

Still, the district manages to muddle through, eschewing child psychologists and electronic gadgets and such to rely on the three Rs and a handy ruler. No one worries why Jonathan can't read. He CAN read, it is expected of him. The school and town library await him. He has his duty.

In any event, it works. In 1960 the top men at both West Point and Annapolis were Highland Park grads. It was greeted with a few smiles and a "Good show, old shoe" or two, but otherwise not much. After all, they only did their duty.

Then there is their football. Any fall afternoon hundreds of tads can be seen overflowing the school playgrounds getting ready for the Big Time—the Highland Park Highlanders, Class 4A.

Friday night they turn out to sing "Hail to the Fighting Scotties" and cheer mightily. It was good enough for Bobby Layne and Doak Walker, perhaps because Jayne Mansfield played in the band.

Decades ago, when there was no stadium lighting, HP fathers used to park their cars in a row at night, lights on, and let the lads get in a night scrimmage. This brought on cries of foul from opposing teams, since cars back then were scarce, but failed to stop the practice.

As might be expected, crime in Highland Park simply is not discussed. There isn't any. When a cook stabbed a chauffeur to death during an altercation in a pantry, two HP police took one look at the body and one commented: "He was the meanest man in Highland Park." And that was that.

For years the friendly neighborhood judge ruled over the town's court, giving little sermons to speeding teen-agers and generally keeping a benevolent hand on the community. But occasionally someone forgot the code, as when the local mother parked in a non-parking zone and got a ticket.

"How do you plead, Lillian?" asked the judge.

"Guilty, I guess," said the housewife.

"Dadgumit," he exploded. "You're supposed to say 'Not guilty.' Now

I gotta fine you $5."

Justice along Turtle Creek may be different, but it is fair.

In the early part of World War II it was common knowledge that an otherwise kindly and friendly fellow who lived near the police station was a Nazi spy. He had a two-way radio in his basement, but that was his business.

The police knew, but did nothing about it. After all, he never got traffic tickets and was kind to his children. Besides, Highland Park was not exactly a hotbed of espionage and all he could tell Berlin was how the Highlanders had pulled it out in the last quarter.

Finally, however, the feds moved in and took the poor fellow away. After the war he came back, and lives there still, a pillar of the community.

He only did his duty, you know.

The Garenne saga

PARIS—"It all happened right here," says Marcel Chopine, walking down the concrete steps and onto the platform of the Paris subway. "He came running down here, paused for just a moment, and I could see his face. I shall never forget the look on that face."

Crowds push by Chopine, nudging their way into a waiting subway car. No one pays much attention to the neatly, if conservatively, attired lawyer from the suburbs. Nor does he pay much attention to them. Chopine is years away right now, remembering a cold, dark winter morning right here, when he was the only one around, until the brief and unexpected appearance of M. Garenne, the Wild Rabbit.

It is February of 1944. The Allied Fifth Army is knee-deep in Italy, the Russians are moving forward on the Eastern Front, but here in Paris, the Nazis are still in firm control. It is terror as usual. Marcel Chopine has fought them, ending up near the Pyrenees, his infantry platoon still fully armed and plugging away, until the order comes to surrender.

He returns to his job here in Paris, chief driver for this section of the Paris subway, or "metro" as they call it. Chopine notices that the French railway trains run close to the subway tracks, and he has many contacts in the business, so it is only a matter of time before he has an underground in the underground.

"It is nothing," he shrugs. "We get only about 10 minutes' notice that a German train is coming along. Just put down the cartouche, the cartridge. Bang." He flings his hands wide to show the results of his nothing. Three of his men are captured, but not Chopine. He is still alive and trying to stay that way. His wife hangs a white shirt on the line if it's safe to come home at night—a red one if the Gestapo is waiting.

That is the way it is this February morning in 1944. Snow has fallen in the night, maybe six inches of it. Chopine is busily at work in the southern part of Paris, on the line from the Luxembourg Station south to Massy-Palaiseau, helping the driver and checking the line, which runs above ground here. It is about 6 a.m. and still dark when the train, running south-bound, pulls into the stop at Antony where all trains, express and local, pull in.

His train is on the right-hand side, and the left track is empty. To get from one track to the other there is an overhead walkway, just above the platform, and Chopine chances to look up. There are three German military policemen, one holding a rifle, coming over the walkway. And there is a fourth person, a civilian, with them. He is carrying a load of clothes in each hand and is walking with some difficulty. Chopine makes out that his pants keep falling down because he has no belt. This can only mean one thing: a prisoner.

As the German carrying the rifle turns to look away, the prisoner tosses his two bundles to the two remaining guards who do the natural thing, they catch them. He turns and races across the walkway and bounces down the 15 steps to a landing, then down the 12 steps to the ground. He stops, a man literally in fear of his life.

The doors to the subway are closed and since—unlike New York City subways—there are no doors between the cars—the escapee jumps onto the coupling between two cars. Up above, there is stamping and confusion, quickly followed by the sound of three angry guards racing down the steps yelling, "Wo ist der Gefangener?" Where is the prisoner?

"I blew my whistle once to stop the train," says Chopine. "The driver looked back and I gave him a hand signal, too. The prisoner is still standing on the coupling, not knowing what to do, and I tell him. 'Fly. Fly away,' and motion for him to jump through to the other side of the train and go north. Just then the guards come down to the bottom of the stairs, and they are saying, 'Where is he? Where is the prisoner?' And I say, 'What prisoner?'"

The three guards run up and down the platform, looking for him, then return to Chopine, who is terribly impatient, as he has to get the train on to Massy-Palaiseau, and doesn't have time for wild pursuits of unseen escapees. "I shall get a light," he finally volunteers, and—with the three guards following—begins a systematic search of the south end of the platform at Antony. Nothing, basically because the escapee had taken Chopine's advice and headed north.

"The guards finally figured that they had lost their prisoner, and were quite upset. They had a pretty cozy life in Paris, and now they were wailing that they would lose their rank and be sent to the Russian front." Chopine does not seem to show much remorse.

"They say that the train may go on, but I'll have to go with them to the police station to help them report the escape. It was at the police station that I learned what happened. The prisoner's name was Garenne, which means 'Wild Rabbit,' and he was a member of the French Resistance. He was being taken to the Fresnes Prison by these three guards, and they were all to get off at La Croix de Berny. The guards did not know that it was a local stop only, and they got on an express train which went right by the prison. They stopped here at Antony and were going over the platform to get on a north-bound train to take them back up to their stop when Garenne made his escape."

After he was turned loose by the German guards, Chopine came back to the Antony subway stop. The trains do not run in a tunnel here, but in a deep cut with high walls on both sides. The ground gradually slopes upward at both ends. It was still morning and the heavy snow that had fallen during the night was undisturbed, so Chopine had no trouble in following Garenne's flight.

"He had no shoelaces, and no belt, so I could see where he had fallen four, five times in the snow. He ran up the tracks until the side walls were low enough for him to get over. I followed."

The trail of the Wild Rabbit led down Avenue Jeanne d'Arc two blocks to this small tavern. Chopine went in and inquired if anyone had noticed a fellow running for his life, with no belt or shoestrings. Answered to the name of Garenne.

Who?

Chopine finally discovered that Garenne had, indeed, made it to the tavern where he was given a change of clothes, something to eat and sent on.

End of story. Almost. Chopine continues: "Six, seven, maybe eight years later, my family and I were spending our summer vacation at La Rochelle, on the Bay of Biscay, and one evening I was talking to a neighbor there, a police inspector. I was telling him this story and as I talked, I noticed that the inspector was becoming more and more interested—and upset. Finally, he asked me the name of the man who had escaped, and I told him it was Garenne. He almost shouted, 'Garenne!' Then he began to tell me HIS story."

It seems that the escapee was from right there in La Rochelle, and was a member of the local resistance group. The entire group was rounded up by the Gestapo and every single one of them was executed at Fresnes Prison but one—Garenne. He returned after the war and when questioned about his survival, simply explained that he had escaped from the Gestapo. This was unique, not to say unbelievable, and the Defense Surete du Territoire—Defense of Territorial Security—moved in. They were looking for collaborators, and La Rochelle had just found one.

When hauled into court, Garenne patiently told how he was being taken to Fresnes Prison for his execution when he escaped at the prison's subway stop, La Croix de Berny. He had no idea that actually they had gone one stop beyond, and that it had all happened at Antony. The French authorities investigated the records at La Croix de Berny and interviewed all the employees who had been on duty that February morning. No one remembered a thing, and an escaping prisoner hotly pursued by the German police is not the kind of morning one easily forgets.

Poor Garenne had been imprisoned again and once more faced execution—this time by the French. He was later paroled and had returned to La Rochelle, where no one would speak to him, much less believe his ridiculous story.

After Chopine's accidental conversation with the police inspector, the Case of the Wild Rabbit was reopened and the records at Antony backed him up. He was cleared. Later, Chopine returned to La Rochelle and there once again met Garenne—only this time a little more leisurely.

Red wagon

THE BACK YARD—Gad. It's dead. Beyond repair. There is no hope. All is lost.

Why, after all these years, would my little red wagon let me down? Through countless jobs, through load upon load, it has carried its burden uncomplainingly, even cheerfully. And now, sob, now it is broken.

This particular little red wagon is a Radio Flyer, a snappy if dated title, to be sure. I never called it my Radio Flyer. Indeed, had I asked the family, "Where's my Radio Flyer?" they would have begun looking for a leaflet stuck in the front door with KLEF's schedule thereupon.

No, I never called it that, it was always just, "The wagon." Short, to the point. The wagon it was. Until now. Now there is no more wagon.

Possibly, at this point, you are wondering just why my consternation over a child's toy. A wagon is a wagon is an anachronism, you no doubt are saying to yourself. Piffle, piffle, I say in response. For a wagon is an absolute necessity to the well-being of any household.

All right, to be sure, there is no great amount of tote that barge, lift that bale, around a suburban dwelling. There are no seeds to take out to the back 40, no crops to bring in, no piles of manure to haul from the barn. All you farm brats know that a red wagon, about 3 feet long and 2 feet wide, is no John Deere with back hoe and color-coordinated subsidy.

But that is like saying Denton Cooley is no match for a lumberjack. Each in its own way does its own thing, I say. And around my happy home, a red wagon is a needed instrument. Indeed, I feel that with each home deed, along with the certificate saying that your house is free of termites until noon tomorrow, there should be one other required requisite: a red wagon. It should be ordained by city ordinance.

Why? To haul, of course. There you are, it is 10 o'clock and all is not well. For Doug Johnson has just stopped laughing enough to tell us that overnight it will drop even unto the teens. Frost is on the faucets and snow will engulf our pot plants.

I do not know about your home, but in mine, the alarm goes off. "Frost? Freezing? My pot plants!" (This is my wife yelling from somewhere beneath the downy comforts of polyester paradise.) And I, pulling on faded Levis and opentoed boots, rush out to the back yard to gather in the crop before the frigid locusts consume our livelihood.

Now, how does one get the pots of purple-blue daffodils into the garage? How does a shivering human net all the beige begonias into the warmth of the tool shed in time? With a red wagon, that's how. All the pot plants go into the wagon and the wagon goes into the garage, thus Western civilization as we know it is saved for future generations.

Pot plants are not alone. There is firewood. In most homes, at least in mine, the firewood is safely stowed away back behind the garage. And the fire in the fireplace consumes it with undisguised glee. Logs come in by the dozens, by the score, by the forest. Each one brought in aboard a red wagon. Frankly, I do not see how a family can keep warm in the winter without a red wagon.

Groceries are a prime passenger for the wagon. So are several six packs which your neighbor wishes to borrow for a party. My own red wagon has come and gone over the neighborhood over the years, taking and fetching various items from the neighbors. The distance is too close to warrant the car, too far to warrant the hands. So the red wagon, my own Radio Flyer, is called into action.

Tell me, have you ever had a load of dirt or sand or fertilizer of any origin dumped in your yard? The truck pulls up and in one fleeting instant deposits a mountain in your driveway. And there you are, looking at your new possession. How to move it? The red wagon, to be sure.

My wagon had hauled no less than the Matterhorn from front to back, or back to front.

It holds water, and so it is that various ferns spend their salad days nesting in a pool of cool water, snug in my red wagon. The wagon, with its 3-inch lip, holds the water, and the water feeds the ferns.

Plots of grass? The kind you buy to fill in the holes left by the chinch bugs of yestersummer? No better way to move them to their new homes than by my red wagon. Bookcases? My red wagon was not doomed to spend its eternity out of doors. No, it moved right inside and trundled about the house, taking this here and that there.

And it was a recreation vehicle, as well. This follows a tradition. You see, as a small child, my sister and brothers and I, along with a gaggle of neighbor children, used to pack into our own red wagon, thence to be hauled about the neighborhood.

Childhoods come and go, but red wagons stay on. And in recent times, my own brood was pulled about in my red wagon. They would sail merrily down the driveway and snake coyly out among the traffic, causing brakes to squeal and horns to honk. And mothers to shriek in alarm, forgetting that they, too, were once passengers in red wagons such as that.

Well, my own wagon has had it. Rotted or rusted or worn to death. Like a good horse, simply done in. It has turned its last wheel, hauled its last load, sponsored its last wagon load of giggles and tumbles. Good-bye, my Radio Flyer.

Some may have wheelbarrows, some may have pickup trucks, some may have sleds or slaves, but no home is truly a home without a red wagon.

Why Houston?

It is a fact, one which generations yet unborn will know, that the very first word man ever uttered from a universal sphere other than his own was the word "Houston." Neil Armstrong, upon reaching the moon July 20, 1969, said, "Houston, Tranquillity Base here. The Eagle has landed."

For some unknown reason, Armstrong didn't say, "Clear Lake City." On the other hand, he didn't say "Travis" or "Harrisburg" or "Allen." No, it was "Houston." That is the name of the place. But why? Why not Bayou City or Gawdawful Gulch or Karankawa? Would not our astronauts have arrived on the moon in somewhat the same state if they had radioed back, "Clute. Tranquillity Base here"?

We accept the fact that we live in Houston the same way we accept that we call today "Sunday": It has always been that way. But what if this were not called Houston? Same town, same people, same smog, same mayor dropping by for a visit and a paycheck, but what if this were called "Big Oil" or "Bayside" or "Subsidence City"?

We may curse the humidity and heat and infestation of cockroaches, but let us count our blessings in one area: We lucked out when it came to a name. I shall, as usual, explain. Smoke if you wish.

When Texas was bursting out all over, in a matter of a few years various names were chosen for our towns, crossroads, counties, swamps. The first public use of the name "Houston" came on Aug. 30, 1836, when a notice from the editor appeared in *The Telegraph and Texas Register*: "We call the attention of our readers to the advertisment [sic] of the town of Houston, by Messrs. A. C. & J. L. Allen . . ." The ad itself stated: "The town of Houston, situated at the head of navigation on the west bank of Buffalo Bayou, is now for the first time brought to public notice . . ." It wound up with the promise, ". . . when the rich lands of the country shall be settled, a trade will flow to it, making it, beyond all doubt, the great interior commercial emporium of Texas."

A really fantastic spot, except that when this ad appeared, there was no town. Indeed, a boatload of dignitaries from Galveston sailed up to visit Houston and went right by the spot without realizing it. On the return trip, they found footprints along the bayou and some surveyors' stakes driven in the mud. That was the great interior commercial emporium of Texas.

Just why the Allen brothers chose the name "Houston" for their enterprise is not clear. They had previously tried to buy what is now Morgan's Point, Galveston and Harrisburg, which already had names. But when they staked out this spot, it had no name and they had to choose one. Sam Houston was the best-known man in the country. He also had the biggest ego. So if the Allens needed permission to use his name for their new project, without a doubt they got it. This set the stage for a rather unique situation. When the capital of the republic was moved here, and Houston became president, he signed his official documents: "Sam Houston, president, Houston." Not even George Washington had such an honor.

Back when Texas was getting named, there was no way of knowing which settlements would jell and which would languish in the backwater, with one exception. When the capital was moved to the village of Waterloo, its name was changed to honor Stephen F. Austin and everyone knew it would eventually become important. But look at what happened elsewhere. San Antonio and El Paso had already acquired names which they kept. Galveston was named after Bernardo de Galvez, Spanish governor of Louisiana, who ordered a survey of the

Texas coast. The bay was unnamed, so the mapmakers flattered the boss. It is doubtful he ever saw the place.

Perhaps the worst example is in North Texas, where two major cities were named for people who had practically nothing to do with them. George Dallas was vice president of the United States when Texas was annexed. He never set foot here. Gen. William Worth did come to Texas the same year a military camp was named for him. It became Fort Worth while the general promptly contracted cholera and died. If only those mighty cities had been named, say, Bowie and Travis, or Cattle and Money. Or a package deal: The Twin Sisters. And now ladies and gentlemen, the Deaf Smith Cowboy Cheerleaders! Oh, well, fortune could have just as easily made north Texas' major cities Irving and Mesquite.

It was just luck that our city was named for the most important person around, and became the most important city. But the Allens could have opted for other famous Texans, and today we'd cheer for the Lorenzo De Zavala Oilers or the Three Legged Willie Astros or maybe the Crockett Rockets. They could have named this place for Gail Borden, editor of the *Telegraph and Texas Register*, who wrote an editorial urging everyone to stay put in Texas and not flee before Santa Anna. Then he packed up his presses and fled.

When the Allens decided to name it for Houston, they might have been dissuaded if they had only known there was already a Fort Houston in Anderson County. In that case, they could have called their new town Sam or The Raven or General. Actually, considering what the stakes on the muddy bayou bank became, perhaps they should have called this place Oo-tse-tee Ar-dee-tah-skee, which was Houston's Indian name. It means Big Drunk. That would certainly have been one great stumble for mankind.

Plot and sub-plot

CARTHAGE—Up and down these terraced Tunisian hillsides are rows of small white stones, with triangular tops. They look very much like tombstones, and, indeed, they are. These are the human sacrifices to the gods of ancient Carthage—Baal and Tanit.

In times of stress in Carthage, and apparently there were many, the first-born children of noble Carthaginian families were sacrificed, their bodies burned and the ashes put in these small white marble boxes. The Roman politician, Marcus Procius Cato, used to end every speech, no matter on what subject, with the declaration: "Delenda est Carthago." Carthage must be destroyed. He had his own less idealistic reasons, but any reason at all seems to be adequate.

Today we can only wonder at how a civilization such as this one, with its enormous feats in politics, navigation, commerce and architecture, could be so blind and crude and subhuman. Twenty-seven centuries later, it still boggles the mind.

But this is not the only cemetery in Tunisia. Nearby at Gammarth there is the French Military Cemetery on the Hollow Mountain. At Massicault, Enfida, Mejez and Tabarka, there are 9,074 Britons who died in the North Africa Campaign. Far to the south, alongside a desert road, are row upon row of neat, white crosses, behind a fence. It's a German military cemetery, holding the remains of the sons of the Fatherland, lined up for their final muster.

And here, right over the low, rolling Carthaginian hills filled with marble ruins and shattered mosaics and small children kicking a soccer ball about, is yet another final resting place for the dead. Our dead. It's the North African Cemetery, one of 14 World War II U.S. military cemeteries around the world, carefully prepared and preserved for all the Johnnies who didn't come marching home again.

It is a beautiful, quiet and—oddly enough—colorful place. The sky is a crystal-clear blue, the 27 acres are green and lush, in stark contrast to the surrounding sand. At the entrance there is a large American flag, bending and wheeling in the breeze. And stretching out across the fields are 2,840 bright, white crosses and stars of David, each one marking the spot where an American serviceman lies.

Like a crisp, truncated classified ad, each marker tells a complicated story in a few words. Name, rank, state, unit. Soldiers and sailors and airmen, officers and enlisted men, cooks and colonels, heroes, malingerers, from the 48 states and assorted territories. Young men who can't go home again.

The rows are divided into nine rectangular plots, separated by wide paths. There are neatly trimmed hedges, shrubs, pools, a chapel and a visitors' office, with an excellent ancient mosaic presented by Tunisian President Habib Bourguiba with the stipulation that it never leave the country. On a coffee table in the office is the official history of what happened and why, as best as anyone will ever know.

They did not die here, of course, although some may have fallen nearby, as there was heavy fighting over in Bizerte. But most came from elsewhere, from Oran and Casablanca, from the flatlands of Kasserine Pass, from across the Mediterranean in Sicily, and there are the airmen who were blown up or shot down while trying to bomb Ploesti.

But, perhaps only relatively, these 2,840 Americans are the lucky ones, because along the southeast edge of the 27 acres is a long wall engraved with the names of the 3,724 U.S. troops who simply disappeared. Missing In Action to this day. The Air Force lists its own, from Abromski, Stanley, a corporal in the 32nd Photo Squadron who never made it back to New Jersey, down to Zura, Andrew, a PFC in the 853rd Engineering Battalion, a Pennsylvanian. The Army and the Coast Guard tick off theirs, and so does the Navy, beginning with James E. Adams and winding through a frightfully long list down to a watertender third class, a Texas boy named John A. Zaiontz. Their resting place, as they say, is known but to God.

We have our mosaics, holding our own with the Carthaginians, only ours show invasions and parachute drops and naval shelling, attack and counterattack, flag raisings and deadly defeats. And there is a final note: "In proud remembrance of the achievements of her sons and in humble tribute to their sacrifices, this memorial has been erected by the United States of America."

As was noted, this is a beautiful, quiet, serene place, far prettier than the slabs of white marble and boxes of ashes right over that hill. But one still cannot get away from the disturbing feeling that these two plots have a great deal in common.

Oddball origins

Elmer Valo was born in Ribnik, Czechoslovakia. I'll let that fact sink in for a moment. It has always hit me as unique, perhaps even extraordinary.

The importance is this: Valo was a baseball player, that most American of all American occupations. From 1940 until 1954, Valo played outfield for the Philadelphia Athletics. This was before the deluge of Latin talent; this was back when virtually every player hailed from Marvin Gardens, New Jersey, or East Armpit, North Dakota. Yet despite this embargo on outside talent, Elmer Valo was born in Ribnik, Czechoslovakia! Fantastic.

Valo is an example of the fact that not everyone is born where they should have been born. For while we can choose where we live and sometimes where we die, we are not queried about our birthplace. Thus we are quite likely to pop forth in all sorts of strange and wrong places.

Hitler, for example, wasn't a German at all, but an Austrian, born in Braunau. And Napoleon was not French but Corsican, born in Ajaccio to an old Corsican family. As a matter of fact, in his early years Napoleon strongly disliked the French. John Paul Jones, "the Father of the American Navy," was born in Scotland, while Adm. Hyman Rickover, father of our nuclear subs, comes from Makowa, Poland. And Rama IX, the king of Thailand, was born in Cambridge, Mass., where his father was studying at Harvard.

Sometimes things swap out. Alexander Hamilton, who created the U.S. financial system, should have been born in New York City so he could keep an eye on Wall Street. Unfortunately, he harkened from Charlestown in the British West Indies. It all comes out all right, though. Harry Belafonte, that singer of the British West Indian songs, was born in New York City.

Speaking of which, Billy the Kid came from New York City, although Pat Garrett, who shot Billy, was from Alabama. And Ramblin' Jack Elliott, "last of the authentic cowboy singers," was born Elliott Adnopose of Brooklyn, N.Y. Montana Slim, on the other hand, should be called Canadian Wilf Carter.

Capt. Richard King, that hard-riding, hard-shooting Texan who started the King Ranch, actually hailed from Orange County, N.Y. In fact, not a whole lot of famed Texans come from Texas. Houston was born in Virginia, Bowie in Georgia, Travis in South Carolina and Austin in Virginia. Dolph Briscoe, however, comes from Uvalde.

You knew that, but try this: What do Sen. Lowell Weicker of Conn., Claudette Colbert and Brigitte Bardot have in common? They were all born in Paris. None of which explains why Mike Nichols comes from Berlin and Julie Christie from Chukua, India.

Let's try another. What do former New York City Mayor Abraham Beame, Bob Hope, Elizabeth Taylor, Charlie Chaplin and Louis Nizer have in common? All were born in England. For some totally unexplainable reason, George Sanders, Andre Kostelanetz and Ayn Rand were born in St. Petersburg, Russia. I suppose it was because they wanted to be near their mothers.

Everyone knows that George Romney was born in Mexico and Henry Kissinger hails from Germany, but did you know that Arthur Burns, former head of the Federal Reserve System, comes to us from Stanislau, Austria? I thought not.

Golda Meir was born in Russia (Kiev) and so was Irving Berlin (Temum). Myron Cohen came from Grodno, Poland, and Laurence Harvey from Lithuania, of all places. Samuel Goldwyn was born in Warsaw, but Darryl Zanuck came from Wahoo, Nebraska. Honest.

Let's try one more: Saul Bellow, Franklin D. Roosevelt, Jr., Paul Anka, S. I. Hayakawa, John Kenneth Galbraith and Lorne Greene? Right, Canada. So let's get tougher: Juliet Prowse? Bombay. Ann-Margret? Sweden. Olivia De Havilland and Joan Fontaine? Tokyo. Elmer Valo? I thought as much. You're not paying attention, so we'll have to start all over.

Only this time, remember that things are not as they seem. All of which explains why Tennessee Williams was born in Mississippi.

Hardin's date with destiny

So there you are. Late as usual. No matter, pull up a chair, deal yourself into the game and keep an eye on the bar.

But don't talk too much. No one else is, for tension is in the air, as thick as the cigar smoke and the smell of stale beer. This is the Acme Saloon on San Antonio Street in El Paso. It is Aug. 19, 1895, and things are about to happen. If you weren't here to see it yourself, you'd swear this whole thing is a scene out of the Late Show.

Up there at the bar, playing dice with a fellow named Henry Brown, is a man, 5-feet-10 and weighing about 160 pounds. He's got a fair complexion, dark hair and a bushy Pancho Villa–type mustache. He's 42 years old. Some say he's killed a man for every one of those years. He is known to have killed at least 21. Law officers put the number at more than 30. He once said he'd killed more than 40 men, but added that every one of them deserved it, and all died in fair fights.

He is John Wesley Hardin, known as Wes Hardin. Most call him Sir. Hardin is the deadliest gun in the West. He's not a robber, not a cattle rustler, not a bandit. He simply kills people. He looks and acts just like what he is—a gunfighter—yet he's not your usual type of seedy saddle tramp. Hardin's father was a Methodist minister, who named his second son for the church's founder. Hardin himself is a lawyer, who settled in El Paso after defending a relative in a court case.

His bloody trail began in the town where he was born, Bonham. Right after the War Between the States, 15-year-old Wes Hardin got into a fight with a Negro boy who—Hardin said—"came at me with a big stick." Young Wes shot him dead with an old Colt pistol. He fled, and killed three Yankee soldiers sent to get him. His career was launched.

Next, Hardin went to work as a cowboy. With his cousin, he killed two more Union soldiers during an argument, won a gunfight with a gunslinger named Jim Bradley who had accused him of cheating at cards, killed a circus roustabout, then got into a fight with a man who, Hardin said, was trying to rob him. This last shooting got him arrested in Longview, but he escaped while on the way to trial in Waco. Three soldiers on horseback pursued Hardin across the Texas prairie. Hardin, on foot, turned to face the troopers as they charged, and killed all three.

He was considered the most accurate gunfighter of his day. While still a teenager, Hardin developed his own fast draw, which saved seconds in the fight, and his life. He used a cross draw, that is, his two guns were in holsters sewn to his vest, with the gun butts pointing inward across his chest. While his opponent was reaching down to the hip for a gun, then to jerk upward and outward, Wes Hardin would cross his arms, pull his guns out in wide arcs, and fire.

He eventually ended up in Abilene, Kan., and—he says—faced down the town marshall, Wild Bill Hickok, with the "border roll." According to Hardin, when Hickok demanded Hardin's guns, "I said all right and then pulled them out of the scabbard, but while he was reaching for them, I reversed them and whirled them over on him with muzzles in his face, springing back at the same time. I told him to put his pistols up, which he did." Hardin wrote of this later in his rather suspect autobiography, and a lot of historians don't believe him, but it's a good story.

A few weeks later, a gunslinger in an Abilene saloon said he hated all Texans. After killing him, Hardin left town. Back in Texas, he kept getting into trouble and shooting his way out. He killed two Negro police officers, got involved in the decades-old Sutton-Taylor family feud, and finally killed Charlie Webb. This latter shooting was of more than passing notice since Webb was the sheriff of Brown County. On the run again, Hardin and his brother, Joe, headed east. A lynch mob caught Joe and strung him up, but Hardin disappeared. He was pursued by the Pinkerton Agency, the Texas Rangers, several young gunslingers out to make a reputation, and bounty hunters, since he had a $4,000 reward on his head. He was 21 years old.

On Aug. 23, 1877, a train pulled into the railroad station in Pensacola, Fla. On board were Wes Hardin and several outlaw friends. Several men got on the train and one came walking down the aisle. John Wesley Hardin looked up to see the fellow carrying a 7½-inch-barrel Peacemaker. That could mean only one thing: Texas Rangers. "Texas, by God!" Hardin yelled, and began his dreaded cross draw. Alas, his guns got caught in his suspenders. The Ranger, John B. Armstrong, watched the fastest gun in the West trying to untangle himself. "He almost pulled his breeches over his head," Armstrong reported. A Hardin cohort shot at Armstrong, who turned, fired once, killing the fellow. Hardin was still standing in the aisle, trying to untangle his guns. Armstrong reached over and knocked him in the head. Hardin came to, two hours later.

Well, that put an end to things. Hardin got 25 years hard labor in the Rusk Prison at Huntsville for killing Sheriff Webb. As a prisoner, Hardin tried to escape, led revolts, got whipped and was put in solitary. After a few years, however, he changed his ways. He became superintendent of the prison Sunday school, studied law and, on March 16, 1894, after 16 years in prison, was pardoned by the governor.

He came out a changed man—for a while. He practiced law in El Paso and was praised as a fine citizen, and he spent a lot of time writing the story of his life. But Hardin just seemed to find trouble. He began drinking heavily, gambling, and started running around with Mrs. Martin

McRose, whose husband was hiding out across the river in Mexico. Something about cattle rustling.

For three weeks now, Wes Hardin has been boozing it up, making life tough for the police. A few nights ago, Hardin was arrested by several El Paso police officers, including young John Selman (or Sellman). After being released, Hardin threatened to shoot Selman if they should meet. But it was the police officer's father, Old John Selman, who came gunning for Hardin. Old John has been on both sides of the law for years, almost getting lynched for cattle rustling at least once. Now he is constable of Precinct 1, but still a dirty guy.

Old John came in here earlier and Hardin said to meet him outside in the middle of San Antonio Street. Hardin said he'd come "a smoking." Old John waited for a couple of hours, but no Hardin. Now it's shortly before midnight here in the Acme Saloon. Everyone is waiting for something to happen. Hardin is still here at the bar, playing dice. Now the door opens, and in comes Old John Selman. He is walking over to Hardin, who does not look up.

"Four aces to beat," says Hardin. Then he glances up into the mirror over the bar, and sees the reflection of Old John behind him. Hardin's hands just begin to move toward his single-action .45-caliber Army revolvers when Selman fires. Bang! The bullet splits open the back of Hardin's head. He starts sliding toward the floor as Selman continues to fire.

"Another of the Few Bad Men Laid Low in a Saloon," The Houston *Daily Post* will headline. And the El Paso *Daily Herald* will report, "For several weeks past, trouble has been brewing and it has been often heard on the streets that John Wesley Hardin would be the cause of some killing before he left town."

He never did leave town. He'll be buried here tomorrow. In Hardin's trunk, they will find 360 pages of closely written manuscript, the story of his life, as he saw it. Constable Selman will be acquitted, having convinced the jury that it was self-defense. But he, in turn, will be killed in less than eight months by a town marshall "in a personal difficulty."

And here, on the dirty floor of the Acme Saloon in El Paso, lies John Wesley Hardin, the most dangerous man in Texas. He died with his boots on, but missing a goodly section of his brain.

Book-of-the-month eviction notice

THE DEN—Closing in on me. Ever tighter. They come at me, pace by pace, page by page. The walls are leaning forward. Too much brandy? Too much work? Why does it seem that my life is suddenly clamped between hard covers? I'll tell you why. Too many books.

There are some who say that you cannot have too many books. To them, volumes mean virtue. Paper with ink on it is equated to gray with matter in it. They like to point to the hundreds of thousands of books they have. Beware of a man with lots of books. It simple means he has no taste. But right now I have too many. I am hosting a party with an endless guest list—everyone who is no one is here. So it is time once again to prune. "All right!" I bellow to the dozing crowd, clapping my hands loudly. "Up and at 'em! It's move-out time."

"Not again," Conrad mutters from beneath his potted palm.

"Oh, give me a man, a stout-lanced man, who marches on to Falkland," Kipling says, waving one hand in rhythm while the other raises a gin and tonic.

"I'm not kidding this time," I say, wandering among the loutish lot. "I'm cleaning house."

Chekhov gazes blankly out the window, ignoring me completely. Maugham makes a pass at Hemingway, who smashes him in the face. It is good. The smash is good, like a brick hitting a melon. After the wine, it's good to smash someone smaller than you.

"Sturm und Drang," sighs Goethe, twitching slightly.

"See there?" I say, accusingly. "You can't even spout your lines properly. It's not 'Sturm und Drang,' it is *Sturm und Drang*. You're supposed to italicize those words to show that you are intelligent. Never use English words when you can dig up an obscure foreign phrase and put it in italics. It shows everyone how smart you are, you ninny."

Faulkner moves over to the bar and pours himself another drink. "I seem to recall one afternoon down by the Chichimugwee Creek, when Alfred DeLeon, he was the second cousin of Ella Mae who ran off with the . . ."

"Oh, shut up," snaps Spillane, pulling out another deck of Luckies. "I'll slap you across the forehead with my .357 Magnum, making your teeth splatter on the wall like dice tossed in an alley crap shoot. Then I'll pump five smoking round holes in your belly, letting you lie there sprawled on the maroon carpet, seeping life into the fibers."

"Very sharp," I say, "but it won't work. This place is getting piled high with books, and I can't find any of you when I want you."

"I'm over here," says Churchill from behind a cloud of cigar smoke.

"I know where you are, Winnie," I reply. "And frankly, you're getting to be a bore. Always the same thing about that 'Noble, keen-browed Anglo race, braced against the foe.' You've got too much room. All of you think you are the only ones who are worthy to occupy my shelfs. Well, you're not. There are a lot of good writers coming along, and I want to make room for them."

"That's *shelves*," says Mencken, snatching a cigar from Churchill.
"Huh?" I say.

"It's not *shelfs*," Mencken says. "It's *shelves*."

"That shows what you know," I retort. "You italicized an English word. Don't you know any snappy foreign phrases? Are you so *gauche* that you have to resort to italicizing English words?"

"English words are the most exquisite of all," growls Churchill. "Incidentally, I feel creative today, so give me another shelve and a halve."

"Do I have any volunteers to depart peacefully?"

Silence, broken only by Shakespeare's pen. "What's that?" I ask. "You're supposed to be bailing out, not adding on."

" 'Tis my latest ditty, dedicated to you," Shakespeare says, dipping his quill. "I call it Ode to the Hockey Puck. It goes:

There once was an envious writer,
Whose pen was not all the mighter,
He tossed us outside . . ."

"Hold it right there, Willie," says Marlowe. "If everyone is going to think I wrote it anyway, then you aren't going to get away with rhyming *writer* with *mighter*. It's *mightier*."

"Think *you* wrote it," the Bard says, tossing down his pen and pulling out a deck of Luckies. "Why, I'll slap you across the ears with my broadsword, splattering your guts across her long, tanned legs and rising, heaving . . ."

"You all are italicizing English again."

"And you are repeating yourself," says Homer.

"Not really," objects Ann Landers. "It was good advice before, and I only thought it was worth repeating. That's not wrong. After all my reputation is all I've got."

"That was, word for word, the same excuse you gave in 1954," says Thackeray.

"I have a feeling I'm losing control of the situation," I sigh.

"Losing control? When did you ever have it?" Twain snorts over the laughter.

Plague of puns

Then there was the monk who opened up a Colonel Sanders franchise and became a Kentucky friar. That comes to us from Carole Marmell of Houston, and is the opening shot in a barrage of puns, spoonerisms and generally forgettable prose.

Such as this from P. W. Johnson of Sweeny. Mr. Jones, accompanied by Mr. Smith of the rental agency, was inspecting some beach houses in hopes of renting one for the summer. The last house on the list was the most appealing, but as they approached the house a pretty young girl came out of the door and sat on the porch. "I like this house the most," said Mr. Jones, "but it seems to be rented."

"No," replied Mr. Smith. "The house is lassed, but not leased."

That should explain what they do all day in Sweeny, Texas. Meanwhile, back in Houston we have the notorious Scott L. Weeden, who has cluttered up this column before. He returns today with a question: "If *pro* is the opposite of *con*, what is the opposite of *progress*?"

"How about some duck jokes?" Weeden asks, and without waiting for a reply continues: "What do you need to kill a sitting duck? A quack shot." You really have to admire his courage, don't you? OK, here is another one: "What do you serve to a sick duck? Soup and quackers." And, thankfully, this final one: "What do you call a duck sued for malpractice?" Pregnant pause. "A quack quack."

We now move onward, and none too soon, to Harry Dalton of Houston, who reports that he has just come back from a little country in the Far East called Taylesmania, obviously inhabited by the Tayles. The citizens there are nomadic, and their main source of food is sheep, but a terrible drought has made food for the herds difficult to locate. So the nomads have to be kept hustling around the countryside with their sheep, or as the country's ruler put it: "We really move our Tayles for ewe."

Dalton, go to your room. Besides we have to make way for the unforgettable Bernus Wm. Fischman. He informs us of a friend who owns a large ranch in West Texas right on the Rio Grande. At the point where the river flowed through his land, there was a sharp bend and very dangerous rapids. The rancher had a small but sturdy raft which he had long dreamed of negotiating through the rapids.

The rancher's friends warned him that his boat was no match for the powerful river. Undaunted, he set out on his adventure. At first the little raft did well, but soon the merciless river pounded and thrashed the boat apart. As the rancher pulled himself to shore, barely escaping with his life, he realized that this was a case where his bight was worse than his barque.

Calm down. Calm down, I say. For Bernus Wm. Fischman is not yet through. He now tells us about the famed Fonda family—Henry, son Peter and daughter Jane. But Fischman says that there was another son most people never hear about. Hargrove. Now, Hargrove long ago realized that he was not the actor type, and had no desire to bathe in the reflected glory of his famous family, so he went off to Australia. For 20 years there was no communication between him and his family. Then, last year he turned up in Hollywood, a very successful sheep rancher and investor.

Proving once more that absence makes the Hargrove Fonda.

A small parish church in Haiti had a deputy pastor, Father Ree. He tried to get the parishioners to turn their backs on voodoo, which was still practiced throughout Haiti, but they wouldn't listen. One day an ancient voodoo witch decided to set Father Ree straight. She appeared at the church door with a doll, the likeness of the young priest. She uttered incantations, stuck pins in the doll and finally rubbed a sticky chocolate goo on the doll's feet.

Immediately, the priest began to writhe and cry out in pain. Mysteriously, his toes began to break out in awful welts, pimples and boils. The witch had produced in one man the shrill of Vicar Ree and the acne of the feet.

YOU PROBABLY NEED SOME MONEY

You Probably Need Some Money

Hi, Mr. Newcomer:

So you're dead broke in Texas? Sorry. There's a lot of that going around. But this handy pamphlet should help you out in these times of need. First, on behalf of the people of Texas, let me tell you how glad we are that you have come down to join us. We don't have many deadbeats around, and every town needs at least one. We sincerely hope you enjoy your stay with us, find a job and settle down to a long and fruitful experience.

Welfare payments: You probably need some money. In that case, let me acquaint you with Texas' welfare code. We are a rich state with a fat surplus in the treasury, and thus you probably expect a fat welfare check. Well, it doesn't work that way. You see, one reason we have such a fat surplus in the treasury is that our welfare payments are practically non-existent. Of the 50 states, we rank 49th, behind Mississippi, in welfare. Needless to say, there is a growing movement to change that dismal state of affairs. Perhaps you have already seen those "Move Over Mississippi — We're Number 50!" buttons. They are selling quite nicely.

You qualify for welfare only if your lawyer and accountant can convince a jury and judge that you are deserving. A minimum of 10 character witnesses is required, including at least one college president, a U.S. senator and a religious leader above the rank of archbishop. If you win the case, the state will appeal to the Governor's Committee on Welfare, which meets every other year ending in '08. No payment will be made until then. If you win your appeal, a deposit will be made to your numbered bank account in Zurich. It has been argued by the ACLU that not every welfare recipient has a numbered bank account in Zurich, so the Legislature recently amended the law to include Geneva. Some observers say such laws limit welfare to those who don't need it. Some observers are very observant.

You may be one of the lucky ones from Portsmouth, Ohio, who got more than $200 to leave Portsmouth, Ohio, and come to Texas. That money was part of a $300,000 federal grant, and there is the distinct chance that more of it came from Texas than from Ohio. You see, Texas is the very last among all the states when it comes to getting money back from Washington. For every $1.46 we send, we get back a dollar. One reason is that the U.S government is deliberately using 1970, rather than 1980, census figures. Texans also are paying almost one-third of the windfall profits tax, all by ourselves. This shows the caliber of representatives we are sending to Washington to look out for our interests. Would you like to go to Washington? We'll pay you a lot more than a lousy $200 to go, and even more to stay.

How to get a job? That isn't easy. It helps to have a medical degree or be able to tackle Earl Campbell. Also, you stand a better chance if you are the legal heir of Howard Hughes, own land on the West Loop, brought several Baggies of white powder with you or can strip down a BMW while it's still moving. If not, there is still hope. Check the want ads of Michigan's best-selling paper, *The Houston Post*, and be sure to keep the paper. You may have to sleep on it tonight. When you spot a position suitable to your skills and experience, get your shovel and go to the place of employment. Note: To get there, use our fantastic bus system.

A few tips when applying for work: Texans love to hire Yankees who remember their roots, so begin the conversation by explaining how much better things were back in Cleveland. Next, show how well you fit in: Gripe about the weather, traffic, prices, potholes and Oilers. Also, it helps if you note your long activities as a union organizer. Top it off with a good Texas joke. We do love those. In College Station, for instance, they love Aggie jokes. Elsewhere, try: "We'd be carrying on this conversation in Spanish if there was a back door at the Alamo." (If you are carrying on the conversation in Spanish, forget the advice about Cleveland.)

Best buys: Ski lodges in Pasadena. Their salesmen are easy to spot; they hang around savings and loan associations on Friday afternoons, wearing ski masks. Say the key words, "Freeze, I'm the law," and win dinner for two. Other bargains are tickets to a Bud Adams appreciation dinner, tickets to a KLEF rock concert and a Klan franchise in the Third Ward.

Texas law: Police, sheriffs and the Texas Rangers all answer to the honorary title, "Pigs." If that fails, try "Redneck." The secret handshake is to grab the officer's badge and say, "Did this come with a fill-up at a participating dealer?" Instant action is guaranteed. If you find yourself in Houston, get off to a good start with the HPD: Explain that you're a good friend of Kathy Whitmire, having engineered her support by the Gay Political Caucus. In small towns such as La Grange, tell the sheriff that Marvin Zindler sent you. In the Valley, when meeting a border patrolman, remember always to speak Spanish and smoke hand-rolled cigarettes. Also, it is a custom to offer them money.

Some final words: We know with these few tips you will not be dead broke in Texas for long. Well, at least not broke. If, however, you still cannot find work, you can always hire out as a missionary to the savages, bringing solutions down here for all our problems. We have lots of missionaries in Texas and just love to hear them tell us how we are doing everything wrong. The best place to do this is in a beer joint late on Saturday night. Just kick open the door and tell everyone to shut up, you're from Up North and have come to Texas to show us how it's done. To get their attention, the key word is, "Draw!"

Tick-tick-tick

The first thing I want you to do is figure out your age. Your exact age. Just jot it down. "32 years, five months and six days," or "17 years and 301 days." I find it easier to use months. Do it either way.

No, I am not figuring up your astrolog. Nor the first draft of your epitaph. It is to help me with a great idea to make a fortune. I call it my Humiliation Calendar, but you might call it your Success Timetable. It depends strictly on how you stack up. Let me explain:

It all began with Stonewall Jackson. The other day, Sound Off ran a photograph of Jackson, and—as usual—he looked like a tired old man. But beneath the photograph was the notation: "1824–1863." Idly, I ticked off the years and discovered that Jackson, a three-star general, never saw his 40th birthday. Further research showed that he was killed when he had lived only 39 years, three months and 19 days.

Then it hit me: I have outlived Stonewall Jackson. At least, I have now spent more time on this earth than he did. Yet Jackson was a lieutenant general and I never made it past lance corporal.

Thus was hatched my latest get-rich scheme. A desk calendar, keyed to how old you are, so that each day you flip the page and it says: "Sunday, July 23, 1983—If you were Alexander the Great, today you would have conquered the world." Or: "Good morning! When John Glenn was your age, they held a tickertape parade in his honor down Wall Street and that afternoon he had lunch at the White House."

Mine own notation for the day would read: "Take out garbage. Buy shoelaces." It just doesn't have the same ring. This is why I call it my Humiliation Calendar. On the other hand, if you have already had your own tickertape parade down Wall Street, then you can smile a condescending smile and think of how you one-upped John Glenn.

OK, now that you have figured out exactly how old you are, you might want to make these entries on your calendar at the appropriate places:

When Thomas Jefferson was 33 years, one month and 25 days old, he was chosen to write the Declaration of Independence.

Capt. William Bligh was 34 years, three months and 28 days old when his crew on the Bounty mutinied.

What did you do when you were 21 years, seven months and 14 days old? If you were Billy the Kid, you were getting killed.

Sam Houston was 43 years and fifty days old at the Battle of San Jacinto when he defeated Santa Anna (42 years, 1 month and twenty-nine days).

Actually, a special desk calendar could be prepared for any career military man. He flips open his desk calendar and reads: "George Washington was your age today—43 years, three months and 21 days—when he was elected to command the Continental Army." Or: "Today you are 35 years, three months and 18 days old. If you were Napoleon, this morning you would be crowning yourself Emperor of France and most of Europe." It would certainly make an aspiring officer work a little harder.

Here are a few more ages of accomplishment to put down on your calendar:

Alexander Graham Bell was granted a patent for the telephone four days after his 29th birthday.

Thomas Edison successfully used the electric light bulb when he was 32 years, 8 months and thirty-six days old.

The day after Marie Curie's 44th birthday, she learned that she had won the Nobel Prize for chemistry.

When the Wright brothers soared into the history books at Kitty Hawk, Orville was 32 years, three months and 29 days old. His older brother, Wilbur, was 36 years, seven months and thirty-one days.

That would be rather depressing, wouldn't it? Some 32-year-old aeronautical engineer sits down at his desk at Boeing, flips open his desk calendar, and suddenly realizes that Orville Wright was exactly his age when he became the first human to make a sustained flight in a powered airplane. And this poor snook is trying to design an armrest so that the stereo headphones can plug in beside the ashtray.

Alexander Hamilton was 49 years, six months and one day old when he was shot by Aaron Burr (48 years, five months and four days).

Gen. George A. Custer was 36 years, six months and 21 days when he was killed at Little Big Horn. Others who met an untimely death include Clyde Barrow (25 years, one month and 30 days) and John Dilinger (31 years and 30 days old).

For all those who think athletes are over the hill at an early age, remember that Jackie Robinson didn't even sign up to become the first Negro to play major league baseball until he was 26 years, eight months and 23 days old.

As for aspiring writers, if you haven't written your own "Comedy of Errors" by the time you are 30 years, eight months and 5 days old, you are behind Shakespeare's pace. Get busy. In politics and government, Barbara Jordan was the keynote speaker at the Democratic National Convention when she was 40 years, four months and 20 days old. Hirohito was slightly older—40 years, seven months and eight days—when Japan attacked Pearl Harbor.

If you are in your early 40s, you might want to figure that when you will be 43 years and 236 days old. That's how old John Kennedy was when he was inaugurated president. Teddy Roosevelt was even younger: 42 years, 322 days.

Anyway, that's my latest plan to make a bundle, although at my current rate of progress I shall become rich when I am 134 years, four months and 23 days old. Eat your heart out, Stonewall.

What a SHOC

THE STREET CORNER – "Ssssst, laddie-boy, just sign right here."

"Huh?" I query.

"I'll accept that as approval," says this familiar-looking but seedy fellow, holding a pen and several sheets of paper. "So I'll just put your name down here."

"Wait a minute," I say. "It's you. Heinrich Armtwister, lobbyist extraordinary. Last week you were getting up petitions to declare Gen. George Patton the designated hitter. What's it this time?"

"Laddie-boy, this time it's for real. I represent SHOC. We pronounce it like 'Shock.' "

"I'll bite. What's SHOC?"

"It's the Society to Help Our Capital. I'm the executive director, founder and currently the only member. But we'll grow."

"What is SHOC trying to do, Mr. Armtwister?"

"We are of the opinion that Washington is not yet ready for self-government, and needs our constant advice and supervision."

"Come again?"

"It's as clear as those soup stains on your tie, laddie-boy. Washington needs our help since it obviously can't cope by itself. Take the Senate."

"What about it?"

"The U.S. Senate is obviously in violation of the Voting Rights Act. Of the 100 members, there is not a single black or Mexican-American."

"So?"

"Look, the major minorities of this country have no representation in their own Senate. That's because senators are elected statewide. SHOC will insist that senators no longer be elected at-large, but by single-member districts. At least some of them. We may let them have a combination of the two plans. Perhaps 60 from single-member districts and the other 40 at-large. Or maybe to insure more equal representation we'll expand the Senate to 2,300 members."

"How will they know which plan to use?"

"We'll let them vote on it."

"I thought you said they weren't capable of deciding."

"They're not. That's why we'll put just one question in the ballot. And we'll decide who wins. Saves time and confusion."

"Mr. Armtwister, you don't have both oars in the water."

"There's more, laddie-boy. Do you realize they call their football team the 'Redskins,' but they don't have a single Indian on the team? That's clear discrimination."

"Or at least false advertising."

"They also don't know much about running the federal government. I'm lining up several oil men to teach them constitutional law."

"It seems only fair, Mr. Armtwister. I remember when Congress was telling Exxon which way to drill an oil well."

"What did they recommend?"

"Down."

"Then we have their action on the Panama Canal."

"What's that got to do with anything?"

"Simple. By deannexing the Panama Canal Zone, Congress has diluted the Panamanian voting strength in this country. SHOC demands that the deannexation be left off the ballot. When we let them vote, that is."

"I'm all for the deannexation, Mr. Armtwister, if we could tack on a small amendment to include Texas."

"All the world is watching to see how we handle these boat people."

"Mr. Armtwister, I don't think these are the same boat people. You see . . ."

"Also, SHOC feels that Washington's tax votes should be tossed out. Our plan is to let the people of Houston decide these things for them. Like which schools the congressmen should send their children to. When they can vote and on what. And we demand the House start using bilingual ballots. Norwegian and Croatian."

"Hold it! Mr. Armtwister, you've had some strange plans before, but this one is the worst of them all. Why should the people of Houston have anything to say about how a city operates hundreds of miles away? That's their business. Besides, what makes you think Houston knows more about Washington's problems than do the people up there? We're no smarter than they are."

"Wrong again, laddie-boy. SHOC feels that we know best what's good for them. They need our advice and consent to live their day-to-day lives."

"I don't see them asking for it, Mr. Armtwister."

"Exactly my point. They are so backward they don't even realize how much better we can run things for them than they can operate by themselves. We need to tell them where to build their jails, how to run their police department, when and how to set their tax rates."

"Frankly, Mr. Armtwister, I don't think the people in Washington will go along with your plan. Like I said, they live hundreds and hundreds of miles away from us. They know what's best for them. We don't."

"Ah, but laddie-boy, it's just as far from Houston to Washington as it is from Washington to Houston. And there's a well-beaten path from there to here."

"So?"

"Well, of all the cities in the country, Washington should understand and agree with SHOC's three rules."

"Which are?"

"We know better than you."

"That's one."

"The farther you get from a situation the more you know about it."

"And the last rule?"

"If God thought Americans could take care of themselves, he wouldn't have created seat belts, erasers or Congress."

A quiet man dies

DALLAS—Mister McCulloch is dead. You never knew him, but you knew someone just like him in your childhood.

He was a serene, quiet, cheerful fellow who never made waves, but rather slipped into the galley and simply grabbed the oars to row along in the good ship Civilization. I can't remember a time when I didn't know him. He lived across the street and was always there, puttering around the yard, watering the lawn, sitting on the porch, and mostly engaging in the lost art of listening. Mister McCulloch was the world's greatest listener. No matter how stupid the comment, how inane the observation, how redundant the conversation, he sat and smiled and listened and somehow made you feel important.

He was a lawyer, and when my mother suddenly became a widow, she turned the entire mess over to Mister McCulloch without a second thought. Trust was too mild a word. "When Arch McCulloch runs off with your money," she would say, "then it's time to give up, because the whole world will be rotten. He's the last honest man."

You know those people who somehow get things done without ever working up a sweat. No fuss, no feathers, it just all falls into place. That's him. When we needed a new YMCA building, who got the nod? When his old fraternity brothers—the Phi Gams—needed someone to oversee things, Brother Arch got the job. And, last year when it came time for the national fraternity to honor its outstanding alumnus—that small handful picked from throughout the country for a job well done—there were the high and the mightly, and one other fellow. Arch Who?

I was well into high school before I discovered that Mister McCulloch was not only on the local school board, but was actually its president—a position he held until his death. As usual, he had arrived at such a task without ever wanting it. It just seemed to seek him out, and when he was discovered, he gave up and dug in. At a time when school boards were the battle pit for every conceivable neurotic complaint, my neighbor held forth with a no-nonsense gavel.

He advocated the revolutionary concept that teachers should teach, students should learn and parents should be there when needed. He firmly believed that the teacher was lord and master of the classroom, that we still had time to learn the three Rs, and that the best formula for teaching was intelligence, patience, love and an occasional ruler laid squarely on the posterior.

He maintained this for more than a score of years and kept his school district at a peak that can be equalled by few and surpassed by none. For those who attacked with theories, frills and gimmicks, Mister McCulloch would simply break out his ultimate weapon—a good teacher armed with a piece of chalk. The combination worked wonders.

Mister McCulloch had a wife and four children. One son was my friend, so I spent a lot of time at their house, back in the days of ceiling fans and radios. On those ridiculously hot August afternoons we would come in out of the sun to sit on the McCullochs' front porch and sip lemonade. And we would wile away the blistering hours listening to baseball games on the radio. All would come to an end a little after five o'clock. Mister McCulloch was due home—it was time to get ready.

He would get off the bus and slowly walk down the sidewalk, smiling and waving at his neighbors. Years later, somehow, he wound up with a different means of transportation. My mother called my sister in California with the news. "Who would you guess would be the last person in the world to buy a Cadillac?" she asked. Without a moment's hesitation, my sister fired back: "Mister McCulloch." She was right. Yet he could have left each day in a golden carriage with liveried coachmen and it would still have seemed only proper and understated.

He must have had a temper. He must have shouted at his wife, spanked his children, driven too fast and double-parked, but if he did, it was the best-kept secret since the Manhattan Project. Mostly, he came home each day shortly after five o'clock, and began puttering around the yard. Watering in the summer, raking in the winter.

Others made the headlines and rocked the boat and streaked through our lives with a whiz and a bang. After they left, there was always a Mister McCulloch around to set things right and somehow make sure that Tuesday followed Monday. For while we must have our cymbals and kettle drums, our brass and our first violins, it is the oboe that we turn to for the true pitch.

Sweating out a lunar eclipse

THE FRONT YARD – Cars drive by, and I can see them slow down as the occupants gape in awe. I can only guess as to the conversations we have started:

"Why are those people out there?"

"Maybe they're on a picnic."

"At 11 p.m.?"

"That's when the ants are asleep."

Actually, my family is out here, spread upon the lawn in the middle of the late night, for two simple reasons. One is that tonight is the night of the big eclipse. It is a time to show the small fry the wonderment of nature when the bodies move about the heavens in mysterious ways, short-cutting the planned scheme of things. One does not often get to see how the moon looks after taxes.

The second reason is that our air conditioning is broken. This happens only on suffocatingly hot nights. I called the repairman, who said he could come out here as an emergency, immediately conjuring up visions of financial failure on my part. I opted to wait until the morrow, when the price drops to the ridiculous.

"When is the repairman coming?" one of my offspring asks from the curb.

"Tomorrow," I say brightly. "He shall be here at the crack of noon. I know, because we solemnly agreed on 9 sharp."

"Why did the air conditioning break, Daddy?"

"See the moon up there?" I inquire.

"Yes."

"Notice how the bottom is getting dark?"

"Yes."

"That is called an eclipse. It comes from the ancient Greek, *ec*, meaning *air*, and *lipse*, meaning *conditioning*."

"Oh, come on."

"All right. *Lipse* really means *cooling*. I was just trying to keep things simple. Anyway, whenever the moon is shaded by the sun, our air conditioning system falls apart. It's been that way since 238 B.C. Or 220 A.C., depending upon your system."

"Then why are all the neighbors' air conditioning systems working?" my daughter asks.

"Because our system is lunar-powered. Theirs are gas- or electric-powered. They are burning up our natural fuels, strip mining Wyoming, leveling the forests and contributing to the fall of the American Way of Life. This neighborhood is lousy with commies."

Just then, Sam, one of my neighbors, comes jogging by, out for his midnight stroll. "Hi," he says. "Outside to watch the eclipse?"

"Not really," I say. "We like to roll around the front yard near midnight. Prevents hemorrhoids."

"Oh," he puffs.

"But watch out for the eclipse," I advise. "You might turn into a werewolf and become covered with hair."

Sam waves and puffs on by, counting his pulse.

"It's hot in there," announces my youngest, coming out on the lawn.

"You people are getting soft. When I was a boy. . . ," I begin.

"Not again, Daddy."

"When I was a boy, we never had air conditioning. We had high ceilings, big fans and I slept in my underwear."

"That explains a lot," says a son.

I ignore the creep and continue. "Air conditioning is a relatively new invention, and a bad one. It thickens the blood, deadens the senses, increases the profits of HL&P. Maybe even when we get the machinery fixed we shouldn't use it. Keeping cool is all in the mind."

"It's not the heat that's getting me," says my youngest. "It's the drums, the incessant drums. How long can we hold out, captain?"

"Don't get smart," I explain. "When I was a boy, we knew how to stay cool."

"Yeah, your gardener did the yard."

"That had nothing to do with it. We could stay cool. Particularly during an eclipse."

My wife speaks up. "Maybe we should get a room in a motel."

"Great, but what would we do with the kids?"

"I mean, maybe we should all move to a motel for the night, where it would be cool."

"It is cool, " I say. "Feel the breeze?" I am greeted with frowns all around. "Look, the pioneers who came to Houston had to contend with mosquitoes, con artists, carpetbaggers, disease and hurricanes."

"Houston's a stickler for tradition, Daddy."

The moon is losing its bottom half. "The ancient Greeks used to think that an eclipse was caused by the angry gods," I say. "To pacify them, the Greeks would put more quarters in the meter until Fornicus, the god of utility companies, smiled."

"Says who, Daddy?"

"Says Plato," I explain.

"Was he one of the Marx Brothers?"

"No, dummy," my eldest says. "Plato is Italian for saucer."

My wife gets up and heads back to the house. "I'll see if the loaves in the front hall are ready."

"That's very funny," I say. "When I was a boy, my father never allowed us to sweat. He would make us. . . ." My sentence is drowned out by a noise, louder and louder. It is the mosquito fogging truck, which comes lumbering down the street, spreading gases to and fro. We race back to the front door as the fumes follow us step for step.

"I feel like a California fruit fly," gasps a child.

"It's part of the eclipse," I explain as my family coughs and chokes in chorus. "Plato said it was caused by disrespectful children." My family pays me no mind and wanders off. Just then I glance out to the street to see Sam jog by again. He spots me and waves a hairy paw.

Machu Picchu choo-choo

THE TRAIN TO CUSCO—Promptly at four o'clock the train leaves the tiny railroad station at Puente Ruinas, which is down at the base of Machu Picchu. Puffing and panting and blowing out thick black smoke, the narrow-gauge train of a locomotive and about six or eight cars chugs toward Cusco, 112 kilometers away.

But that's 112 kilometers as the condor flies, and neither I nor the train is a condor, so we must wind slowly over the mountains and down the valleys, across the outback of Peru. The trip up from Cusco this morning took four hours and seven minutes, not bad for a three-and-a-half hour trip. Now we go back the same way we came, the train having been turned around in a round-house alongside the track.

Here we go. IthinkIcan IthinkIcan. The first part of the trip follows along the Urubamba River, which is really the only way to get through this part of the world. There are no roads, only a few rickety-looking foot bridges across the river at this point, and all around, the Andes soar up into the fog, effectively cutting us off from the rest of the world.

About halfway up on many of the mountains there are slight ridges, furrows. They run horizontally and at first appear to be natural formations. Then the light dawns: these are terraces built by the Incas several centuries ago and still standing. They would build stone walls then haul up soil from the valley below and plant their crops. Archaeologists have found these terraces as high as 22,000 feet, which is pretty rare air for gardens. One courtyard at 20,700 feet had been cut and leveled and packed with almost 100 tons of earth from down below, or about 4,500 loads.

Incan rules decreed that the finest farmland in the empire would be used to produce food and fabric for religious purposes—the empire was really a theocracy—and most of that was burned as offerings. The second best was set aside for the rulers and nobility, and put in storehouses in case of war or famine. The local tillers of the terraces got what was left. And they got to keep up to 10 llamas per household. They had no money, so in lieu of taxes, each family had to work it out. This was not so difficult as it might seem, since then, and now, farmwork in these altitudes scarcely takes up 60 days a year. The rest of the time was devoted to the local WPA project, which around here was terrace building.

IthinkIcan IthinkIcan. The train slowly climbs higher for, although Machu Picchu is high, Cusco is even higher. The trip goes from 6,462 feet up to 11,207 feet at Cusco. That's a climb of 4,745 feet. Along here the altitude is still relatively low and the vegetation is thick, almost a rain forest. Quite pretty, it is, but not many people. Just a few huts here and there and occasionally a small village.

Gad. Out in the boonies without so much as a *cerveza*. No, wait. Here comes a small boy down the aisle of the train selling luke-warm beer. There is no point in debating the matter. He's got a monopoly. Other vendors come along selling cookies and crackers and sandwiches and guidebooks. Here come two armed guards. Curious. Not a bad trip, actually, and not a bad train. It may not be up to Amtrak, but it's a lot nicer than some I've been on. The scenery now changes to less vegetation as we get higher, but the mountains seem to get larger than ever, with snow on the tops in the early spring.

We stop on a siding and I ask why. It is to let another train come by, and sure enough, after a while it does. It is the train from Cusco, packed with Indians who have gone in for the weekend market. They are loaded down with baskets and purchases, along with whatever they took to sell and didn't. Bags and baggage, children and chickens. We crank up again and soon come to a pretty little village, right by the river.

A WASPish girl with her brown hair in pigtails comes bounding out of a gate and rushes down to the train. Soon a WASPish young man in a beard and a U.S. Army jacket saunters out of the gate, looks idly at the train and wanders back in. Now what in the world are two norteamericanos doing here? Peace Corpsmen? Hippies munching cocaine leaves without some overenthusiastic cop peering over their shoulders? Maybe it's Bonnie and Clyde in hiding. After all, Butch Cassidy and the Sundance Kid met their maker not too far from here, just to the south in Bolivia.

No matter, for off we go again. Here comes the kid with the warm *cerveza. Uno más, por favor.* The scenery is disappearing in the dark and we seem to be going rather slowly now. We stop again. For no reason. The two guards get out and muck about, chatting with the locals. Ah, here is a train employee getting back on as we take off again.

"Pardon me, señor, but what's the problem?"

"Problem? No problem. Just a leetle problem. A leetle part is broken," he says, holding up his hands to show that it's quite leetle.

"What part?"

"It is—how you say?—the brake."

IthinkIcan IthinkIcan. We are going slowly through the night as the guards wander up and down the aisles. We are now far behind schedule but—all things considered—I'd just as soon not go too fast, anyway. But why the guards? I seek out my fount of information again.

"Why the guards?"

"What guards?"

"Those two guys with the 45's strapped to their hips."

"Oh, it's nothing. Just—how you say—bandidos."

"What bandidos?"

"It's nothing. They don't get on much anymore."

"How much is 'much'?"

"It's nothing. Only a leetle thing."

Need for "Alamo"

At dawn yesterday the Alamo fell. It ended 13 days unparalleled in our history because the overriding fact was that the Texans didn't have to stay. They could have left. As a matter of fact, they were ordered to leave by Sam Houston, who felt the fort was indefensible.

But they stayed, and for one very simple reason—they knew that the longer they could delay the 4,000 troops under Gen. Antonio Lopez de Santa Anna, the better chance Texas had for success. They also knew that they would never know if they were right, but they obviously felt that it was worth the risk. As the West Berliners say, they voted with their feet.

The defenders numbered slightly more than 150 until a group of 31 volunteers from Gonzales under Capt. Albert Martin fought its way through the Mexican lines and into the fort. Now it may sound strange today—fighting for the opportunity to meet certain death—but if it does, then we are the poorer for it.

So these men, about 185 or so, from all walks of life and from all over, decided it was time to stand up and be counted. The garrison's commander, Col. William B. Travis, put it down neat and clear in the last letter from the Alamo. If you are a native Texan, you probably haven't read this letter since the third grade or so. If you are new, then don't feel left out. You have traveled a well worn path and are in exceedingly good company. Once more with feeling:

Commander of the Alamo
Bejar, Feby 24th, 1836

To the People of Texas & all Americans in the world—Fellow citizens
& compatriots—

I am besieged, by a thousand or more of the Mexicans under Santa
Anna—I have sustained continual Bombardment & cannonade for 24
hours & have not lost a man—the enemy has demanded a surrender
at discretion, otherwise, the garrison are to be put to the sword, if the
fort is taken—I have answered the demand with a cannon shot, & our
flag still waves proudly from the walls—I shall never surrender or retreat.
Then, I call on you in the name of Liberty, of patriotism & everything
dear to the American character, to come to our aid, with all dispatch—
The enemy is receiving reinforcements daily & will no doubt increase
to three or four thousand in four or five days. If this call is neglected,
I am determined to sustain myself as long as possible & die like a soldier
who never forgets what is due to his own honor & that of his country—
Victory or Death.

William Barret Travis
Lt. Col comdt.

P.S. The Lord is on our side—When the enemy appeared in sight we
had not three bushels of corn—We have found in deserted houses 80
or 90 bushels and got into the walls 20 or 30 head of Beeves.

Travis

On the dawn of the 13th day, Santa Anna began what was to be his
final assault. As a red flag fluttered from the church in Bexar and the
band played "Deguello," the massive army marched forward. No quarter.
In horrible fighting, they finally breached the outer wall of the courtyard
and poured in, slaughtering every single defender.

The cost to Santa Anna was between 1,000 and 1,600 of his best troops,
13 irreplaceable days, and eventually, the Battle of San Jacinto, his own
army, his own freedom, and Texas. Not a bad morning's work for the
Texans.

All of which brings us to today. One must cringe at the thought of
the members of that small garrison sitting up on some cloud peering down
at their Texas. What must they be thinking? What must they be saying?
What is the distance from the Alamo to Abilene? In men?

Imagine for a moment facing the jury box where men in coonskin hats
and leather jackets sit—holding their rifles and powder burns—explaining
to them that they died for the glory of unsecured loans and bank stock.
Invite Davy Crockett over some evening to watch the campaign speeches
on the tube—the televised copouts. Sit on a siding with Jim Bowie and

114

watch the campaign train roar by, and note his expression. Tell Travis all about the last session of the legislature—then duck.

Ah, the last letter from the Alamo—as drawn up by the House Investigations Committee: "We find no wrongdoing on the part of Mr. Santa Anna, a freely elected and highly responsible leader. His demand for a surrender has been answered with appreciation and the master key to the front door. If our call for support is neglected, we shall do something, or other. Maybe. If at all. Then again we may bug out the back."

And finally, imagine Sam Houston—a bit tipsy, perhaps, with scowl on face, hand on cane, floppy hat low over sunburned forehead—walking into the voting booth with you. Watch his face closely as you explain the list of candidates, their histories, their deeds, their headlines.

We need enough good men—150 in the House who once more are joined by 31 men from across the way—in the Senate. Add to them governor, the lieutenant governor, and so on. Alas, it appears that once again we need about 185 men who will stand up and be counted.

But where are you, Travis, now that we really need you? For we no longer answer the surrender demand with a cannon shot, we are no longer determined to sustain ourselves as long as possible & die like a soldier who never forgets what is due to his own honor & that of his country.

Perhaps it is time once again to remember the Alamo.

Stalking commies in Amarillo

To: Director
Central Intelligence Agency
Langley, Va.

From: Felix T. Mildew
Agent-in-Charge
Palm Springs, Calif.

Subject: Operation Putty Nose

As per your instructions, chief, I wound up my successful plot to overthrow Dominica, induced PATCO to join Solidarity and now have thoroughly investigated the need for the CIA to resume domestic spying operations. I realize this has to be trotted by Congress for advice but not consent, but we should have no trouble in rounding up the necessary support. (See: Operation Hoover.) Under separate cover I am sending along several interesting Polaroids that should at least get majority support from the House Intelligence Committee. The horse is on the left.

As for justification of domestic surveillance, that should be no problem. I mean, there is subversion all over the place and there are commies *everywhere.* I, personally, have spotted them on the golf course in Daytona Beach, along the strip in Las Vegas and on the slopes at Aspen. Throughout my in-depth investigation into communism in America I have . . . uh, excuse me, chief. There's a knock at the door.

Sorry. It was the bellboy with the ice. Now, where was I? Oh, yes. Here is a brief list of known communist agents who should be followed, their phones tapped, mail opened, and neighbors quizzed:

All members of the Save the Whales Committee (a front for the Save the Baby Seals Committee).

Lead-lined Indians who do acid rain dances.

Friends of Sargent Shriver.

All members of the media. (Show me a press club and I'll show you commiesymps to the core. There's a weathergirl in Omaha who I, personally, plan to investigate.)

Anyone named Veik (that's Kiev spelled backwards. Picked that up the other night while watching Password).

And, obviously, anyone who objects to our resumption of domestic spying operations. Really, what are they trying to hide, eh?

Come to think of it, I didn't order any ice.

According to your memo, chief, I see where we plan to resume "special activities" or, as we called it in the trade, "sneaking dealings" inside the United States so long as it doesn't influence U.S. policies or politics. Now come on. What's the point of, say, rigging an election or smearing a reputation if it doesn't influence policy? It's that kind of handcuffing of our intelligence community which has so greatly helped the International Communist Menace. See if you can't get that changed. Use tape made in Chicago hotel at ACLU convention if necessary.

Also, this continued ban on break-ins and electronic bugging is really going to hurt. Check with Legal Dept. to see if Fourth Amendment covers Democrats, too.

Odd. There seems to be a black wire running out of that ice bucket. Must remember to check it out.

Agent Staff Flag in Flagstaff reports strange dealings in that area and suggests we increase his office by 45 and double his budget. I agree. Flasgstaff is a known hotbed of international intrigue. Agent Armadillo in Amarillo reports that security at the nation's only helium plant is minimal. He urgently requests reinforcements and a replacement. Wire reads: "If I have to spend another January in Amarillo, I'm going bonkers." Will have it decoded immediately.

I keep hearing a ticking. That's curious. Anyway, suggest we set up a full-fledged domestic infiltration agency (Code name: Domestic Infiltration Agency) to coordinate burrowing into suspected enemy operations such as the Sierra Club, Chrysler and the Dallas Cowgirls. As a first step,

I have secured a skybox at Texas Stadium. (It's on expense account disguised as "Miscellaneous Aerial Observation—$47,500.") Also, plan to join Agent Orange in Cotton Bowl this Saturday. Any time you find thousands of people screaming "Go Big Red!" it bears watching, and the CIA never misses a thing.

Yr. Ob't Sr'vt
Felix T. Mildew
Agent-in-Charge

P.S.: Just received your latest message. No, I don't see any reason to beef up our Cairo office. The problem is in Dayton.

Shortest route to New York

THE AIRPORT COUNTER—"I'd like a plane ticket," I say to the clerk.
"Right," he says, turning to his computer screen. "Where to?"
"New York."
"The city or the state?"
"The city."
"The one by the Holiday JFK or the one by the Holiday LaGuardia?"
"I don't care. Either."
"Right," he says, typing furiously. "That'll be Flight 198. Houston to Atlanta to New York. You have a confirmed reservation."
"Uh, wait a minute. I don't want to go to Atlanta."
"You're not going *to* Atlanta. You're just going *through* it. Same plane."
"I don't even want to go through it. Just straight Houston–New York."
"It's a quick stop," he says.
"No. I have spent so much time waiting for flights in the Atlanta airport that I could legally vote for Andrew Young."
"But you stay on the plane."
"No."
"It hardly slows down. Just runs along the runway and takes off again."
"I said no!"
"Well, you don't need to get surly," he says, punching some more buttons. "OK, Houston to New York."
"Great."
"By way of Chicago."
"What?"
"And, of course, Atlanta."
"Look, do you have a direct flight to New York? If you do, put me on it. If not, I'm leaving."
"OK, OK, but you'll regret not going through Atlanta. Beautiful city."

He hits a few more keys. "Smoking or non-smoking?"

"Smoking."

"Cigarettes, pipe, cigars or those funny little things you roll yourself?"

"Cigars."

"Sorry, FAA rules prohibit smoking cigars on planes."

"Then why did you ask?"

"Just curious. You have yellow teeth. How about the chewing gum section?"

"Fine."

"Take two pairs of pants. Now, we have a special 10 percent discount under our Air Fair plan."

"Fantastic."

"And that puts you right in the middle of the Fourth of July Special."

"What Fourth of July Special?"

"For an Air Fair discount, you have to order your ticket six months in advance."

"But I want to go now. Today."

"Today? That's impossible, sir. I mean, it just isn't done."

"Do it."

"I don't think our computers are programmed for that." He punches a few more keys. The machine starts shaking, then groans. Smoke seeps out of a seam. It goes dead. "I hope you're happy," he says to me angrily. "Now I have to do it all by hand. Do you have a pencil?"

"Here."

He starts writing on a paper bag. "Would you like to take advantage of our Trip the Flight Fantastic Plan? Half off."

"OK," I say. "I'll do it."

"And the names of the other 34 in your group?"

"But it's just me. No group."

"No group? Do you have an eraser?" the clerk asks. I hand him one. He rubs the bag for a moment, then resumes writing. "May I see your God Is My Co-Pilot Club card?"

"I'm not a member."

"You get free drinks."

"No, thanks. I don't drink."

"Then you should join our High and Dry Club."

"What's that?"

"Special low-cost tickets. You get to wait in our special lounge, and during the flight the pilot lets you take over while he goes back and has a few drinks."

"No, thanks. I'm really not interested."

He scribbles some more on the paper bag. "All right, here you are. Houston non-stop to New York."

"No Atlanta stopover?"

"None at all. Of course, as part of our Beginners' Luck Special, you do have to fly over Oklahoma City."

"Why should I do that?"

"The air traffic control trainees handle this flight all by themselves, and they can't figure out where you are unless you start dead center in their radar screens. But it's a quarter off the regular fare."

"That does it!" I shout, storming off.

"OK, OK. Don't get mad," the clerk says. "Here you are, Houston–New York, direct line, no stops. How do you want to pay for it? Credit card, company billing or travelers' check?"

"Cash."

"What? Haven't you caused enough trouble? Well, all right, but you'll have to fill out this form and list three references."

I fill them out, pose for front and side photographs, then grab the ticket and examine it closely. It looks correct. "Thanks."

"Have a good trip," the clerk says as I walk off. "Oh, by the way, while *you* go straight to New York, your luggage goes to Atlanta."

Makes you shutter

AUSTIN—Photography is the world's most popular hobby. No one can even guess how many cameras there are in the world today, how many photographers, how many pictures, and how many times in the past men and women on top of mountains, diving into oceans, crying, smiling, dying, have been told: "Just one more."

Yet, back in the distant ages someone, somehow, somewhere, took the world's first photograph. And perhaps even today we can determine who took it and where and who owned it. So our search takes us—of all places—to this quiet southwest corner of the campus of the University of Texas, to the Humanities Research Center, past armed guards and up elevators and past scrutinizing secretaries to the Photography Collection on the sixth floor.

And finally to one Joe Coltharp, the curator, a spry, enthusiastic gentleman—the type which should be required of every museum and gallery in the world. He shares the thrill of discovery as it hits each visitor. He is guard, guide and cheerleader. Joe Coltharp could take you through hell and you'd plead: "Just one more time."

"The basis of what we have is the Gernsheim Collection," says Coltharp. "Helmut Gernsheim was a German who lives in France now although he has a Swiss mailing address. He is a photographer. He has taken some nice photos but he's not in the great class. But he was an excellent collector of photographs. I understand that he offered his collection to the Royal Society in London, which couldn't afford it. Then I heard that Wayne State University in Detroit was going to buy it and build a special museum for it. That fell through.

"Former President Harry Ransom had been following all of this and stepped forward. He bought the collection in 1964. I don't know the price, but the collection is priceless. No one can put a price on it today. Since then we have added on and now we have the Goldbeck Collection. He specialized in large groups of military forces. Here is one he took of the entire U.S. Army Panama Canal command. We have the Smithers Collection. He lived in Alpine and was a photographer who hired on as a mule skinner with Pershing when he chased Villa. His photos are fantastic." Coltharp holds up a shot of the U.S. cavalry cresting a ridge, swords and pennants flying. "Then there's the work of Jimmy Hare. At the turn of the century it wasn't considered an official war unless Hare was there. And a lot of Texana from all over the state."

Coltharp gets up from his desk and walks down a hall. "I am the only one with a set of keys, and when I take them home at night I never put them in the same place. What we have here is one of the top collections of photographs in America. No original ever leaves here unless it is hand-delivered and with a guard. We are not so much a museum as a research facility." He gestures to a room. "We check all parcels at the desk, and no one touches our material unless he wears white, cotton gloves. You can't be too careful."

He arrives at a heavy steel door, fumbles with some keys, and opens it. Inside is a sign warning that, in the event of fire, the area will be sprayed with toxic gas. It might kill the researchers, but it will save the photographs. "We have about 150,000 photos at least. We don't know for sure. We have this library on photography, about 10,000 volumes. Here are photo albums. This is the personal album of Lewis Carroll."

He opens new drawers and old album covers amidst an unbelievable collection of historical materials, and the funny thing is that practically no one knows they are here. This is the personal photo collection of John Foster Dulles: Nehru, Adenauer, the signing of the UN Charter and one autographed simply: "Elizabeth R." Here are microfilms—not so modern after all. This one was attached to a carrier pigeon and flown out of Paris when it was surrounded by the Communards in 1872.

In this drawer are photographs of the first war ever photographed in detail—the Crimean War in 1854. Not prints, but the originals by Robert Fenton. Here's a daguerreotype, by Daguerre. Shots made of the moon and shots made on the moon. The works of William Henry Fox Talbot, who copyrighted so much that he held photography back by 20 years, Coltharp says.

120

"This is a copy of 'Pencils of Nature,' printed in 1844. It was the first book which contained photographs," says Coltharp, opening a drawer. "They could not print photos with the type, so each book has them pasted in. This is the copy of 'Idylls of the King.' It was the first literary work illustrated with photographs. It is extremely rare. We have three of them."

Coltharp waves toward a mountain of cabinets. "We have the entire photo collection of the *New York Journal-American*. Negatives and prints. We got 129 filing cabinets full and haven't gone through a lot of them yet. It will take years. We have almost everything. Yale University asked if we had any historical pictures of mules, for some reason. We checked and sent them back 125 prints."

Then there are the cameras, between 1,700 and 2,000 of them. Ancient wooden boxes, motion picture cameras, big, little, new, old. Shelves and shelves of cameras. Roy Rogers. Boy Scout. U.S. Navy. And exposure meters from 1862 to 1948. Finally, Coltharp walks over to a shelf. On top is a cardboard box marked: "Glass." He pauses a moment, then says: "And this is the crown jewel." He takes off the cardboard, and here it is.

The world's first photograph.

Sitting here on a metal shelf in a building in Austin, Texas. At first glance it looks like an ornately framed silver plate. There are no whites and blacks. Just silver. But it is not silver at all. It is pewter. A plate 8 by 6½ inches, and you have to get up close and then get the light at an angle to see anything at all. Then you see it: rough and smooth, lines and shadows. It is a view of a courtyard in Gras, France, taken by Nicephore Niepce in 1826 from the window of his workroom.

Niepce was a man of means and an inventor who was in suspicious partnership with Louis Daguerre, generally thought to be the father of photography. But it was Niepce, not Daguerre, who took this, the world's first photograph. And it's underexposed, no doubt causing Niepce to yell: "Just one more."

He had been experimenting with lithography and tried to get a permanent image on stone, copper and zinc, without much luck. He and Daguerre kept up a correspondence, each trying to pry information out of the other while revealing little of his own work. Then in 1826, Niepce tried yet another experiment. He coated a polished pewter plate with bitumen of Judea, which becomes insoluble after being exposed to light. He left the lens open on a bright summer day for about eight hours, then washed the plate with a mixture of oil of lavender and white petroleum. This dissolved the parts of the bitumen which had not been hardened by the light. And on that summer day in 1826 – 11 years before Daguerre's initial success – Nicephore Niepce made the world's first photograph.

The story of the plate itself is interesting. It was lost for decades, put in a trunk in England, and eventually found by none other than Helmut

Gernsheim. Today it sits here in a helium-filled glass box in a room with 50 percent humidity under the watchful eye of Joe Coltharp. So our search ends here, except for one final question which must be answered: Who *owns* the world's first photograph?

You do.

English it is

It has been said time and again that Americans are lousy linguists. We have never had much interest in learning another language and it's getting worse. Only 8 percent of our colleges now have foreign language requirements, compared with 34 percent in 1966 and 85 percent in 1915. Fewer than 25 percent of us can read, write or speak anything but English.

The only exception to that trend is the huge number of people coming up from Mexico, bringing with them their language and culture. And, unlike earlier waves of immigrants, these new arrivals insist on the right to give their children a bilingual education in the public schools. This has been expanded by Federal Judge William Wayne Justice of Tyler. He wants bilingual courses offered to a greater number of Mexican immigrants, and to offer it through the 12th grade.

It is not clear just why the Spanish-speaking among us should be treated any differently from the millions of other immigrants who came ashore over the centuries speaking scores of languages. Indeed, if I were of Hispanic heritage I might be a little insulted that the government feels I'm too thick-headed to attain the same goals as the others: "Thanks, Judge Justice, but I'm just as swift as any Swede, so don't patronize me by ordering all these extra goodies just for me." Yes, I think I'd be slightly insulted by that decision.

It's a good thing that such legal decrees did not exist in previous years or today we might be speaking a babble of languages. As it is, we opted for English. Not by any majority rule, since the largest number of immigrants came from Germany. But English it is.

Still, in our never-ending desire to feel inferior, we constantly hear it pointed out that the average American can only speak one language while the average European can speak two or three. Unquestionably, we would have an advantage if we could speak other languages, and I'm all for it. I've tried it myself. As a matter of fact, I met my wife in Russian class. So don't send me hot letters saying I'm against learning other languages.

But I do get tired of being constantly told how much better off the average, say, German, is because he can communicate in several tongues. The fact is that in most of the world they speak various languages not because they *want* to, but because they *have* to. I recall a French businessman explaining that virtually every letter he wrote, every con-tract, every document he handled, had to be in French, English and Ger-man. Now this is no boon. This is a serious drawback to getting anything done. If you doubt that, consider doing your own thing three times over.

We have the advantage, not the disadvantage. In this country, an ad campaign to sell toothpaste can be done in one language. To cover the same area in Europe you would need about 25. Hollywood can turn out a movie in English to show to virtually all 230 million of the American people. To show to an equal number of Europeans, the movie has to be dubbed or sub-titled over and over, and even then you lose some of the flavor. Television and books and newspapers around here flow freely across state lines without missing a nuance. You can't do that in much of the world.

A businessman in Los Angeles can pick up the phone and cut a deal with his counterpart in New York. No sweat. A businessman in Lisbon calling Moscow (which is on the other side of Europe but 24 miles closer to Lisbon than L.A. is to New York) would first have to hunt up a translator. His colleague in Moscow, for self-protection, would have to do the same. So don't let anyone sing you the praises of being bi- or tri-lingual in other parts of the world. It's not a help, it's a huge, unavoidable hindrance.

In light of Judge Justice's ruling, we might wonder what kind of Texas our grandchildren will have. Will every book, speech, sign, warning, have to be in two languages? Our ballots already are in English and Spanish. Will our laws and courts be bogged down even more by translations? There is nothing wrong whatsoever in promoting our heritages, but when it serves to split us into factions, watch out.

Theodore Roosevelt once said, "There is no room in this country for hyphenated Americanism. . . . The one absolutely certain way of bring-ing this nation to ruin, preventing all possibility of its continuing to be a nation at all, would be to permit it to become a tangle of squabbling nationalities."

Judge Justice's ruling might well make it easier for newcomers to get in the mainstream. I certainly hope so. But if it only perpetuates the inabil-ity of young Texans to speak our language, get a job, climb the ladder, then the judge is not doing them any favor.

Roosevelt had some thoughts about that, too: "We have room for but one language here, and that is the English language, for we intend to see that the crucible turns our people out **as** Americans, and not as dwellers in a polyglot boarding house."

We tend to forget that language differences have torn apart many a country. Today we can see the problems in Belgium and, just to the north of us, in Canada, where a great and good nation may very well be split and harmed because its citizens can't agree on what to call a spoon.

I remember once flying back from Paris and going over Montreal. I turned to my seat companion, a Frenchman, and said, "Did you know that Montreal is the second largest French-speaking city in the world?" He nodded, then responded: "Yes, and isn't it a shame."

Observations

Put down your pens and swords, your Whigs and wigs, your grape and shot, and gather 'round. Yes, it is that time again, when we honor the greats among us who have made 1776 a year to forget. Indeed, here we are, a bit more than halfway through the year, and already we have enough winners for an awards ceremony.

So the parchment, please, as we present the Awards to Celebrated Citizens—the Mrs. Olsens among us at the Boston Tea Party of life. First, and certainly least, we honor the town drunk and former corset-maker, Thomas Paine, whose 47-page pamphlet, *Common Sense*, has sold hundreds of thousands of copies. Paine, broke as usual, hasn't realized a cent from his writing, having ordered his partner and printer, Robert Bell, to donate Paine's half of the profits to buy mittens for the American soldiers in Quebec. To Paine we give our Glove Thy Neighbor trophy.

Moving onward, to the French government, which has temporarily (eight months) abolished its *Corvée* policy of mustering up forced labor for road repairs, we give our Drive Friendly—Or Else Trophy. And to Russia, which has only just now signed a treaty with Denmark giving up her claims to Holstein, we present our There Is Nothing Like a Dane combat ribbon.

Finally overseas, Austria has abolished torture, and to the royal court we give our Welcome to the 18th Century trophy.

Now let us come back home, or almost, to Canada, where an American army has been fighting to free that enslaved area from the King's yoke, whether it wants to be freed or not. To General Benedict Arnold, commander of what's left up there, we present our Up Against the Wall, Redcoat Mother trophy.

Least Remembered Line of the Year: "We hold these truths to be sacred and undeniable. . . ."—Thomas Jefferson, before it was changed by Ben Franklin.

Best Remembered Quote of the Year (Gallows Humor Div.): "When the hanging comes, it will be over with me in a minute, but you will be kicking the air for an hour after I'm gone."—Portly Benjamin Harrison, upon signing the Declaration of Independence, to another signer, Elbridge

Gerry, who was both small and frail. Gerry refused to see the humor in the statement.

Least Remembered Man at Philadelphia: Timothy Matlack, a penman, who transcribed the final copy of the Declaration.

Best Remembered Reluctant Quote of the Year: "You write 10 times better than I do."—John Adams, deferring the job of writing the Declaration, to a young colleague from the South, Thomas Jefferson.

Let us now honor Silas Deane, our sneaky political agent to France, who—for the first time—utilized invisible ink to convey secret messages from Paris to Philadelphia. He used a tannic acid solution, writing between the lines in his letters, which could be read when the paper was dumped in ferrous sulfate. To Silas, we give our coveted Deane's List Trophy, along with our Cloak and Swagger medal.

Sergeant Thomas Hickey, hanged for treason in New York on charges of conspiring to kidnap General Washington and deliver him to the British, receives our Hang Loose Award (Come, Let Us Treason Together Div.). General Washington, who has been authorized by Congress to muster up to 2,000 Indians to fight for the colonies, wins our Home of the Braves plaque (crossed fingers over a field of broken promises). And we note in this area that Britain has signed an agreement with three separate German states to send mercenaries to fight for the British against Americans. In all, 29,166 men will come, and to them we give our God Is an Englishman (But a German Will Stand in at Cost-Plus) award.

Strangest Recruit in a Rather Strange Army: Private Yankee Doodle, who stuck a feather in his hat and called it macaroni.

To Benjamin Franklin, who was appointed our envoy to Madrid but refused to go, we present our The Reign in Spain Is Plainly on the Wane Trophy. And to Benjamin Franklin (the same), who was named an envoy to Canada to bring the 14th colony into the fold, but didn't, we give our Canada Try ribbon.

Least Statesmanlike Move of 1776: On March 23rd, Congress authorized privateering.

New Jersey, of all places, wins our award for giving "all inhabitants" of adult age, worth 50 pounds or more, and residing in their county for 12 months, the right to vote in general elections. For the next 14 years, New Jersey will not realize that this means women—yes, women—can vote. Fortunately, the law will be rewritten limiting voting to "free, white males," as, indeed, it should. New Jersey wins our Barefoot and Pregnant trophy.

Britain's General Thomas Gage offered a general pardon to all leaders of the rebellion except for two, whom he still wants to hang: Samuel Adams and John Hancock. Since the general has refused to sign such a pardon, we give him our Put Your Thomas Gage Right Here trophy.

To George III, whose statue in New York's Bowling Green has been melted down for Continental bullets—42,088 by actual count—we give our Get the Lead Out combat ribbon.

Least Important Event of the Day: This morning, Thomas Jefferson bought seven pairs of gloves for his wife, who is sick. He also paid three pounds, 15 shillings, for a new thermometer.

But now let's get down to the biggie award. John Adams wrote to his wife right after the July 2 vote approving the Declaration of Independence: "I am well aware of the toil and blood and treasure that it will cost us to maintain this Declaration, and support and defend these states. Yet through all the gloom I can see the rays of ravishing light and glory. I can see that the end is more than worth all the means; and that posterity will triumph in that day's transactions." So to Adams, and Franklin and Jefferson and Washington and all the rest of that crew, who is leading us to God knows where, we give our Floundering Fathers trophy (Give Us Liberty Or Just Forget the Whole Thing Div.). Now let's hear it for our winners.

Texians pull through scrape

WEST OF THE BRAZOS—This is the time of the Runaway Scrape. The name does not have a very triumphant ring. It does not conjure up visions of lightning charges, heroic victories and magnificent highlights of mankind. Nor should it. For the Runaway Scrape was a time of mud and blood, of obscene butchery and frightened families, of panic and chaos. And it happened here.

This is Central Texas, roughly the time between the fall of the Alamo on March 6 and the victory at San Jacinto on April 21. A short time, as the modern calendar turns, but eons for those who were running for their very lives, with weighted wagons trying to cross bloated rivers, and Santa Anna's legions hot on their hides.

The scene is very simple: It is the spring of 1836 and Texas, foolhardy in the extreme, has decided that it is a free republic no longer under the rule of Santa Anna. Anglo settlers and Latin landlords alike have already banded together at Washington-on-the-Brazos, just up the way, to declare on March 2 that Texas is now and forever shall be free. It takes one day to draw up the document, one day to sign it. The delegates are in agreement, they live under despotism, there is no freedom of religion, no public schools , the Indians have been incited against them, there is no protection, and "it is the right of the people to take their political affairs in their own hands in extreme cases."

The fact that this is an extreme case is not up for debate. In the midst of their learned discussions on the rights of mankind they get more gamey news. The Alamo has fallen, and with it, their sons and brothers and neighbors. The delegates vote to ride to war, but are held back by more sober minds who feel that the army is better off without facing an invasion of politicians, and besides, they have to hammer out a government. This they do, creating a Texas constitution worth fighting for. On March 16, faced with the news that Santa Anna has crossed the Colorado at Bastrop, the Constitution is ready for signing. Texas' first civil officers are elected after midnight, and at 4 a.m. the convention is adjourned so the lawmakers can join the Runaway Scrape.

It is just in time, for Texas and Texians are moving out. It began even before the Battle of the Alamo down around what is today Corpus Christi in January when news came that the Mexican Army was crossing the Rio. Then it began to snowball. On March 11, Sam Houston moves his army east across Texas to the Colorado River and orders all Texians to do likewise. That was the bugle calling retreat. By March 17, the day after the Constitution is signed, Washington-on-the-Brazos is deserted. San Felipe de Austin, the biggest city around, with five stores and 30 houses is burned to the ground by its inhabitants, and left. Richmond is abandoned by April 1. All settlements between the Brazos and the Colorado are emptied. Before April 13, San Augustine and Nacogdoches are left bare, as the inhabitants flee toward the east.

It is a cold and wet spring and the rivers which bar the way to safety are swollen to dangerous heights, but still the Texians come. Women and children mostly, for the men have gone the other way, to join Sam Houston's little army as citizen soldiers. The men gather at Gonzales, at Harrisburg, at muddy crossroads and hamlets, Indian fighters and traders and ranchers and farmers. Some go to join Fannin at Goliad, where they are captured and 427, including 90 too wounded to be moved from their beds, are executed.

The Runaway Scrape continues. Wagons, horses, a few cattle, children and dogs, trudge eastward before the Mexican Army. Many die on the road and are buried where they fall. Disease runs through the soggy camps. Doctors are scarce since they, too, have joined the army. Most Texians burn their homes before they leave, so that Santa Anna will find nothing to take.

The going is no better for the Mexican army. Cannons and ammunition, horses and wagons, have to be shoved through the mud and wrestled across streams. The rivers prove almost impossible, and sappers work around the clock to set up crossings. Yet the Texas countryside warms on occasion, the spring flowers begin to peep out, and Mexican soldiers are touched by the beauty of it all. Indeed, Colonel Gonzales Pavon orders his men not to harm what's left of the town of Gonzales, because he wants his regiment to set up a colony here after the war.

"If the banks of the Guadalupe, going from Bejar (San Antonio) to Austin are extremely beautiful, because of the winding of the river, and undulation of the woods, ali of which created a beautiful contrast with its green valley, the area in which the town of Gonzales was situated is no less pleasant," José Enrique de la Peña, an officer with Santa Anna, writes in his diary.

What little is left behind by the Texians is quickly snatched up by the Mexican soldiers. Cattle, pigs, chickens, all are popped in the pot by the army chefs. The few buildings left standing become barracks for the Mexican soldiers. Things are looking up: "Had we been well organized, the Texas campaign would have been a delightful trek, a series of pleasant days in the country interspersed with military maneuvers," de la Peña writes.

That trek was long ago, but these are the river banks they marched to. These are the fields where they camped. They are the places the pioneers and privates saw during the Runaway Scrape. So much happened here, and we overlook most of it. We remember only the Alamo and Goliad and San Jacinto. We forget General José Urrea, who captured Fannin then pleaded for his life. We forget Elijah Stapp, who kept on working as a delegate at Washington-on-the-Brazos while his family possessions were being destroyed by the invaders marching through Victoria. We forget the time the Guadalajara Battalion, dug in on both sides of a riverbank, looked up in amazement as a Texian steamboat tooted through camp.

Golden time

THE DEN—It is the bewitching hour. In my home, that means a few choice minutes when my wife and I get together to discuss the day. It's the cocktail hour.

I suppose that, if one could set up a daily calendar, the span from 5 to 6 p.m. would be the ideal time for the cocktail hour. But the simple fact is that I am usually not home then, nor—from looking at the freeways—are most other husbands in Houston. Five and six o'clock may come and go, still the work day flourishes.

But eventually, at whatever time into the night it is, the husband comes home through the traffic, up the driveway, out of the car and through the bicycles, skates and garbage spilled by the neighbor's dog. Then, after having slain the dragons of work and transit and reentry, the father goes into his bedroom, there to disrobe and get into something comfortable.

That, in itself, is a symbolic shedding of the day's worries.

Then one must solve several familiar problems. The case of the lost lunch money. The need for new tennis shoes. The flea powder and the chinch bugs. My wife, meantime, is busily bustling about in the kitchen preparing dinner. Children, neighbors' children, dogs, neighbors' dogs, come and go. This is the storm before the calm.

Yet, little by little, order is restored. Sometimes this requires frowns or fisticuffs, but, eventually, things get quiet. And once the immediate problems are solved, once the casserole or souffle or Hamburger Helper is on low, it is that golden time of the day—the cocktail hour.

To be truthful, the name is wrong, false advertising, because "cocktail" connotes alcoholic beverages. It can be Dr Pepper or Sprite or a tall glass of iced tea, no matter. And it's rarely a whole hour. More like 20 minutes.

Yet, whatever the drink and however long the time, it's a part of the day to which I look forward. My wife and I sit down. When the weather is cold, we stay indoors with a fire and a little soft music. But if the weather is right, such as many evenings this time of year, we go outside. No matter the place, it's the time and the atmosphere which are important. So it is that we sit down, and go ahhhhhh.

That is a signal. At that very moment, small people come into the room with spelling tests and he-hit-me problems. Now I invoke the law of the land: They may come in and sit down and join the conversation, but do not bring their baggage of problems with them. It's cocktail time. Parents have rights, too.

I tell my wife and she tells me what happened today. A bringing up to date. A let-it-all-hang-out time. It's great therapy. We go through everything, the creeping crabgrass, the insolent driver, the rotten shopkeeper, the obscene telephone call.

Or, on the other hand, the funny things that happened, the joke told by a friend, the cute quote, the ironic situation, the fortune which arrived in the mail if we only buy a lot on Lake Slime. Other subjects to cover include report cards, the Oilers, what a gallon of milk cost early in the day and have you read any good books lately. I also inevitably bring up the West Loop, taxes and how long is it until my vacation. The cocktail hour is a good time had by all. I love it.

I cannot say with certainty how this splinter of time developed, it simply evolved. Because in earlier days, when the small people were wee, there just wasn't time. Dinner was a major production of shoveling Pablum, and the following baths were enough to exhaust an army. Next, my wife and I ate supper. By then the 10 o'clock news was on and the day was over.

If you have a house full of small children and are wondering just how in the world you and your spouse will ever find time for the cocktail hour, take heart. You see, as the children got older, we discovered—to our delight—that they could get along by themselves. We could say, "It's time to eat," and we'd all sit down and eat. We could say, "Go take a bath," and didn't have to follow along to make sure they didn't go down the drain. Year by year, they took more care of themselves, they didn't need us anymore. Thus, not by design but by age, we had some moments alone.

Like right now. Some of them are into homework and, far from bothering us, don't want *us* to bother *them*. So we come here, my wife and I, to the den. I turn on the music, fire up a cigar. Then we sit down and say ahhhhhhh. What's been happening? How did the day go? I recommend it highly.

Flying that kite

THE FIELD—This is the big day we've all been waiting for. Our first (and no doubt last) Indian Guide Kite Flying Contest. Man against nature, father & son against father & son. Hate, kill, stomp, bleed. This kite-flying is dirty business. Whoever said "Go fly a kite" obviously never did.

We arrive shortly after 1 p.m. as the sun is getting downright hot on the asphalt parking lot. Fathers and sons are already scattered hither and yon trying out their kites. With me are Little Brave and Lobo. Little Brave is my eldest son. Lobo is the kite. There is no question which is which as Lobo says LOBO in large red letters across his top. Beneath it is a full moon and down at the bottom is a lobo howling at the aforementioned moon.

"I don't think we'll win," says Little Brave, surveying the opposition. And indeed, there is some sophisticated hardware afloat here on the parking lot. Big kites, little kites, red, yellow, hot pink and pale chartreuse kites. This town is full of weird kite-flying talent.

"Remember what we say in the Apache tribe, Little Brave. It's not whether you win or lose, it's how you slay the game. That's an old Indian expression I learned from an old Indian."

Little Brave snorts. The red youth of today is not properly respectful of his parents. As a matter of fact, my son is no smarter than my father.

"Let's give Lobo a try," I say. "Here, you hold the kite and I'll get it up for you." He holds the kite and his wise old father, Scratching Bull, lopes off across the macadam prairie. And lopes and lopes. Lobo lopes after me, showing no interest in being airborne. Forty-five miles later, Scratching Bull is bushed.

Little Brave strides up. "Here," he says patiently. "You hold it and I'll try." I stand more or less upright and Little Brave walks backward a few steps as that damned kite takes off like a Saturn rocket. He casually plays out the string to the end. The kids today have absolutely no respect.

"Bring it down easy," I say. We must be careful with Lobo since we made it from the ground up, so to speak. The rules said we could buy the sticks but we members of the Apache tribe cut them—we like to go native all the way. Besides, the Indian Guides consider us some kind of outcast since discovering that our last tribal project made firewater.

It is time to gather around the man in charge, Superchief. "First is the tribal kite-flying," he announces. We Apaches grin that inscrutable red-man's grin, for we know we are a sure thing. Our ultimate weapon is the neighborhood surgeon, Running Sores, who is a kite builder extraordinary. If NASA had hired Running Sores, it could have saved millions on rocket propellants.

The large tribal kites are lined up for the contest. Some are bigger than the Apaches' entry, but none looks so sleek, so smooth. "The first kite to go up on 150 feet of string and stay up for 10 seconds wins," says Superchief. We stand by as Running Sores holds his huge white box kite up with one hand. In the other he holds an old Indian kite-flying aid, a rod and reel.

"Go!" shouts Superchief. The mighty kites rise slowly and, one by one, do an imitation of a Zero at Coral Sea. All but ours. The entry from the mighty Apaches soars onward and upward till death do us part. Running Sores slowly plays out the line till the huge kite is only a small white spot hovering somewhere over downtown Beaumont.

"Hooray, hooray!" we Apaches cheer as one. Break out the firewater, we are once again king of the Indian nation. Watch out, roundeyes. Wounded Knee, here we come. Ah, here is Superchief with his clipboard. We cluster around to watch as he breaks out the plaque.

"And to the Apaches, third place."

Silence.

Angry looks.

"Third place? How could we finish third out of one? We've got the only kite up there! Superchief scores with forked pencil. Hate, kill, stomp, bleed!" A mutiny is brewing among the Apaches.

"The two others got theirs up first and they stayed 10 seconds," says Superchief. He always has a way of shooting down our noble anger with cold facts. "Now it's time for the individual kites."

We line up in sullen silence. Due to our test flight, Little Brave and I decide we will have a better chance to win if Scratching Bull stands there and holds the kite while Little Brave works the string.

"Just keep out of the way," Little Brave says with childlike candor. Scratching Bull does as he's told.

"Go," says Superchief and I let go. Lobo falls to the ground like a spent sparrow. I raise it again, and this time Lobo sails into the Great Spirit's domain for about three seconds, then turns downward and crashes into the ground, breaking into so many parts that not even Running Sores could mend it.

"We lost," says Little Brave. Scratching Bull, in his infinite wisdom, jumps up and down on Lobo's head. "It's only a game," says Little Brave softly. We gather up Lobo and get into the car for the sad journey home. Once back in the tepee, Scratching Bull unpops a beer and sits down to console his shattered dreams.

Odd, there is something going on outside. It is Little Brave in the street holding on to the end of a string. At the other end—grinning madly—is a mended Lobo sailing merrily among the clouds. It is a day Scratching Bull shall remember for as long as the rivers flow and the sun shines—whichever comes first.

What war?

JERUSALEM—This is the story of how I covered the war. It all began one evening right here at the bar. I had spent the day in pursuit of the best Israeli red wine, only to find that what I had been drinking *was* the best Israeli red wine.

Two other journalists had been in here earlier, both saying that something was afoot. "It looks big," said *Newsweek*.

"Bigger than big," said the *Guardian*.

"What looks big?" I asked.

"Nothing," they replied, leaving me with the check.

"They mean the war," said Akmed, the bartender.

"The war? There's no war on."

"It's early in the week," said Akmed.

The next day while I was wandering through the souk, a man came up to me and gasped, "Fat Man. Tell Fat Man that the Jordan flows both ways."

"Did he have this dagger in his back when he approached you?" the taxi driver asked me later.

"Not that I noticed," I replied.

"Did he say anything?" the taxi driver asked me on the way back to my hotel. "Anything before he died?"

"The inspector's dead?"

"No. Maurice."

"Who's Maurice?"

"He was the fellow in the burnoose with the dagger in the back," the driver said, stopping the car so he could hold the .38-Magnum in his other hand. He clicked back the hammer. "One more time. Did he say anything?"

"Yes, yes, he did," I replied. "He said . . ." Just then the bomb went off under the hood and put an end to both our conversation and the cab driver. Competition must be pretty fierce among Jerusalem cabbies.

"There's nothing up," I was assured by an official Israeli government spokesman the next morning. "Besides, we couldn't fight a war right now if we wanted to."

"Why not?" I asked.

"All the TV crews are covering the Falklands."

"Actually," said a diplomat at the U.S. Embassy, "a war right now is out of the question. Israel couldn't afford it. Don't you know the U.S. is in the middle of a recession?"

"If Israel invaded another country, what would the U.S. do?"

"Do?" said the diplomat. "Why, we'd be appalled. Angry. The president and Congress would take swift action against Israel."

"How?"

"They'd say tacky things about Menachem Begin. And wait a couple of days before sending the next shipment of F-16s. It would require firm action on our part."

I went down the hall to the CIA office. "I have no new information," said the head spook. *"The Washington Post* hasn't arrived yet."

"But I keep hearing that the Israeli Army is on alert. That it is going to march at 1 a.m. tomorrow—the Third Parachute Regiment leading the attack."

"Which way?"

"Down, I suppose. Don't parachutes go that way?"

"Which *direction*. Who is Israel going to war with?"

"Aren't you supposed to know things like that?" I asked.

"We can't be expected to know everything," said the spook. "Now I've got to go. The wife and I are taking a weekend vacation."

"Where?"

"The Beirut Holiday Inn."

It was clear that nothing was happening. Still, there was no point in taking any chances. It might be my big opportunity to cover a real live war. I immediately took the first step any foreign correspondent takes in such a situation: I bought a safari suit. They won't let you in press conferences at the foreign ministry of any self-respecting country unless you are in a safari suit.

"It starts tomorrow," said Akmed at the bar late that night.

"What starts tomorrow?"

"Excuse me, stranger," said a tall blonde, sliding up to the bar. "Do you have the time?"

"For what?" I asked.

"The time. Like what time is it?" she panted breathlessly.

"It's midnight. Why?"

"Oh, just an hour to go," she said, slinking off. Then she turned. "Do you know which way the Jordan flows?"

I said I didn't, and she left.

"Maybe it flows both ways," said an overweight fellow sitting at a corner table. I hadn't seen him before. He was perspiring profusely while swatting flies with last month's *Brangus Gazette*. "Can I buy you a drink, Mr. Ashby?" he said.

"How did you know my name?" I asked, reaching for my No. 2 pencil and my Big Chief tablet.

"It's written on the receipt from the Tel Aviv Sears pinned to your safari jacket," he grinned.

There was something about him I didn't like. Probably because I'm partial to flies.

"What do you know about the war?" the Fat Man asked.

"What war?"

"Very good. Cautious. I like that in a man."

"I can't see that any war is on the way. Israel would never attack a neighbor."

"You're absolutely right," said the Fat Man over the thunder.

Meanwhile, at the bar, two American diplomats were saying tacky things about Menachem Begin.

A fellow squirrel

THE YARD—He's out here somewhere. I know he is. If he comes walking by, I can spot him at 20 paces in a fog. His name is Earl, and he's really not very hard to identify. Funny little grin. Beady eyes. Brown hair. Furry tail. Doesn't like cigar smoke.

Oh, I should note that Earl is not your run-of-the-PTA neighbor. He's a squirrel, actually. But don't hold that against him, because, otherwise he's just your average fellow. Likes a good dirty joke, J&B and Walter Cronkite. And he's partial to avocado.

Earl came into our happy little family quite by accident, as, indeed, did most of the other members. It all began one quiet evening last spring when I was out for my stroll. Down the street, there seemed to be a crowd of the Munchkin Mafia, the wee tads in the block who stopped stripping cars long enough to form a circle around something on the ground.

That something turned out to be a tiny baby squirrel which apparently had fallen out of its nest, or possibly was thrown overboard by design because of terminal halitosis. I came upon the scene as the gang was trying to decide which lucky family would shelter the baby.

"You should just leave him alone," I said in my woodsy fashion. "Its parents will come back and fetch it eventually, even as your own do, albeit reluctantly." This idea was greeted with sullen stares all around. "Then one of you will have to take it home."

Thus I departed under the hail of stones, giggling slightly over the thought of the poor slob who would be up all night taking care of a baby squirrel. That night I stayed up, taking care of a baby squirrel.

Earl the Squirrel, as he was christened, was slow on the uptake. We almost lost him, to be truthful. He wouldn't eat. The vet said that Earl would take to a dropper and canned milk, which was ordered up posthaste. After a few worrisome days, Earl showed signs of life, and began to nibble a bit on some lettuce. Then he took to cracked and peeled nuts. Then to boiled water and more milk and peanuts and avocado. Fresh avocado. At a half-buck a whack.

"This is outrageous!" I stormed. "There isn't room in this house for me and that damned squirrel!" A quick look around the table told me that I should not poll the delegation as to who was leaving, so Earl moved in, lock, stock and avocado. Actually, he was a cute little fellow, popping around the house, snoozing in this cage, nibbling on Lafite Rothschild '29. I am dead set against trying to domesticate wild animals, remembering what happened to Adam, but Earl had an ingratiating talent for getting his way. When I commanded him to stop wetting on the rug, he would act as though he couldn't understand a simple English sentence. When I declared that he must get into his cage, he would run up my pants leg and take a nap. I was in no position to argue.

As he grew in wisdom and stature and favor of God and man, Earl would go outside for brief climbs. We would open the door, and with strong urging ("Earl, you're a squirrel, for God's sake, go out and climb a tree.") he would venture into the outback. Five minutes later, Earl would be scratching at the door again, ready for J&B before dinner.

This insanity lasted into the summer, and we really forgot to notice him. This would lead to phone interruptions ("Hold on for a minute, I've got to get the squirrel some avocado."), followed by strange pauses on the other end of the line.

But all good things must come to an end, thankfully. It was in midsummer, and Earl was out for his after-dinner stroll. Every evening he would stay out longer and longer, sometimes past his bedtime. This time, he went out and, quite simply, never came back. We looked, we whistled (if you ever want to feel stupid, go outside and whistle for your squirrel), but nothing. Earl had reverted back to his own, eschewing anchovies and J&B and avocados with a twist of lemon and perhaps a dash of salt, if you don't mind. He was gone.

There was a great gnashing of teeth and tearing of hair and wearing of sackcloth and ashes even unto the fifth and sixth generations, but no Earl. He was back in his tree. Sayonara, Yankee Dog. But I have no doubt that next spring, one evening just before Walter Cronkite, we will hear a scratching at the door, and there will be Earl, with Earleen and seven little squirrelettes, ready for their J&B and peeled avocado. With a twist of lemon, if you don't mind.

The sole survivor

THE CABINET—Good grief, what is this?

I know what it is, actually. I've always known, it's just that this sort of crept up on me. An old friend I had not expected to see. It is a glass. A wine glass. Of indiscriminate form, sort of square with the proper stem flowing down to the base, a round base. If you saw it, you would not rise up and shout, "There, by George, is a wine glass!"

Over the years, it has been pushed back to the rear of the muster because it does not mix and mesh with any of the other $1.50 wine glasses. It is a cut above—and years before—the others. And it is the sole survivor, the last boat from Dunkirk, the rear guard of years past.

We bought six wine glasses when we lived in New York City, bought them at Bloomingdale's, and I can even tell you what kind of a day it was, but I won't since clearly you couldn't care less. We bought them, all six, made in Belgium, and they came in a box with partitions to keep the glasses from banging together. A sort of six-pack, it was. A dark brown box with six wine glasses made in Belgium. It was a major investment for newlyweds trying to live on the $3,600 a year my wife made as a teacher and the $110 a week I was bringing home from *The New York Times*.

We used them, when we could afford wine, and we used them when we couldn't. I drank iced tea from those glasses.

Over the years, one by one they got broken, just how I do not remember, but they did not go together in one big crash. Mostly the dishwasher ate them. All but this one. Well, today I can't really use a single wine glass that does not look anything like the others. It is the bastard child of the cabinet, but it shall never be thrown away because it is an old friend. It just keeps getting pushed to the back of the shelf, and when we die our children shall go through the cabinets and say, "What's this? A lone wine glass? Out it goes." Then it, too, shall meet its maker.

You probably have something similar. Maybe several. A spoon. A toy. Not the usual newspaper clippings and photographs that are easily decipherable to others, but rather things which, by themselves, are meaningless to anyone else. Merit badges. Dog collars. Rosebud. A remembrance of times past, times that were good no matter how bad they were. A blanket that kept away the witches. A robe that kept away the cold. Or maybe just a good book, probably—in today's bright light—a very bad book, but at the time a most valued friend.

It does not have to be tangible. It can just as easily be an expression. A smile. A bright autumn afternoon or a dark winter morning when the wind shuffles the leaves and the water drips from the drainpipe. Old friends, come back for a visit.

We all have a few around, their numbers culled out by time, by each move, by each fire or flood or divorce or death. A few recollections that get shunted aside by the day-to-day life in the 1980s. But then, ah, but then, most unexpectedly they pop up. A saying. A picture. A song. Play it again, Sam.

They always bring back pleasant memories, or we would have tossed them out long ago. No one wants to keep around reminders of bad times. Christopher Robin. Robin Hood. Nancy Drew. Robin Roberts. It does not even have to be of childhood. Panmunjon. 3-D. The Dallas Eagles vs. the Fort Worth Cats. I had a '51 Ford. Blue.

I used to chuckle at my father's Baylor letter sweater. Green and gold. He always kept it, long after he couldn't fit in it. I could never figure out why he kept it, moth-eaten and ragged. One day he didn't make the trip, and the team bus was hit by a train.

You have them around, even if you don't know it. How much is that doggie in the window? Ask not what your country can do for you. I have a dream. Sorry about that, chief.

The New York World's Fair was in town, mainly because it was New York. Friends came to visit us and stay at our apartment. Some of them we even knew. A West Texas rancher came in his pickup and when we said there was no room in the inn, he rolled out his bedroll on the floor. We talked about Texas and drank wine.

I wonder what we shall recover and recall decades hence? Astro stubs? Anderson bumper stickers? Longnecks? In 1999, what will we stumble across that shall relight those good old days of neutron bombs and save-the-whales?

Whatever it is, it will come as a surprise on a busy day when all sorts of things are happening. And suddenly, there it is. A wine glass, the sole survivor, Rosebud.

Mourning after

So this is what it's like, right? This is the big time all you 18-year-old Texans have been waiting for. Drink time. Hats and horns. Huzzah. Huzzah.

Yes, indeedy, the laws have been changed and last night was the first time you could legally enter the corner tavern and partake of demon rum. So you did, didn't you? Sauntered in with all the ease of Marvin Zindler in La Grange, walked up to the bar, carefully put one foot on the brass rail and in a loud voice, said: "Barkeep, a double Scotch and bourbon."

Then you had another, and maybe one more, right? Remember how the walls started moving about and the floor began its curious buckle? And for some unknown reason your great and wondrous thoughts on life, death, God and the Great Chinch Bug Conspiracy just wouldn't come out right.

Then you left, and through the grace of the Houston Police Department you finally made it home. And into bed, where you tried to sleep while keeping one foot on the floor. All of which brings us to this morning. The morning after the night before. Your eyes look like a Gulf roadmap, and your mouth tastes like the Red Army marched through it, in muddy boots. And some idiot is running a metal lathe either under your bed or between your ears—it's hard to tell. All in all, you are in line for a mercy killing.

So here you lie. Your eyes won't focus and your brain won't function. You are broke. And something happened to your watch, although you can't recall exactly what. You have a strange bruise on your forehead and odd stains on your knees. Finally, somewhere in the back of your brain is a vague recollection of standing on a piano and reciting "To a Louse."

This drinking bit isn't exactly what it's cracked up to be, is it? And all those funny Phil Harris and W. C. Fields jokes don't seem too humorous, do they? You waited for 18 years for this? You could have waited another 18.

Well, all is not lost. Here are some handy rules to avoid feeling like the fire marshall on the Hindenburg. Take notes, and try to stop those dry heaves while I'm talking.

First, never drink during the week. Coming in hungover on Monday morning is permissible, but not on Tuesday, Wednesday, Thursday and

Friday. As a matter of fact, if you come in hungover on Tuesday, there is a definite chance that they won't be needing you on Wednesday.

Never drink before the sun goes down. It is a medical fact that this causes scurvy in mice, so there is no telling what it will do to you.

Never drink with mice.

When the bartender says, "Do you want a Delaware punch?" don't answer. It's an old joke and not worth explaining.

The Seagram 7 are not on trial for conspiracy.

Not only is it a felony to take a loaded gun into a bar, if you shoot and miss, it can be downright dangerous.

You may order Black Label or White Label without feeling like a bigot. You may even order a Pink Lady, but there is no guarantee you'll get one.

They do not carry White Lightning at the Old Capitol Club.

Never order a Horse's Neck for the Godfather.

Be careful not only where you drink, but when. For instance, never drink in an Irish bar on St. Patrick's Day, a Mexican bar on Cinco de Mayo, a black bar on Juneteenth, or a Republican bar next election day.

When someone at the next table asks why you think you're old enough to drink, do not reply with the old cliche: "If I'm old enough to fight, I'm old enough to drink," because all you've done so far this evening is drink.

If you're a Teasip, learn the lyrics to "I've Been Working on the Railroad." You can never tell when a very large Aggie will ask you to sing your school song.

If you ask the bartender the age of the wine, and he looks at his watch, forget it.

If you can say, "Harvey Wallbanger," you can order one, but if you have to point, then you've had enough.

Along these same white-lines, Grand Marnier is pronounced "grawn mon-yea" and champagne, of course, is pronounced "sham-pain," but if you have trouble with Tom Collins, it's time to quit.

There are several other ways to know when you've gone into the twilight zone, and from the looks of your poor, trembling body, this is the most important part of the lecture. Stop drinking when:

You agree with John Mitchell about Watergate.

You forget how to finish "To a Louse."

No one cares whether you finish.

You see eye-to-eye with your left shoe.

You run out of money.

You can't get your index finger out of your ear.

You can't find your ear.

The bartender stops asking you for your I.D. and starts reminding you that there is a Senior Citizens' Happy Hour every Thursday.

The puns bowl

A fellow moved to a ranch in Wyoming and began noticing that his neighbor down the way had an interesting thing going for him. Every morning the neighbor would send his horse, a beautiful roan, out into the woods, and every evening the horse would return with a string of moose following.

The rancher would simply lean out of his window, aim his rifle, and pick off the moose. The new fellow thought this was a great idea, so one night he stole the horse and the next morning sent it out to the woods to do the usual job. That evening, however, as the new arrival waited expectantly with his loaded rifle, the roan came trotting into the corral with nary a moose following. Just then the horse's owner appeared, demanding to know what was going on, and the new fellow explained that he had only borrowed the horse in hopes of nabbing some wild meat, but added that the plan didn't work.

"Of course not," said the rancher. "Don't you know that a stolen roan gathers no moose?"

That's right. It's time once again for puns and such. For instance, J. Walter Rogerson of Houston heard about a London jogger who got drunk and was weaving down Disraeli Avenue. The jogger was causing a huge traffic jam with his antics, so a bobby pulled the drunk over, asking: "Mate, is this any way to run Disraeli Road?"

The *Mensokie*, a publication from the Central Oklahoma Mensa group, reports—as quoted by the local Mensa bulletin—that two knights were attempting to cross the bridge over a moat, but each time a huge yellow hand would reach out from under the bridge and mighty fingers would flick the knights off their mounts. Finally, one knight had his page slip over the bridge. So the second knight ordered his page to do likewise. Successfully across, the young aides rescued the damsel in distress, proving, of course, that you should let your pages do the walking through the yellow fingers.

This same publication also tells us that the late Aristotle Onassis was visiting Beverly Hills a few years ago and was photographed while visiting the former home of Buster Keaton with a real estate agent. The photo was captioned: "Aristotle Contemplating the Home of Buster."

A big league umpire was notorious for making his decisions adamantly and nastily. The players nicknamed him "The Brute." One day, the umpire invited his little boy to sit on his lap, but the lad refused, saying: "The son never sits on the brutish umpire."

Deeon Tucker has a real-life, homegrown pun, which was unleashed on the world in early December of '75 at a Bay Area Drug Abuse Control Committee meeting. A discussion was under way as to whether

Crisis Hotline, with which the committee worked, should enter a float in the Clear Lake City Christmas parade, and, if so, what kind.

Someone suggested the float should be a huge telephone, and since the Hotline logo was "the warm fuzzies," someone else suggested that the director dress in a furry outfit and perch on the top of the phone. At this point, another member spoke up: "And suspended above it could be a giant syringe, and we could name our float, 'The Furry with the Syringe on Top.'"

Moving ever onward, we come to the notorious Scott L. Weeden, who is obviously a twisted person, for he has now sent in his latest effort. To wit:

A little girl had a teddy bear that was cross-eyed. A visiting aunt asked what the little bear was called. "It's called Gladly," said the little girl.

"That's an unusual name, isn't it?" asked the aunt.

"No," said the little girl. "It's Gladly my cross-eyed bear."

I think I've heard that one before, but it's still funny.

A rather clumsy construction worker named Irving Womwear slipped off a 17th-story construction site but was temporarily saved from death when his suspenders caught on a beam sticking out into space. As poor Irving swung back and forth, a crowd gathered below. Then Irving's foreman got an idea. He stuck a spanner into a bucket of tar, reached out, stuck it onto Irving, and pulled him in.

And the crowd yelled as one: "There's a tar-sprinkled spanner saving Womwear!"

I DIDN'T ORDER THIS

I Didn't Order This

MONACO—This is Jimmy'z (yes, with a z). It is *the* place in Monaco for everyone who wants to see anyone who's someone. Jimmy'z is a discotheque, with blinking colored lights above the small, crowded dance floor and music loud enough to climb.

The room is dark, but light enough to see around. There is a long bar against one wall, low tables and comfortable chairs about. Up against this wall are two tables kept empty and reserved for our party, an exclusive bunch of hangers-on, hosted by Freddy the Platinum King.

I am one of the latter, and shall explain just why I have come to this expensive dive. It is because, believe it or not, there has been a Murder in Monaco (a little chilling disco music, if you will). Yes, in this lap of luxury, this litter box for fat cats, there has been a murder, and I intend to find out whom done it.

The victim was an antique dealer, found dead in his shop. But it was a murder with class. He had been hit over the head with a bottle of the best champagne. And not just any bottle, you understand, but a full magnum. That's about twice the size of a regular bottle.

The police, of course, are baffled, for there has not been a murder in Monaco to speak about since the Grimaldis dispatched their arch-enemies, the Gibelins, in 1297 and took power. Well, the police may be baffled, but I have seen enough Agatha Christie movies to know that the murderer is still among us, which is why I am combing this principality, leaving no 500-franc chip unturned, to find the culprit. I've already checked the gambling casinos, the bars, the hotel lobbies, and now I am here at Jimmy'z, scanning the crowd.

The culprit could be my host, Freddy. (You think I'm making up all of this—I'm not.) But he is a friendly, laughing fellow. Freddy is British, a widower, he nightly comes here with an entourage and dances with young girls till the dawn. "Are you rich?" I ask subtly.

Freddy smiles. "Let's say I'm comfortable."

Smash! Tinkle-tinkle. There is the sound of glass being broken and the feel of dampness. My right arm is covered with champagne—a very good champagne. I hear loud voices and glance over my shoulder to the other table. A dandy looking young lady is being wrestled out the door by somebody's heir while waiters hustle around mopping up. She is apparently shouting at Robertino Rossellini, the Love Child of Ingrid Bergman and Roberto Rossellini. The Love Child has a beard. How time flies.

She is yelling something. Could it be: "I'll do you in like I did the antique dealer!"? No. My French is not very good, but I think she's saying the gray flounder is on the mantel.

I return to my suspicions. Sitting across from me is a large fellow with a bushy black beard. He says his name is either Akmed or Ahmed, the noise being so great I cannot understand. He offers me a glass of champagne from a magnum before him. It, too, is very good champagne. I thank him and he says, "Perhaps there has been a misunderstanding." That baffles me entirely.

Old men with young women come in. The young women in Monaco are issued uniforms: deeply tanned skin, sprinklings of gold jewelry, and tight white clothes. Everyone of them looks exactly alike, which—in this case—isn't all that bad. The music loudly grinds on.

A fellow about my age across the table says he lives in Monaco but is from Beverly Hills. Yet people from Beverly Hills don't speak with a British accent. He is taking the Concorde to New York for a business meeting, then on to Philadelphia and to California. "A board meeting of a company," he explains.

"What do you do for the company?" I ask.

"I'm chairman of the board." He offers me some champagne. A magnum of Möet and Chandon here costs the equivalent of $90, so I reluctantly accept. Perhaps he'll just hand me the bottle and a straw.

I hear the familiar smash. Tinkle-tinkle. Once again my right arm is wet with champagne. It's showtime, folks. I turn around to look. The same girl is being wrestled out the door by the same scion. Do they do this for the tourists every hour on the hour? Rossellini is mopping up his face. He was supposed to have been dating Princess Caroline, but currently she is in Hawaii with Guillermo Vilas. Maybe that's what the fight is about.

"No," Freddy the Platinum King informs me the next night before we head back to Jimmy'z for more research. "The girl is from Buenos Aires. She was mad at Prince D'Armberg. It seems the prince had told her father something about her—something bad. And it got back to her. At least that's what she says. Had nothing to do with Robertino."

It is another evening at Jimmy'z. Above the shouting I keep listening for the smash-and-tinkle, but nothing. The two tables are thus far empty. "No one comes here till 2," I am told.

Who did it? Who did in the antique dealer? Was it the sun-tanned, good-time girl on the dance floor? I saw her twice at the casino, once giving an elderly gentleman a huge wad of cash. Maybe she's a cop. Or could it be the loud-mouthed American journalist? If there were a fight in the antique shop about an upcoming exposé, I'd side with the antique dealer any time.

The colored lights blink on and off. The music gets louder. At this point the lights are supposed to go out, followed by a shot. But nothing happens. Suddenly a waiter appears at my elbow, puts down a champagne glass and begins to pour me a drink. He is holding a magnum bottle of Möet and Chandon. "I didn't order this," I say.

"It's a gift to you from a friend," the waiter smiles.

Fighting sisters

BRAY'S BAYOU—They are probably right down here somewhere. Possibly just beneath my feet, resting and rusting and waiting for orders.

They are the Twin Sisters, two cast-iron cannon that led an exciting life, met a mysterious death, and may yet be resurrected. They are idle right now, but once they were two angry young women, blasting grapeshot and chains and sawed-up horseshoes across a soggy plain just to the east of here known as San Jacinto.

The Twin Sisters were all Texas had in the way of artillery at the battle, and were brand new. They were a gift to Texas from the good people of Cincinnati, Ohio, who knew that the Texans needed all the help they could get. At a meeting on Nov. 17, 1835, one Robert T. Lyttle had proposed "that, as in the case of the patriotic Greeks, the South Americans and the Poles, we have right to cheer them on by our sympathies, and to aid them in supplies. . . ."

So two six-pounders were made by Greenwood and Webb of Cincinnati. Since the U.S. was neutral, the cannons were listed as "hollow ware" and were slipped down here. They were each about five feet five inches long, had a four-inch bore and weighed in at approximately 800 pounds.

On the day before the Battle of San Jacinto, the Sisters got into a fight with a Mexican cannon twice their size, the Golden Standard. Thirty Texas artillerymen trundled the pieces forward for the duel. The Texans had never fired the cannons before and were probably trying to figure out where to attach the bayonet, when the Mexicans opened up.

The Standard's first shot hit the Sisters' commander, Lieutenant Colonel James C. Neill, in the rump. The Sisters answered in kind, hitting Captain Fernando Urriza in the rump. Then they went to work, killing two mules, and wrecking the Standard's limber, which is the front part of the gun carriage.

So much for the first artillery duel. The next day, April 21, 1836, the Twin Sisters were put in the middle of the Texans' line and were hauled up the hill by manpower. George Hockley was now in charge, since Neill was still nursing his rear guard action. Then General Houston, in his usual urbane manner, gave the order: "Halt! Halt! Now is the critical time! Fire away! God damn you, fire! Aren't you going to fire at all!"

Boom.

After the battle, the Sisters were used to guard Mexican prisoners and were later sent up to Austin to stand off the Indians—who never showed up. They were fired every now and then on ceremonial occasions, and when Texas joined the Union, were sent to a U.S. Army depot in Baton Rouge, La.

Now comes the War Between the States and Texas asks Louisiana for the Sisters again. One was found rusting in a scrap foundry, the other in the hands of "a gentleman living in the Parish of Iberville." The Louisiana legislature earmarks $700 to fix them up, and returns them to a grateful Texas. The Twin sisters, back in action, see duty in Galveston, then are brought back to Houston.

After the war, in July of 1865, a Yankee soldier billeted in the old Kennedy Building just off Old Market Square notices the Sisters on a vacant lot next door. A month later, five returning Confederate soldiers get off the train in Houston and one of them, Henry North Graves, 19, spots some Confederate cannon lined up along the railroad track, bound for a Yankee foundry and destruction.

Graves finds the Twin Sisters among them. He and his comrades— John Barnett, Ira Pruett, Sol Thomas and Jack Taylor—immediately decide to save the Sisters for Texas, or as one Rebel puts it: "We'll bury them so deep no damned Yankee will ever find them." Joined by a Negro named Dan, they return that night and silently steal the Sisters. They burn the woodwork, then roll the barrels down to the bayou.

Which bayou? Apparently Bray's Bayou. And apparently right here, somewhere, they dug a hole and pushed the cannon in. Then they swore an oath that none of them would reveal the Sisters' location until it was safe to do so. In 1895, Graves and two of his old diggers returned to the scene, but couldn't find the spot. Graves tried again in 1920, still no luck.

Since then others have tried, and the cannons have been variously reported as in a Washington, D.C. Navy yard, in New Mexico, lost in the Gulf and dumped in Buffalo Bayou. No one really knows for sure, but probably they are down here somewhere, beneath the grass and trees and abandoned hot water heaters and cables and railroad ties.

Just resting and rusting and waiting for General Sam to shout again: "Fire away! God damn you, fire! Aren't you going to fire at all!"

Rainy day refuge

THE PLAYROOM—We all have things, places, songs, faces that suddenly transport us backward in time to our childhood. For some it's the face of a nanny or early companion, for others it's a doll or a book or just an expression. For me, it's here. The Playroom.

This is the third floor in my mother's house, high above all else; just one huge room with two smaller cubicles off to one side. This was children's territory, where adults were not expected nor wanted, buffered from reality and rules by a steep staircase unfit for longer legs. It was a comfortable nest anytime, but was particularly suited for rainy afternoons. Indeed, like a true Pavlovian, when it rained, I would head for the Playroom, close to the clouds but out of harm's way.

It hasn't changed that much, actually, since those days. A disorderly, private, dusty Brigadoon, open only to Pooh and Hans Brinker and Monkey Blocks. Have you ever made a house out of Lincoln Logs with the singular intent of wrecking it? You build it perfectly, see, then you roll a ball into the walls and it collapses with a delicious, small Rrruh, like a dog clearing its throat.

Here is an elevator I made with help from one of my brothers, back when Truman was president and America could lick the world, only we wouldn't because we were good and true and fed the DPs. It was made with an Erector Set that came in a red metal box. The box is here, scratched, but sturdy. I wonder if small boys still build elevators?

A box filled with plastic fences, used to hold in plastic cows. Dolls, belonging to my sister, I suppose, although I never remember her playing with dolls. From the ceiling hang more boyish things—a chinning bar and a punching bag frame. The chinning bar is still there, but the bag has long since disappeared. I remember when we put up the bar how my mother was afraid the whole thing would fall down, ripped from the ceiling, and how her sons would bounce around on the hard wooden floor. We had to tap the ceiling carefully to find the studs, but even then, Mother wasn't very happy.

This little room here, lined with shelves, holds the world's only collection of *Life* magazines read by a small boy on rainy afternoons. We had the first *Life*—with the picture of Boulder Dam on it, as I recall—and all the hundreds of others that followed. Every now and then a pile would be lugged up and put on the stack, bringing in a bit of the outside world to this side of the looking glass.

A civilian is now in charge of the British navy, name of Winston Churchill. Alfred Hitchcock has black hair. "Sudeten Germans Hear Their Leader." "Czechs Have an Able War Ministry." Sept. 18, 1944, with a cover of Dewey. June 17, 1940, The British are pulling out of Dunkerque, but according to Sgt. Jack Wadsworth, it's still better than in the Great War. At least this time they can get hot tea. "Nazi Paratroopers Land in Holland." " Norway's King Haakon Runs for His Life." Mommy, what's a blitzkrieg?

Later on, I learned. Here's a cartridge belt from our side, and a rusty helmet from theirs. Here's the fellow who sent them both—my uncle, all spiffy in his Marine whites. This is Cousin Budd Burks, who was killed by a ranch hand, and his widow, Amanda, who drove his cattle through Indian Territory to the railhead in Kansas. And this is William Featherston Kuykendal, born Nov. 4, 1804. He's a grim-looking fellow, in a high black silk hat and a long white beard. My father's great-grandfather. Somehow he doesn't fit in with Monkey Blocks and marbles, although he looks as though he'd enjoy a good blitzkrieg every now and again.

A football game, back when football was a game. A worn set of boy's boots. A sign liberated from a streetcar. On one side it reads, "For Whites," on the other "For Colored." More books, more boxes, an unfiled collection of the unwanted.

As my days here grew fewer and fewer, and relatives died off, this became the storing place for what they had left. My grandfather's shaving stand with a hook on the side. His razor strop used to hang here. It had a double headed eagle, showing that it was the same kind used by the czar himself. Grandfather's hat, "T.&N.O. Conductor." My grandmother's knitting, old photographs, old books. By the time they brought my father's stethoscope up here, I was gone.

Winnie-the-Pooh by A. A. Milne. A clipboard. The stamp collection. Prescription pad. Barbells. All the things that used to make up a cozy, cluttered corner, where quilts were rolling hills and small cars were embarked on large adventures. Backward, turn backward, O Time, in your fight, make me a child again just for tonight. Or at least on a rainy afternoon.

Super subterfuge

It is the Super Bowl. The 50-yard line of the Super Bowl, to be exact, about halfway up. This is the Golden Horseshoe of the sweat set, the Four Hundred of jockdom, where everyone who is anyone gathers. Right here, John and Nellie Connally. Curt Gowdy and his family. Steve Kardell and his date. Judge Hofheinz and Ed McMahon and . . .

Wait just a minute. Back up. Instant replay. Steve Who?

Why, Steve Kardell, of course. From San Augustine, Texas. Erstwhile U of H law student, beach bum, womanizer and, briefly, chauffeur. Now the toast of the Zum Zum Gang. Bon vivant. Raconteur. A crop duster among the Learjets.

But to start at the beginning: "My roommates v.ere trying to figure out some way to get into the Super Bowl," explains Broadway Steve. "And they heard that the club owners would be getting chauffeur-driven limousines for the weekend, so they applied as chauffeurs, hoping they'd get into the game that way.

"I wandered down to see how they were doing at the agency and someone says to me, 'Get out to the airport and pick up Art Rooney and his family.' And I said, 'Who's that?' "

Rooney, Kardell is told, owns something called the Pittsburgh Steelers and is one of the most respected men in pro football. Be nice. Grovel when necessary. So Kardell is assigned a brand-new black Cadillac limousine and off he goes to the airport.

He pages Rooney, and up steps a small, jovial Irishman in a cloth cap. It's Mister Big himself. Kardell leaps to the task of gathering up the Clan Rooney and baggage. Then he smartly leads the way to the limo and immediately makes his mark by not being able to open the trunk. A passing cabbie shows him how. Next he finds that there is too much baggage, and has to hire a taxi to follow along.

It is beginning to appear that Kardell is not exactly the world's foremost chauffeur and he decides to throw himself on the mercy of the court. "Mr. Rooney," he whines, "I really don't know what I'm doing." By now, Rooney himself may have had suspicions in that direction.

"That's all right, Steve," he says happily. "I usually take taxis anyway. We'll just stick with you and you stick with us."

Kardell is so overwhelmed that, after dropping off the Rooneys at their hotel, he proves his skill by driving all the way to the garage before realizing that he still has their luggage in the trunk. Rooney's suspicions are confirmed.

Friday night. Party time. Kardell takes the Rooneys to the Astrodome for an NFL blast. Strictly upper-upper, with guards manning the offensive line. Kardell pulls up, trying to look as pompous as possible, lets out the Rooneys and prepares to wait out the night. "Come on in," says Papa Steeler.

The guards look a bit perturbed but say nothing as Kardell parks the limo then bellies up to the bar. Boss's orders. Alan Shepard, Howard Cosell, Steve Kardell—all the biggies. After all, any friend of Mr. Rooney's is a friend of mine. Cosell is just explaining how he is a shoo-in for the Senate when Rooney inquires if Steve is ready to go.

Saturday. Shopping at the Galleria. "They were really impressed with it, but they couldn't find a Steeler scarf or pennant anywhere, even at Neiman's."

Evening. First to Mass—even owners have owners. Then off for another round of business parties. An ABC get-together at the Warwick and there is Kardell, discussing the effect of blackouts on no-shows. Any friend of Rooney's. Onward to the Petroleum Club. "Come on in, Steve." More crab claws and champagne. Ho-hum. At the end of the evening, Rooney allows that he is hungry. Does the native guide know of a good place to eat?

Off to Tony's, where the doorman is adamant: No reservations, no table. Kardell slips in and in his best chauffeuresque manner announces that Mr. Rooney is hungry. A table for eight (seven Rooneys and one Friend) coming up. "They said it was the best meal they ever had in Texas," Kardell, the Big Mac gourmet, says.

Super Sunday. By now Kardell is one of the family, so he and his date arrive early at the hotel for brunch. This way, Lamar Hunt can ask his advice on the future of pro football. Kardell's knowledge of shortcuts and back alleys is so famous that Rooney has chartered a bus to get them to the stadium.

And that is why the Natty Bumppo of Super Sunday and his date are sitting here on the 50, being briefed by a Cleveland Brown on the upcoming play. Any friend of Mr. Rooney's.

"I used to be a Dallas Cowboy fan," sighs Kardell, taking off his glass slipper. "Go Steelers, go."

"High Noon" courage at 2 a.m.

Charles Caleb Colton said courage is generosity of the highest order. Ovid said it conquers all things and gives strength to the body. Cervantes said it lies just halfway between rashness and cowardice, while Churchill said it is rightly esteemed the first of human qualities because it is the quality which guarantees all others. And Washington Gladden said simply that courage is better than fear.

Napoleon, who saw a host of courage and cowardice in his time, noted on Saint Helena that there was one kind of moral courage he had very rarely met: "the two o'clock in the morning kind."

"I mean unprepared courage, that which is necessary on an unexpected occasion, and which, in spite of the most unforeseen events, leaves full freedom of judgment and decision."

I must confess that Napoleonic proverbs were not on my mind that dreadfully cold night in Manhattan. I had just gotten off work, had successfully fought my way across Times Square to the subway shuttle and was standing on the subway platform beneath Grand Central Station awaiting the local.

Like other passengers, I am swathed in overcoat and galoshes and am carrying the needed reading material so I won't have to look at anyone else. The local finally thunders by and squeals to a stop and we all get in.

I sit down on one side and right across the aisle another fellow about my age slumps into a seat. He is redheaded, not too large, with a big overcoat wrapped around him, collar up, dark pants and black shoes. And he is tired. Lordy, he is tired. He isn't even reading, just staring at the floor. Just as the door is about to slam shut, I hear a commotion and this tall youth flies in, holds the door and two others jump aboard.

They are trouble. You can spot it immediately. The first one in is tall and, I still remember, kind of skinny and with high cheek bones. He is obviously the leader. The two others are shorter and I really can't recall much about them.

They are talking in loud voices, using language heavily laced with purple prose. The door shuts and we lumber northward toward 50th Street, the purple gang standing up in the aisle, although there are several empty seats, bouncing about and cursing and generally making themselves obnoxious.

Now, every subway rider knows instinctively what to do on such occasions: nothing. Like a horde of armadillos, we each roll into tight mental knots, bury faces in newspapers, and say absolutely nothing. Not even a glance their way. Not a whimper nor a thought that can be construed as an ungracious gesture toward the youth of America. We all do it, about 20 of us. All, that is, but the redheaded fellow sitting across from me. He is in the Twilight Zone. He stares at the floor, the picture of a man who needs a good night's sleep.

We leave 50th Street, me and my co-riders snug in our own cocoons. But we are not to be let off so easily. The tall one moves up to an elderly lady and tries to make conversation. She doesn't even look up. Smart woman. These lads are not in our orbit. They are either drunk or high on hash or Lord knows what.

It sounds like the worst cliche lifted from a pulp detective paperback, but they reminded me very much of a pack of wild dogs. Snarling, yapping, bouncing about, three large young men looking for bad trouble. We hit 59th Street and a few passengers got off; some smart ones simply walked out the door and stood on the platform waiting for a later, but safer, subway.

The rest of us stayed put. I had only one more stop so it was worth the risk. The doors stayed open. Gad. We are not moving. We are staying right here for some reason. With that foul mouthed bunch, who are laying it on heavy. The tall one is talking at the top of his voice, tossing out every juicy word his sub-par IQ can dredge up.

Again, no one moves. Discretion is the better part of valor, Falstaff said, and he lived to a ripe old age. The gang begins bullying another passenger, who is trying to ignore them. Things are getting sticky. You can never find a cop when you need one.

Then the redheaded fellow, who had been dozing off and on, sighs audibly, and slowly, painfully, stands up. He arises with the terrible effort of a man who would give all that he had just to be left alone.

As he stands up in front of me his overcoat swings open to reveal the dark blue uniform of a New York City policeman. He is a cop. An off-duty cop. The salt stains on the lower pants leg show that he had been either directing traffic or trodding a beat all evening out there in the snow and slush and 15 degree weather. Eight hours. Now he is off duty and heading home, his tell-tale hat has been left back in the station house locker room.

Had he not stood up, no one in the subway would have known who and what he was. But he knew, and that was enough. Home and hot toddy and warm bed would have to wait for a minute. There was one more small job to do. He pulled out his nightstick and headed down the subway car.

It was deathly still. It was Gary Cooper in "High Noon," walking down the deserted street, only it was for real. The subway refused to move, making only a low whirling purr. The three looked at him, then at his billy club.

I peered up over the headlines and noticed that everyone else in the car had done the same. What the hell was going to happen? They could jump the cop and beat him to jelly and not a soul in the car would have seen a thing, officer. The trio looked at one another for about 10 years. Then the cop gestured with his stick toward the still-open car door.

"Out," he said. They meekly obeyed. The car doors shut and suddenly their courage skyrocketed; they shouted obscenities at the cop as the subway continued its journey up Manhattan. The cop trudged back to his seat, wrapped himself in his coat, and went back to sleep.

It was the bravest thing I ever saw. Like "High Noon," I suppose, but actually it was about two o'clock in the morning. Napoleon was right.

To the Corps

Each fall I attend the State Fair of Texas, and each time, at about 3:30 in the afternoon, there comes across the fair, above the thousand noises of throats and goats, a familiar rat-tat-tat. Ratty-tat-tat. It is the drums. And bugles. I stop whatever it is I am doing and heed the call to arms, for it is the U.S. Marines Drum & Bugle Corps and the Silent Drill Team marching to the parade ground. Each time my family nods in acceptance and we agree to meet somewhere else in about an hour. I go my way, they go theirs. But this year it was time to make a change. This year it was time to take my sons.

So the female side of the family headed onward, while the males reported for duty. We got there late and had to stand at one end while most of the crowd sat on bleachers. No matter, because this was a time I was looking forward to in the same manner as my well-rehearsed and still unused birds-and-bees speech: Fear mixed with terror.

You see, I would like very much for my young sons to follow a family tradition and join the Marines. But I shall not talk them into it, because, well, because I don't believe in the John Wayne School of Recruiting. The Corps is not dress blues and sabers. It is not the professional training, no matter what the ads say. The only profession I was trained for is limited to a few civilian organizations which make offers you can't refuse. And it is not the money, which for me came to $86 a month. It is not the glory of combat. Anyone who glorifies war is sick.

Yet after all, it is better to serve, to give and to defend, than to—for transparently convenient reasons—bug off to Canada. American sons and their sons and their sons have stepped forward and marched off so that others could gripe about it. I want my sons among the givers, not the takers. The Marines' posters are right about one thing: No one likes to fight, but someone has to know how. We live in the real world.

On that brilliant autumn afternoon at the State Fair, when they asked, "What did you do in the war, Daddy?" my answer was easy: "Due to great planning on my part, absolutely nothing." But when they wanted to know why Daddy joined the Marines, I was hard put to say. It wasn't that I didn't know, it was that I couldn't say exactly. And, besides, what if it came out like a sales pitch? What if they bought it? What if some day in some ridiculous place, one of these children in Marine green got his tail shot off for God and Wall Street? No, I will not sell. Nor will I let my assorted brothers, who became Marine officers and thus didn't do much, give them a sales pitch. That is not the way to become a Leatherneck. You cannot have anyone else to blame for the price you must pay.

The Corps attracts some people as easily as it repels others. But it does attract. It attracts those who ask not what their country can do for them. It beckons those with no purpose they can define but with the deep and unrelenting desire to be bigger than themselves. And, for some reason I could never understand, it attracts Texans. More than half my platoon in boot camp was from Texas. I thought it odd until I discovered that no one else did. It seemed to be always that way. Indeed, the Republic of Texas had Marines. They led the Big Mutiny of 1842 and thus aren't mentioned much.

Should my sons join up? A very good question, one not easily answered. There are other good branches of the military services filled with fine people. There are safer spots than beaches, more rewarding classes than Fox Hole Digging 810. On the other hand. Yes, on the other hand. Perhaps we do not demand enough. There is the very good chance that we underestimate our children, who might well be capable of courage and sacrifice and goodness we, ourselves, can't handle. There were sons clinging to the riggings on John Paul Jones' ships. There were sons at

Iwo Jima, at Inchon, at Hue. And I'll bet every single one of them had a father somewhere who thought it impossible. I'll bet their sons did, too.

The corps has scores of traditions, and one is that when the *Marine Corps Hymn* is played, no matter what happens, you stand at attention until it is over. It is a body salute to the good men and true who came before. On that autumn afternoon at the fair when the program was winding up, the final order came, "Pass in review!" The drums rattled, the bugles howled, and then came the *Marine Corps Hymn*.

As the crowd got to its feet, the troops marched by and then wheeled away across the fairgrounds with the music following behind. The crowd scratched, milled about, and then wandered off, but the song kept coming. Undisciplined as usual, my eyes darted about. I was fully expecting the beloved voice of my drill instructor, Daddy Webb, to scream: "Keep them eyeballs at attention, idiot!" But no such order came, so I sneaked a look. The officer in charge, resplendent in his blues and saber, was still at attention. A black sergeant in camouflage uniform had his boots at a sharp 45-degree angle. Two other Leathernecks across the parade ground stood stiff.

One old fellow, God knows who he had fought, was still at attention. Another, slightly younger, a WW II gray, with authorized belly. And near me, a young man whose wife was chasing a toddler. His credentials were, in half a word, 'Nam. Here and there, left behind by the crowd, stiff as starched khakis, were a few good men. It is that which makes it worth the price. Like making love, you can't explain it, you have to experience it.

CB jackal

EAST OF LULING—Plugging back toward Houston with a station wagon full of dirty laundry and equally dirty children, we look like an Okie family trying to get to California before our dried beans give out. All I need are chickens and bedsprings tied to the roof.

In other cars, plowing along IH 10 through the night, the scene is very much the same, with cartons and kids rising over the back seats and up the windows like a high tide hitting Baytown. Up front, the father grimly grips the wheel while wondering if he can hang on until the relief of Monday morning at the office. And over on the other side of the front seat, riding shotgun, the wife and mother, head tilted back, dozing.

We all move forward, like lemmings marching to the sea, running about 55 miles an hour except when that urge, born into us all, takes over and we accelerate down and zoom up, hitting 60 for a few wild, carefree moments, until reason takes over and we return to our mundane existence.

Yes, mundane, average, even dull, for we all dwell here in the right-hand lane, the vanilla brick road. But over to the left, ah, over there is where the action is. It is a lane totally given over to cars, trucks, wreckers and campers, which lord it over we poor peons to the right. Over there, the parade thunders by, each vehicle carrying a distinctive marking as clear and gaudy as the Caddie fins of the '50s. It is the new highway status symbol: The antenna of a citizens' band radio.

There they go, streaking down antenna alley, linked through the air-waves by bonds thicker than blood. I had not realized how many there are on the open roads these days until I began counting. It seems as though every other, every third at least, vehicle on the highway today has a CB antenna sticking up, whipping and prowling through the airwaves. Now, why, pray tell, would someone want to plunk down all that money for a mere gadget? Because, in a word or two: The Fuzz.

Yes, nothing in business history has so helped an industry as has the 55-mile-per-hour limit helped the CB business. They must be working night and day at the factories trying to fill orders for the American motorist who wishes to know in advance where the Highway Patrol is lurking. "Smokey," the cops are called.

Their every movement is pinpointed by a band of citizens which feels that laws are for other people. Well, in this case, they are right. Speeding laws are, indeed, for other people, those over here in the right-hand lane.

We are too law-abiding, or in my own case, too chicken, to take our chances and beat the fuzz at the 55 m.p.h. game. So we muck along over here, simmering silently in our own self-pity, never daring to go much over the speed limit for fear that Smokey is waiting 'round yon curve. For we do not know where the cops lurk. It is a secret known only to those over on the left.

Whzzzzz, they go by, 70, 80, their antennas upright and attuned, waiting for word of a bust. Every now and then it comes, and you can see the brake lights suddenly brighten the skies as the word is passed on the CB: "Smokey at 12 o'clock high!" The CBs slow down to a lawful 55 and slide by Checkpoint Charlie, then slowly crawl over the next hill and hit the accelerator with grace and glee.

I am passed by a pickup truck, antenna alert, then a truck, ditto. Whzzzzz. Here comes a car doing at least 80, and sure enough, it has that tell-tale tail pointing outward, ever on the guard. But this particular car is being closely followed by another phenomenon on the open road: The CB jackal.

This is the motorist who is too cheap to buy his own radio, but simply dawdles along the highway until he spots the necessary antenna. By the speed of the moving vehicle, the CB jackal can tell that the driver is ever on the alert for Smokey, so he just pulls in behind and stays on the rear bumper. When the CB slows to a crawl, so does the jackal. Painless and cheap.

Whzzzzz, they go by and disappear into the darkness. The lion and jackal. Past Waelder we go, the lemmings inching toward the sea. We are now approaching the notorious Flatonia Fuzz. It is here, under the overpass, that the Texas Highway Patrol balances the state budget.

But not tonight. For the CBs are thundering upwards of 75. Obviously, if the cops were waiting, the robbers would slow down. But they do not, so it is clear that the way is clear. Onward we go, down IH 10, the quick and the dread.

By now the lion and the jackal are probably pulling into their respective driveways so they can go in, mix a drink, pick up the morning paper and complain loudly about crime in the streets.

To Schulenburg, which twinkles up ahead. Traffic moves forward, up and over the . . . ah, blinking red lights in the road. The cops have caught another one. The patrol car pulls the culprit over, then flashes a spotlight at a second car, and pulls it over, as well. That's hard to do. One cop car pulling over two cars. They nudge to the side of the road as my little pack of motorists creeps by at 54, just to be sure.

The cops have the drivers out of their vehicles by the time I get to the scene, and are busily writing out two tickets. One to the lion, one to the jackal. I laugh uncontrollably, then—while the authorities are busy elsewhere—silently slip up to 60. Even the jackals have jackals.

Stranger to demon rum?

HUNTSVILLE—Did Sam Houston drink? I had always presumed he did. Like a fish. When one thinks of Sam Houston one thinks of a man who did almost everything. He didn't live life, he consumed it with insatiable gusto.

Anyone who went through three wives, two states and the Mexican Army must have nipped a bit every now and then. But, then again, how can one be sure? Perhaps he was only associated with demon rum in the public mind because his portrait hung behind virtually every bar in Texas for almost 100 years. And this is not such a bad idea for supporters of sobriety. Maybe the legislators in their wisdom should require that General Sam's portrait go right alongside the liquor license. For it would take a strong man indeed to quaff drink with the General glaring down in profound disgust.

Now, some may say that this is a rather minor question to kill time on and perhaps it is, but anyone who spends hours watching 22 strangers fight over a piece of inflated leather should not throw stones.

The problem began a while back when my blind faith in General Sam's drinking capacity was dealt a shattering blow by an article I came across in the March 30, 1861, *Harper's Weekly*. (All right, so I'm behind in my reading. There are advantages to being a procrastinator. You are probably getting ready to put your Christmas decorations up, right?)

The story was speculating as to whether Texas would secede from the Union, not that the magazine seemed to care: "Its (Texas') people comprised among the worst vagabonds and scoundrels in the world. When a man was so infamous and hopeless he could not ship on board a whaler, he went to Texas."

But *Harper's* liked Sam Houston—who at the time was governor of Texas. It ran a large Mathew Brady photograph of the General, and told a bit about him, explaining: "Probably no man in this country has led so adventurous a life as Sam Houston." The unsettling news came toward the end: "Governor Houston is a man of very simple habits and genial manners. He eats no flesh and drinks no wine. His ordinary dinner is a plate of oranges or other fruit, and a glass of milk."

All the other facts about him seemed to be accurate, so maybe I was wrong. Poor Sam, accused of hitting the bottle all these years when actually it was a glass of milk. Just to make sure, however, I find myself here in Huntsville going through Houston's homes and museum, a heap of Houstoniana, looking for a definite answer.

Item: Houston is in Arkansas, going to Texas. He becomes friends with John Linton one night on the road and they agree to a "sacrifice to Bacchus." They get a drink with each article of their clothing they throw into the fire. Houston wins, passes out.

Item: Houston is living with the Cherokees where, he later recalled, he "buried his sorrows in the flowing bowl . . . gave himself up to the fatal enchantress."

Item: The Indians called him Oo-tse-tee Ar-dee-tah-skee. A Cherokee word, but meaning what? Raven, perhaps. Houston gets in an argument with a clerk, his faithful Indian companions agree to second him in a duel. Both men miss. Much later Houston learned the Indians had not put lead balls in the guns.

Item: New Year's Day, 1838, Houston makes a New Year's resolution not to "touch, taste, or handle the unclean thing until the first of January next." A friend, reporting this momentous decision by the Texas president, commented: "I am in hopes that he will refrain from intoxication for the short term of one year, which will do credit to himself, and be a fine thing for the Republic of Texas."

Item: That May, Houston wrote that both he and a friend were totally reformed: "Neither gets 'tight'."

Item: May, 1838, Houston takes a group to inspect the Texas Navy at Galveston. J. A. Biggs and Brother submit their bill: dinner for 63, $315. "Liquor at the Bar for Company, $33."

Item: Houston presides over the building of his city, Houston, the Republic's capital: two taverns, some log cabins and a few saloons. An observer noted that drinking "was reduced to a system, and . . . the Texians being entirely a military people, not only fought but drank in platoons."

Item: This presents problems. Houston and Ashbel Smith, the surgeon general of the army, and some friends drink for hours, then collapse. Later in the night Houston sends his slave, Esau, to a slave's nearby shack for a glass of water. Esau reports there isn't any.

"Esau," says Houston, looking out the window, "can you believe that this is I, Sam Houston, protege of Andrew Jackson, ex-Governor of Tennessee, the beloved of Coleto and his savage hosts, the hero of San Jacinto and the President of the Republic of Texas, standing at the dead hour of midnight in the heart of his own capital, with the myriad of twinkling stars shining down upon his unhappy forehead, begging for water at the door of an old wench's shanty. And. Can't. Get. A. Drop?"

Esau shakes his head in sad agreement. They are surrounded by taverns and pubs, by barrels of booze, and there is not a drop of drinking water in all of Houston, Republic of Texas. "That's just right, Marse Gen'l," sighs Esau. "We sure ain't got no water."

Item: Oo-tse-tee Ar-dee-tah-skee is Cherokee for "Big Drunk."

Item: John G. Tod of the Texas Navy, trying to determine if Houston is for Texas' annexation. "When sober, he was for annexation, but when drunk he would express himself strongly against the measure."

Item: Houston marries the daughter of a Baptist minister and builds this fine, white home here in Huntsville, surrounded by pecan trees. Here is a samovar given Houston by the people of New Orleans. Houston kept it filled with wine. He fathers eight children, hard to do on a diet of oranges and milk.

Item: Houston makes a speech in May or June of 1853 in Nacogdoches opposing both Sunday blue laws and prohibition. "I do not object to total abstinence. I believe that total abstinence is the only way by which some intemperate drinkers can be saved. I know it from my own personal experience."

Item: Houston's second son, Andrew Jackson Houston, is born in 1854 and Houston takes the temperance pledge. Quoth the Raven: "Nevermore." On Nov. 19, 1854, Houston is baptized in the chilly waters of Rocky Creek and causes a sensation. "The announcement of General Houston's immersion," a church newspaper breathlessly reported, "has excited the wonder and surprise that he was 'past praying for.' " It noted that 3,050 clergymen had been praying for him, but without much hope.

"Well, General," a friend remarked, "I hear your sins were washed away."

"I hope so," the General replied. "But if they were all washed away, then Lord help the fish down below."

Going through channels to get cable

THE FRONT DOOR – Knock-knock.

"Who's there?"

"Wire."

"Wire who?"

"Wire you not on the cable?"

I open the door and there stands a fellow with a clipboard.

"I'm not on the cable because I live in Houston, a sleepy fishing village on the bayou that is among the last to get cable TV."

"How come?"

"I'm not sure. You'd have to ask the federal grand jury. Something about City Hall and a few good friends."

"Well, worry no more because this is your happy day. I'm here to tell you that you – yes, *you* – Mr. Occupant, are now eligible to get the wire. I'm Pinky Smedley of Sable Cable. 'We tie your tubes.' Here is a card showing what we offer."

"A table of available cables from Sable? What are they?"

"Channel number 1 tells you what's on all the other channels. Channel 2 is Channel 2. Channel 3 tells you what's on Channel 1."

"Sounds fantastic."

"Channel 4 is the Hispanic channel. Channel 5 is our Black Is Beautiful Network. Channel 6 is the Gay Rights Network. Number 7 is the children's channel. And Channel 8 is your regular Channel 8."

"Uh, I don't mean to be picky, Pinky, but so far I'm still waiting for something I'd pay to see."

"Oh, it gets better, Mr. Occupant. We have Ted Turner's network, which gives you day-by-day play-by-play of the Atlanta Braves."

"I'm an Astros fan. The sole survivor."

"Back a winner. You also get Channel 21. That's non-stop commercials. And Channel 19 is the Matsushita Network. It's Japanese."

"Not interested."

"You have to take it. Matsushita owns Sable Cable. In accordance with new Japanese laws, there is a revised series on World War II: *How the East Was Lost.* The first show deals with American aggression at Pearl

Harbor."

"What's it called?"

" '*Tora, Tora, Tora*—That's an Irish Lullaby.' "

"No, thanks."

"Next week's show is *The Bataan Joggers*."

"What else do you have?" I ask.

"Channel 17. Non-stop music."

"I've already got that."

"You've got the cable?"

"No, a radio."

"Ah, but this is different. We show album covers, too. This week they are featuring the love theme from *Patton*. Then we have the local government access channel. It covers the voting, the debate, the important decisions being made that affect Houston's future."

"I didn't know they were televising the Houston City Council."

"No, this is coverage of the Houston Realtors Association."

"Anything else?"

"We've got Channel 81. The Mideast Urban Renewal Network, brought to you by Brown & Beirut. Then there's Channel 11."

"What's that?"

"KHOU-TV. You've never seen it?"

"Of course, but I thought . . ."

"We've got other channels. The Dukes of Hazzard Driving School. The Bigot's Network, and our movie channels."

"OK, now we're talking. I only want them."

"To get them you've got to take all the others first. The movie channels are extra. But they're good. On Channel 43, we have *Rocky II½*."

"You mean *Rocky III*."

"No, Channel 43 only shows the first half of the movie. The second half is on Channel 44."

"I've got to subscribe to both of them?"

"It's a bargain, Mr. Occupant. To get Sable Cable, we only charge $5 a month."

"Not bad."

"Of course, there are certain extras. Like installation. That's $45."

"OK."

"You want it inside?"

"Of course I want it inside."

"Oh, for $45 we just toss the wire into your backyard. Running it inside is another $112."

"Right."

"Then there's the deposit for the little black box: $25."

"Do I get interest on it?"

"No."

"Do you realize at today's interest rates how much Sable Cable is going to make from the millions of interest-free dollars it will hold?"

"Around $2,233,418 a month, we figure. I suppose you want insulation on the wires, to get better reception."

"At least the color will be better."

"Color? I didn't mention that . . ."

"OK, OK. What does it come to?"

"I'm not through. And our weekly script book so you can follow along."

"What do I need a script book for? What's the matter with the sound?"

"Oh, you want sound?"

"Yes."

"Do you want the pictures and the sound to be from the same channel?" he asked, tabulating on his hand calculator.

"Naturally."

"In English?"

"Vulgar" Texans

There is a new book out, called *I Think of Warri*, by one Robert J. Attaway. I have not read the book nor have I ever met Mr. Attaway, nor do I particularly wish to.

But I do want to call to your attention an ad for the book which its publishers, Harper & Row, recently ran in *The New York Times Book Review*. To wit:

"Warri is a hellhole of a city in Nigeria—steaming with heat, raucous with taxis and bars and prostitutes, luring vulgar Texans in search of oil riches. Written in the tradition of the young Graham Greene . . . etc. etc." The part which bothers me is the "vulgar Texans" bit. A small point, to be sure, but bothersome nevertheless.

First of all, this description of things Texan may be only in the mind of the fellow who wrote the ad. But then, copywriters, as everyone knows, are not famed for their truthfulness, else we must believe that all cars save gas, all clothes come out white-white and children really run into the space capsule just before launch yelling, "Dad! Dad! I've only got two cavities!"

But let us assume that the copywriter has accurately caught the spirit of this book: that the bars of this particular hellhole are crowded with vulgar Texans, rubbing elbows with raucous taxis and prostitutes and being watched over by Peter Lorre, fanning himself behind the bar with a three-week-old *Manchester Guardian*.

But why are the vulgar fellows from Texas? I'll tell you why. Because if Warri was chockablock with vulgar Vermonters, no one would care. If they were from Omaha or Sacramento or Toronto or Huntington, Long Island, they wouldn't be in this raucous hellhole of a city in the first place. No, they would be back home reading books about vulgar Texans.

In a bar in Warri, Nigeria, if the plot calls for some ugly Americans, then Central Casting automatically sends down a gaggle of semi-sober Texans, who throw ten-dollar bills on the bar, make obscene cracks about the barmaid, get in fights, curse Washington, pinkos, queers and commies. Mr. Attaway thought of Warri's worst, and immediately thought of Texans.

All right, let us be fair. Texans can be crude, vulgar, even braggarts. Those on their best manners at the Petroleum Club can be downright obnoxious in Warri and Passy. We have all seen them and cringe at the spectacle. But they are not alone.

I have been insulted by French police, English journalists, Mexican bartenders, Italian cab drivers, Norwegian shipping magnates and the entire City of New York. I have been cheated by hotel clerks in Paris, shopkeepers in Los Mochis, moneychangers in London. I have been lied to, laughed at, looked down upon and frozen out in a dozen different countries in a score of languages and dialects.

By the same token, I have been fed, watered, directed, listened to, actually understood by an even greater number. Cab drivers in San Francisco, lobbyists in Tallahassee, waitresses in the Scottish Highlands, hotelmen in Italy, pub operators in the Shetland Islands, and a cast of thousands, all have come to my aid.

If one can find all types, then just possibly in the annals of traveldom one has also come across some Texans who knew which fork to use, and said please and thank you and can I hire a hundred of your starving, unemployed villagers to work on my drilling rig?

When a Tenneco helicopter goes down in the boonies of Ethiopia, and the local guerrillas grab the crew, who's caught? A fellow from Big Spring, that's who. When a rig blows up in Libya, who do they call to risk his life? A fellow from Houston, that's who. When the storms sweep over the North Sea and the Dutch and the Norwegians and the English head for the safety of the shore, who's out there by himself trying to save the shop? Some good ol' boy from Kilgore, that's who.

But when Mr. Attaway needs some vulgar fellows to spice up his book, who gets the nod? Texans, that's who. I suppose Central Casting could have sent down Van Cliburn and George Bush and Katherine Anne Porter to sit around the table in the back of the bar, but it wouldn't have sold as many books.

Now certainly there are Texans running through the hellholes of the world in search of oil riches, but I am getting a bit bored with the idea that they are all crude and vulgar. And if I were Mr. Attaway, I wouldn't even mention it to the good ol' boy from Kilgore sweating out the North Sea storm. He just might find out how vulgar a Texan can really be.

A&M football

KYLE FIELD, A&M—"Daddy, who's Hullabaloo Caneck?"

"He was an Indian chief who sold this part of Texas to the white man to be used for a school. He got $24 in beads and the Coors franchise, and on still nights you can hear him laughing. Now sit down and watch the game."

We have just missed the kickoff, but the rest of the contest lies ahead this afternoon here at College Station. It is the Aggies against the Kansas State Wildcats. I have brought my little family up here to witness this event as part of their continuing education, and in the spirit of equal time as—up until now—they have thought that all good high school students died and went to the University of Texas.

The action opens predictably enough. A&M fumbles.

"Daddy, which side do we cheer for?"

"We can cheer for the team in the maroon and white. They are the Aggies; the Aggies are they."

"I thought we never cheered for them."

"Normally we don't. But they are playing a non-Texas team, so this time only, it is all right to cheer for the Aggies."

A&M responds to this burst of generosity and chauvinism on my part by fumbling again.

Kansas State scores. 7-0. Now there is a long pass to an Aggie who doesn't drop the ball. Gary Haack. The Aggies have a nice drive going.

"Daddy?"

"What?"

"Why don't you tell these people your favorite Aggie joke? They're Aggies, aren't they?"

"Child, Kyle Field is not the place to tell Aggie jokes. Never, ever, say those words here again, or we shall end up as half-time entertainment."

A&M rolls forward and promptly fumbles. They've got that play down perfectly. The crowd, however, does not lose heart. The Aggies, I must say, are an optimistic lot. If George McGovern were an Aggie, he'd still be demanding a recount. The stadium is full, with 50,027 bodies packed in here—the largest crowd ever to see a nonconference game in Kyle Field. Part of the reason is probably due to the growing size of the A&M student body. There are now 28,038 students here including 8,818 girls. Both are records. The total is up 6 percent over last year while the girl's total is up 22 percent. At least one university vice president believes there is a direct relationship between last year's winning football season and this year's enrollment growth. "Everyone wants to be a winner," he explains.

The first quarter is almost over and A&M sends in a new quarterback, David Walker, who seems to have played this game before. A long pass. A nice run by George Woodward, who was all-district, all-state and all America at Van Vleck. A touchdown. It is now 7-7 and you would think A&M just won the war. Bands play, crowds cheer, volcanoes erupt. The roar must be distinctly audible not too far from here at the home of Dr. Jack Williams, the A&M president. Dr. DeBakey carved on Dr. Williams' chest this summer, so the president is not allowed to go to football games yet. He listens on the radio. Dr. Williams has lost some weight, but looks fine. He just prowls about the house, and reads books. However, he's read every book around, which in College Station is not hard to do.

Ah, the Aggies are moving closer. A barefooted kicker named Tony Franklin slams the ball 42 yards for a field goal, making it 10-7. More huzzahs. Fight, Farmers, Fight!

"Daddy, where are the pom-pom girls?"

"They do not have pom-pom girls at A&M. They have cannons and classrooms, sheep dip and labs, corn and calculus, they've got mangos and bananas you can pick right off the tree. But they do not have pom-pom girls."

Nor do they need them today. Another touchdown and the Aggies lead, 17-7. Good grief, now they've got the ball again, as Kansas State cannot make any headway against the Aggie defense. It's like trying to run against Barbara Jordan in the Third Ward. Now the farmers come back, this time tossing out to Curtis Dickey, the second fastest man in Texas. Unfortunately for Kansas State, the fastest man does not play for them but for UT. I am getting this dreadful feeling that it will take more than one speedster for the Longhorns to win on Thanksgiving.

Yet another field goal by the barefooted kicker, and it is halftime. Here comes the Aggie Band, spilling across the green Astroturf like chocolate syrup across a pool table. No matter who wins the first half and the last half, the Aggies always win the halftime. It is announced that Alabama is leading SMU 28-3. There is no cheering. Perhaps the Aggies have feelings for their opponents after all. No, I spoke too soon. It is back to football, and they show no mercy. A good kick, a nice interception. It is now 27-7.

"Daddy?"

"What?"

"Why don't you yell 'Hook 'em, Horns' like you usually do?"

" 'Hook 'em, Horns' falls into the same category as Aggie jokes here. Unless you wish to be fatherless, shut up."

Into the fourth quarter we go, with Woodward running up the center, then Dickey zipping around the end. Then, somehow, Kansas State scores. I think it was during a time out, and that tends to make the Aggies angry. The band rumbles and roars, the troops scream, "Fight, Farmers, Fight!" and Kansas State must know how Poland felt in 1939. The farmers are out for blood, and when the final gun stops the slaughter, it is 34-14.

"Daddy?"

"What?"

"Are we going to the Thanksgiving game?"

"I doubt if there will be a Thanksgiving game. It would endanger UT's amateur standing."

Stick around

THE KITCHEN—A few minutes of freedom from driving one of the children to the store in time to pick up another from the movie and then take the third one to the store I just took the first one to.

In such brief seconds, I attempt to fix things around the house, specifically, things which break and need to be put back together. My solution is simple. I use this small tube of fantastic super quick-hold glue. It sticks anything. The problem is, as any homeowner knows, the container for the glue. This reminds me of the scientist who invented an acid so strong that it would eat through anything, but what do you keep it in? For glue, how do you get the cap off? You can't because—just like the ads say—this glue will hold anything at all together forever. Including the cap to the tube.

Oh, the first time, when the tube is new, it is easy enough. The top comes right off. But the second time you attempt to open this fantastic product, you can't. So here I am, tube in hand. Twist. Gad. The tube has broken open and this clear, yukkie glue is pouring over my hands. The label warns it will stick your fingers together. No problem. I start wiping quickly. I have 10 seconds. The fingers on my other hand are trying to stick. Quick, keep them moving, like a palsied pianist. Fingers are wiggling. And apart.

Now get a towel or something and wipe this goo off. That does it. The glue dries to a sickly whitish color on all my fingers. There it will stay until July. But no matter, I have survived one of the worst accidents awaiting the happy homeowner: the quick-drying superduper glue getting where you don't want it.

Eh? What's this? It seems, well, somehow, it does appear that the tip of my left index finger is firmly attached to my left middle finger. Yes, right up there at the end. I wiggle them back and forth and gently try to pry them apart. I know it sounds rather silly, but my fingers are glued together. OK, OK, laugh. Certainly it seems ridiculous, but I am not making up one word of this. Really, would anyone admit he had glued his fingers together if he hadn't?

I will not go into details, but I try everything to separate my two fingers. Water. Gasoline. Paint thinner. A thin razor blade deftly slipped between the two so as to cut only glue, not skin. Nothing works. I pull at the fingers only to feel my skin pulling from the bone. Yet there must be a way.

At this point there is only one thing to do. I nip around the corner to see Calpakis the Wily Greek. He is in his garage, putting New Zealand license plates on his car for some obscure reason.

"Hi," I say brightly.

"Not now," says C-the-W-G. "You all had your chance before the Iowa caucus, before the New Hampshire primary. Even as late as Massachusetts, I might have considered running. But now it's too late. Besides, I've got to spray for milkweed."

"I just need some advice," I say.

"Buy gold in 1978. Now leave me alone."

"C-the-W-G, this really funny thing has happened to me. Ha-ha. I mean, it's so funny. Ha-ha."

He looks up from his work. "Stop it. I can't stand the hilarity. Let me guess. You found a parking place at the Galleria."

"Even better," I say. "You see, well, look here." I wiggle my fingers at him, two of them in remarkably exact timing.

"Fantastic," says Calpakis. "I'll hook up the light so you can show me your swan and snake and Loch Ness Monster."

"No, it's not that," I explain. "You see, Calpakis, uh, I've—that is—due to the result of a one-in-a-million accident, I've glued my fingers together."

Silence.

He looks at me. Then at my fingers. More silence.

"I remember the time you got your hand caught in the garbage disposal," he says. "And when you called me up to ask if shingles went on both sides of the roof. Then there was the time you wanted to freeze Saran Wrap for window panes."

"It worked great 'til spring."

"But this," he says, "is a new one even for you. Here, let me see."

I stick out my firmly welded fingers. He examines them like an expert. "OK, don't worry about a thing. I've got a friend."

"I knew you could help, C-the-W-G."

"Take the midnight flight. When you get to the lobby of the Rio airport, wear a red carnation and be reading the *Newark News*."

"Wait a minute! Who is this friend of yours?"

"Never mind. He's good. Take my word for it. He'll even give you a new face. And change your fingerprints."

"C-the-W-G, there's got to be an easier way. Look, the fingers are just glued together there at the end."

He examines them again. "OK, just for you. I'll give you this advice: Go to the drugstore and get some stuff which unglues this superduper glue."

"They make it? Superduper glue separator? I didn't know there was such a thing."

"Actually," he says, "that stuff was on the market first, but it didn't move very well. So they had to invent the glue."

"Thanks, C-the-W-G," I say. "I knew you'd have the answer."

"The answer is no," he says from somewhere near the front bumper. "All of you had your chance before the Vermont primary. Don't come sniveling around here now."

Our heritage?

(There have been a lot of erroneous stories as to just how Texas proclaimed its freedom on March 2, 1836. To straighten history out once and for all, I hereby present the true story of the Texas Declaration of Independence.)

WASHINGTON-ON-THE-BRAZOS—The 59 delegates are gathered here to take up the business at hand, namely setting up some kind of government for Texas with no money, no army, no navy, no laws and an invading force of several thousand heavily armed troops pouring across the Rio bent on destroying Texas.

Chairman Richard Ellis opens the debate: "Men, there has already been a lot of discussion on this matter, angry words, tirades, and we all have our own opinions on this, but I think we should be paid two dollars a day plus 15 cents a mile."

"And expenses," says one delegate.

"What about a staff? I move that we hire a staff," a delegate shouts from the rear of the chamber. "I need a secretary. One who can keep records, write letters, handle constituents and clean buffalo hides."

"Right," Ellis agrees. "Plus offices and franking privileges. OK, that settles that. Anything else?"

"Yes," says a delegate from Brazoria. "What about the Declaration of Independence?"

"I give up," says Ellis. "What about the Declaration of Independence?"

"I move that we have one."

"Objection!" shouts a delegate. "This kind of talk will only make San-ta Anna mad. Then, it's no more Mister Nice Guy."

"Right!" shout the delegates. "We're not traitors!"

"We discussed this matter of independence before we moved here," says Ellis. "Back when we were at San Felipe de Austin."

"This is a screwy place," says Sterling Robertson from Milam. "You people got weird names for towns, like San Felipe de Austin and Washington-on-the-Brazos. Why don't we come up with some normal names?"

"Yeah, like Teetering-on-the-Brink."

"How about Venus-on-the-Half-Shell?"

"I like Frost-on-the-Pumpkin."

"Delegate-on-the-Take."

"Texas-on-the-Decline."

Ellis raps his gavel. "If we might have order, I'd like to get back to the matter at hand."

"Matter-at-Hand. It has a ring," says another delegate.

"All this talk is making me thirsty," says the delegate from Refugio, Sam Houston. "I move that we adjourn to the bar across the street."

"If I ride over do I get mileage?"

Ellis raps for order again. "I think two dollars a day is sufficient."

"That is too much," says the delegate from Bexar, Jose Antonio Baldomero Navarro.

"How do you spell that?" asks the convention secretary and parttime masseuse, Flame O'Fun.

"T-h-a-t."

"No, the name. Hoe-say whatever."

"This is a screwy place," says Sterling Robertson. "Why don't you peo-ple have normal names? I mean, what's a 'Jose Antonio Baldomero Navarro?' It sounds like a Matamoros law firm."

"Right," says the delegate from Jasper, George Washington Smythe.

"I'll say," echoes the delegate from Washington-on-the-Brazos, George Washington Barnett.

"We so move," say a delegate from Bastrop and another from Nacogdoches, Thomas Jefferson Gazley and Thomas Jefferson Rusk.

"I'll go along with the crowd," says a delegate from the Alamo, Samuel Maverick.

"All this talk is making me thirsty," says Houston, opening his desk drawer.

"I move that we need a Declaration of Independence," says a delegate. "We should write it up, then have the other delegate from Refugio, Ed-ward Conrad, print it up for us."

"Why him?"

"Because Conrad is a printer, that's why."

"I'lL b6e glagd to do o i.t." says Conrad.

"Mr. Chairman, I move that we wish Sam Houston a happy birthday. He's 43 today. I want everybody to sign this card. It goes: 'Noses are red, violets are . . .' "

"Where is Houston?"

"He's resting. On the floor under his desk."

Ellis raps for silence again. "The overwhelming vote of this body is that we don't want a Declaration of Independence because Santa Anna has a lot more soldiers than we've got."

"Nonsense," shouts a delegate. "We've got Travis and Bowie in the Alamo and Fannin at Goliad. We're on the edge of victory. I can already see the light at the end of the tunnel."

"The Alamo?" says the secretary, Flame O'Fun. "That reminds me, Mr. Chairman, I've got this dispatch about that place. I think it's fallen or something. It completely slipped my mind. Oh, and Fannin got captured. I was supposed to tell you."

"Mr. Chairman, I suggest we go."

"Wait a minute. Has everybody signed Sam's birthday card? Good. Wake him up and I'll read it: 'When a government has ceased to protect the lives, liberty and property of the people . . . .' Hey, this isn't the birthday card we signed."

"Mr. Chairman, I think I hear drums. Or marimbas. I move that we move."

"Right. We'll move to Harrisburg."

"Mr. Chairman?"

"What?"

"Do we still get 15 cents a mile?"

Tips for news junkies

If you are a bona fide news junkie, such as I, you know the need to be selective in your reading habits. There simply isn't time to wade through all the information available in our daily newspapers. I mean, no one, not even the quickest scanner, reads everything in every paper. So, over the years I have come up with a list of stories, photographs and such in newspapers which I avoid. For instance, life is too short to read any story about Brooke Shields. Or any story about Brooke Shields' mother. I never read anything about Brooke Shields' father, and don't intend to.

Headlines can be excellent warnings for avoiding a story. Never read any story about reptiles that has the headline, "Snakes alive." Also turn the page rather than read a story about a missing pooch, with the headline,

"Dog gone." I skip over stories headlined, "Group slates meeting" or "Man killed." And don't bother reading any story that has a headline ending with a question mark.

If you are reading a story and come across the words, "humankind" or "finalized," move on. (Not in this case, of course. I'm giving bad examples in a finalized form to all of humankind.)

It is not only words that one must avoid, but pictures as well. Do not bother looking at photographs of the polar bear frolicking in the zoo's pond on the hottest day of the year. That particular photograph was the second picture ever made by a news photographer and has appeared and reappeared in every newpaper every hottest day every year. Also, don't bother with the standard spring-day-in-the-park shot. You've seen it a hundred times: The dog catching the Frisbee in midair. That was the *first* newspaper photograph ever made.

One more weather photograph to skip over is the rainy-day-in-Houston shot always taken on a downtown street corner. A woman, looking soaked and pitiful, is standing there with an umbrella turned inside out. That photograph first appeared in *Poor Richard's Almanack* in 1772. It has run on every rainy day since then.

Other standard photographs you might consider flipping by are those showing a group of people, feet on spades, removing the first shovelful of dirt from a construction project. Also, pass on by shots of two men shaking hands while one gives another a check, unless, of course, you recognize one as an Arab sheik and the other as your congressman, and the photo looks a little grainy, as though it was shot from afar.

The sports section has avoidable photos, too, but it also has certain stories that the discriminating reader quickly skips over. First, of course, one should never read any coverage of an athletic contest that does not tell the reader, in the first paragraph, who won and by how much, and in the second graph, how it was done. Your time is too valuable to wade through reams of colorful humor just to find out who won the bloody game.

Also, avoid stories headlined, "Coach cautiously optimistic," or uses the phrase, "America's team." Be sure to pass over the standard George Steinbrenner-is-really-just-a-pussycat interview, along with any story whatsoever that even mentions Al Davis.

The editorial page has some of the best thoughts in the paper, but here again one must exercise caution. Do not, for example, read an editorial that begins with, "Both sides have a point . . ." or one that ends with, "It is a serious question that bears further study."

Do not bother to read an interview with any politician who says there is not enough money in the U.S. Treasury for the Meals-on-Wheels program for elderly shut-ins, but there is enough for cluster bombs to drop on Beirut, particularly if he explains, "It's all a matter of priorities."

The same goes for any executive of a utility monopoly who praises the free enterprise system.

Ditto for a retired general who complains about welfare payments.

Do not go any further into a story about a diplomatic meeting that is called "frank and fruitful."

Shun all book reviews that refer to the author by his or her first name or run the punchlines in French.

Also shun any movie review that clearly is written for other reviewers. Your first clue is when the film is compared to another one you haven't seen.

Obviously, turn the page rather than read a story that begins: "I've got some good news and some bad news."

And never, under any circumstances, read a newspaper story about how to read a newspaper.

Cook's tour—1976

One of Jimmy Carter's chief projects as president, he has told us countless times, is to streamline the federal government. He wants to consolidate, trim, maybe even make cheaper, the Washington bureaucracy.

The problem is that every president since George Washington has been promising the very same thing and all the while the federal bureaucracy just keeps rolling along, not like Old Man River, but like a snowball, getting bigger with every turn. Yet no president can just go in and throw out, for we have any number of hard-working federal employees in useful and necessary agencies. How can Carter tell one from the other? He can't, but I may be able to help him with a brief rundown on people and positions he may not know about. For instance:

The State Department has an officer based in Washington, in charge of cultural affairs for the Cook Islands. State also has a cultural affairs officer for NATO, which has no culture, and for San Marino. Just what the cultural affairs officer for San Marino does all day is not clear, but I think he keeps looking for San Marino.

Members of the Federal Election Commission are appointed.

The International Trade Commission has a section handling only "buttons, buckles, pins, hook and eyes, slide fasteners, peat moss pots, incense, hand fans, fossils, fly ribbons." It also has the memo writer's dream: a Word Processing Unit.

The president of the Panama Canal Co. is an Army major general. The surgeon general of the Navy is not a general but an admiral. However, the Sergeant Major of the Marines is a Marine sergeant major.

In the Department of Labor, the Women's Bureau has at least two officers who are men. The Postal Service has a Graphics Design and Production Division which, one must assume, is in charge of getting pictures for stamps. The Bureau of Indian Affairs has one officer named James Bearghost and another named H. Rainbolt.

The Tennessee Valley Authority has a personnel office on Raccoon Mountain, Tenn. The Veterans Administration has a department which handles nothing but headstones.

The Forest Service, which usually deals with forests, has a staff which handles the Freedom of Information Act and has a Civil Rights Office. For NASA, the Office of Equal Opportunity Programs has more officers than its Office of University Affairs, Office of Energy Programs or its Office of International Affairs. NASA, incidentally, still has an Apollo-Soyuz Closeout Office. I am not sure what it does, but whatever it is that needs doing, we have a staff doing it. Certainly it doesn't cost much, because NASA also has a Low Cost Systems Office.

There is, in the Washington bureaucracy, a Commission on Federal Paperwork. There is also an Office of Latin American and African Geology. One of my favorites is the Officer for Micronesian Status Negotiations. I suppose that each morning he checks to see if Micronesia is still there, then—assured that it hasn't disappeared during the night—goes off to lunch with the cultural affairs officer for the Cook Islands.

Getting its priorities straight, the Air Force has two generals in its Legislative Liaison Office, taking care of congressmen, and only one general in the Office of Information, which tells the rest of us what's happening.

The State Department has a staff handling Art in the Embassies. The Department of Agriculture's library has a law branch.

One of the longest titles around Washington must be the Department of Health, Education and Welfare's assistant secretary for administration and management, Office of Administration, administration services division director.

You probably thought the Alliance for Progress was long gone, but no, like the Apollo-Soyuz shot, its staff lingers on. Along these same lines, the Department of State's Bureau of East Asian and Pacific Affairs still has a section handling Vietnam, Laos and Cambodia. I'm not sure what the staff members do, either. Maybe they talk with another State Department staff, the Office of Foreign Disaster Assistance. Certainly, if ever we had a foreign disaster, it was Southeast Asia.

If they are looking for the cause of these disasters, I think I have found it: The Director of Defense Intelligence is "Vacant." We have a political-economic officer for our Angola desk, which makes sense because our government has no economic or political ties with Angola. But we have a politico-military officer for our Canada desk, in case the Mounties launch an all-out attack on Buffalo.

We have four ambassadors-at-large and an Observance of International Women's Year Task Force. The busiest person in Washington is probably Nancy McDonnell, the State Department's Congressional Travel Aide.

Of all the slots in Washington, without a doubt President-elect Carter will wish to leave untouched the jobs of three State Department officers who handle our relations with Estonia, Latvia and Lithuania, three countries which haven't existed since August 1940. If Carter does wish to consolidate, maybe these staff members can be introduced to State Department officers Michael Durkee, Susan Klingaman and Charles Schaller. These three diplomats take care of our day-to-day international matter of war and peace with, respectively, Andorra, Liechtenstein and Greenland.

It couldn't be

AUSTIN—Teletype wires can be terribly misleading: "Pls advise what you want to do from this end on death of State Rep. Hawkins Menefee of Houston." It's one of those ridiculous mistakes. Gremlins in the wire. The death of State Rep. Hawkins Menefee? The mere idea is absurd.

It is Tuesday. That's the Honorable Hawkins Henley Menefee right there, leaning up against the highly polished brass rail in the House chamber, wearing a light brown suit, a baby face and an angry look. "Eighty-five percent of the state legislature is made up of good, hardworking people. You never hear about them, all you hear about is the 15 percent who goof off. Well, I'm tired of hearing about them."

The state representative from Houston's 84th District shifts his stance slightly, then grins: "I just hope no one asks which group I'm in."

If someone did try to categorize Menefee, it would be an impossible task, for he was an odd sort. Of all people in this seedy self-deluding business of politics, Hawkins Menefee would be elected the Pragmatic Idealist—the son of Don Quixote and Elizabeth I. He was a Democrat, a reformer who admired Price Daniel Jr. Yet he counted as his friend and adviser Rep. Fred Agnich of Dallas, an archconservative. "Agnich and I never agree on anything," Menefee once said. "Sometimes we violently disagree, but he always levels with me."

He was a 29-year-old, 5-foot-7-and-¾-inch bachelor, a guitar player, the party clown with a master's degree who wrote in his thesis: "The world of Texas politics has about it a certain mystique that has both confused and fascinated those who study it."

The death of Rep. Hawkins Menefee? Ridiculous. He frowns out at his colleagues, busily debating the new constitution. "My accountant just told me that it cost me $4,431 last year to be a legislator," he sighs. "I make $13.71 a day as a representative, and look here," he shuffles through a stack of papers. "Our janitors here at the Capitol make $14.61 a day. I make less than a janitor."

It is pointed out the janitor works only five days a week and Menefee is basing his salary on a seven-day week. He snorts: "Anyone who tells you that a legislator doesn't work seven days a week hasn't ever been a legislator. I go home and bright and early the phone starts ringing." This particularly disturbs Menefee since, by nature, he likes to sleep late and work late.

"Advise on the death of Rep. Menefee." It is Tuesday and the representative from Houston's 84th District is pouting: "The other day I broke my cardinal rule in campaigning and cussed." The idea of young Menefee uttering a profanity is a joke in itself. "An opponent got up and started lashing out about all the ninnies in Austin so I got up—I was really steamed—and said, 'Dammit, let me tell you what it's really like.'" He seems relieved to have confessed his sins.

Another delegate walks up and leans against the shiny brass railing and begins to lobby Menefee about an upcoming article in the constitution. This is rather unusual for such an old pro to cozy up so sweetly to a freshman lawmaker, but then, everyone knows the Honorable Hawkins Henley Menefee is a comer. He gets smiles from the powerful and gentle advice from sworn enemies. *Texas Monthly* picked him as one of the 10 best in the legislature.

It is Tuesday and Menefee laments the time he was late for a date and how it nipped a blooming romance. He argues with his good friend, Rep. Neil Caldwell, about the constitution. He grows solemn in discussing the outlook for the new charter, then glances up at the rostrum where a colleague is defending an amendment and smiles: "They're letting him carry that because it's not too important and he's not too swift."

The death of Hawkins Henley Menefee? There must be some mistake. Only Tuesday, leaning against the shiny brass rail, the last angry young man, who still found the world of Texas politics full of mystique and fascination, who would battle up and down these halls for mass transit, clean air, clean government, and still feel guilty about saying "dammit" in public.

Yet the teletype doesn't lie. It was a car wreck. The House Chamber is empty, and eight red carnations lie on one desk. The delegates have stopped their debate of Jeffersonian democracy for two days to contemplate the death of their baby-faced young colleague who knew all the words to "You Stomped on My Heart and Squashed That Sucker Flat."

The comer is gone, and a newsman sighs: "Some of 'em we wouldn't even miss. Why did it have to be Hawkins Menefee?"

Singing our song

All together now, we're ready to sing the state song. OK, ready? "Tex-aaaas, our Tex-aaaas . . . "

Look, folks, I don't like this any more than you do, but it's our duty. I'll hum a few bars and maybe you'll remember the rest of it. Humm-m-m-m-m-m-m, da-daaa-da-da-da-daaaa. Remember now? You don't remember? That's not unusual, because practically no one knows our state song. We know the flag, of course, and so do a lot of non-Texans (although I once saw the Lone Star Flag in a Manhattan store window under "foreign flags").

We know our state tree (pecan), state bird (Mimus polyglottos, the mockingbird), state flower (Lupinus texensis, the bluebonnet). Some even know the state stone (palmwood), state gem (topaz) and state grass (sideoats grama). Yet no one can remember the state song, even though it was taught to many of us in school.

So, since discussion is currently underway over splitting up Texas to give us a voice in the U.S. Senate for a change, this might also be a good time to talk about the state song. (Actually, the splitting itself is a gross violation of our familiar state pledge: "Honor the Texas flag. I pledge allegiance to thee, Texas one and indivisible." But everyone already knows that.)

The official state song is "Texas, our Texas." The tune was written by William J. Marsh who died in 1971 at age 90. The words are by Marsh and Gladys Yoakum Wright both of whom were from Fort Worth. As might be expected, the song is the work of the Texas Legislature, which offered a prize back in 1929. I do not know what the prize was, but "Texas, Our Texas" was the winner, which tells us something about the losers.

Actually, as state songs go, ours is not a bad song; it's just not a very good one and the proof is in the pudding: "Texas, Our Texas" has been with us for 46 years and no one knows it. That seems to be an adequate test and fair by any standards. So we must now drop the other shoe. We need a new state song. Easy now, easy. How can you defend the old one if you don't even know it? And when was the last time you heard it sung or played? I thought so.

That settled, we come to the next step: How to go about it. We could have another contest, but that would simply repeat the crime. A lot of well-meaning amateurs would crank out a lot of goo about "Oh, off shore rigs that rape and pillage, raise thy cranes above the spillage . . ."

and so on.

We might well go the easy route and adopt a tune already associated with Texas. Oklahoma officially adopted "Oklahoma!" by Rodgers and Hammerstein. Maryland went back a bit further and got the tune to "Christmas Tree, O Christmas Tree." We might even consider "The Eyes of Texas," which most people in and out of Texas think is the state song, anyway. There's "Deep in the Heart of Texas" and the theme from "Giant," which is an excellent tune.

"The Yellow Rose of Texas," however, is the strongest entry in this field. It has historical and cultural ties to Texas history, everyone already knows the song, and it supposedly celebrates a mulatto girl named Emily, our undercover agent at San Jacinto. Thus it brings together all our major ethnic groups. The Czechs and Germans would just have to translate it into their own languages. The French could grow misty-eyed, the Irish could drink to it and the Gypsies could steal it.

But perhaps the best route to follow is to come up with a totally new song, created by professional songwriters. When you want it done right, you should go to the experts, which probably explains why we don't have a new state constitution. OK, so we tell Burt Bacharach and Sammy Cahn and Jimmie Webb and others of that class that the State of Texas is in the market for a new song. It must:

Have a good, catchy tune that people will like and will sing.

Be singable. Nothing like the National Anthem, which goes up too high, and down too low.

Move right along and not drag out before each football game, but must still be heavy and dramatic enough to get the job done.

Be memorable, snappy but not too controversial. Evoke a bit of history without being maudlin. Proud but not boastful. The main requirement is that it must be the kind of song that people want to sing.

Let's get cracking on it. Until then, we'll have to be content with what we've got. Now let's take it from "Shines forth in splendor your star of destiny."

Family of owls is branching out

THE PATIO—It is a nice time to enjoy the backyard. The late afternoon sliding softly into early evening, the temperature dropping into the high 90s. The humidity mildewing my nostrils. The mosquitoes buzzing. But the best part of all is that I am out here alone. There are no dogs or kids causing me to consider becoming either a hermit or a mass murderer, whichever comes first. And there is no owl.

Now, for those of you who do not understand my glee, never having had an owl in your tree, let me assure you that you are fortunate. Those who do not have two owls in your trees are even luckier. A gravel truck could split your spleen and you still would not be even with those who have owls in their trees.

In times past I have had two. The major domo of the lot was a big, ugly, arrogant bird named Owl Capone. He hung around in the branch directly above my patio and let loose when it suited him. The other was his chippie, Owlice. She got equal joy out of making me miserable. Together they ruined my patio. But even worse, owls have the delightful habit of returning to nature that which does not interest them. Unnecessary mouse entrails land neatly in my martini.

To see the last of my owls is to see joy unencumbered. And I have been joyous these past few weeks. Owl Capone and Owlice went to that big speakeasy in the sky. After my fist-clinching and obscene cursing, they left. It is lovely to use my patio without first flushing. It has been sanitized for my protection.

"Oh, *look*," says my wife. The tone in her excited voice suggests something she thinks is important and I don't.

"What?"

"Look here," she says.

I wander back into the den and look out the window at the magnolia tree. Now, I don't know if you have any magnolia trees in your yard, but they kill all the grass and rain large leaves endlessly. I liken them just above floods and just below owls.

I stare at the tree. It stares back. Dead silence. I will be fair. Magnolia trees don't talk much. Well, maybe after a few doses of root stimulator they open up. But generally, they are a quiet bunch.

Nothing. I see nothing. You can feel pretty stupid staring at a tree. Suddenly a leaf moves. It is a furry leaf. No, make that fuzzy. Or feathery. Eh? Feathery? The leaf is an owl. A small owl. Hardy bigger than my hand and not at all like the Goodyear Owls I have seen bending down my branches with their fatty tissues. He shakes, then looks at me. He's kind of cute. Not real cute, mind you, but kind of cute.

So that is what Capone and his bit of fluff have been doing, frolicking among the birchbark. Capone was a horny owl. And this is the result. OK, Owl, *you* send him through Baylor Medical. That's your responsibility. You pay for your pleasure.

"And look over there," says my wife.

I look at some more leaves, which move. Two more eyes are looking at me. Another owl! That makes two! I am running a maternity ward around here.

They are small owls, to be sure, but will gorge on rodents until they are big, and then I'll be right back where I was, with those fat beasts up there, ruining my late afternoon binge. One owl is cute. Two owls are not.

I am sulking on the patio contemplating possibilities. Should I get a B-B gun? Bow and arrow? No, they eat those for breakfast. Perhaps the Argentine navy has an extra Exocet missile they'd let me borrow right after their victory parade through downtown Buenos Aires. Fire when ready, Gridley.

"Oh, *look!*" That tone of voice again. Back into the den to peer out the window up into the magnolia tree. There's one. Good Lord! Now there are three! I'm over my quota. I charge into the yard.

"Begone! Begone! Buzz off!" Six beady eyes look at me in disgust. Clearly father and mother have already briefed the little nippers on the landlord's eccentric habits. They refuse to move. One by one they close their eyes and go back to sleep. I can't even keep them awake, much less make them go on.

Is there a law against owlicide? I've got three in my tree. And there is the chance that their parents will come back from an orgy in the swamp. An entire family.

I could chop down the tree, but they'd just move to the condo in the pines. Poisoned rats. Maybe that would do it. Or a feather-seeking Sidewinder. What are owls afraid of? Is there a scare-owl? It's certainly not me. I know. I read somewhere that owls are terribly afraid of nuclear fallout. No, that would be overkill.

Sulk-sulk. Well, it could have been worse. Owls often lay more than three eggs, I mean, I could have . . .

"Oh, *look!*"

Courting talk

So you want to learn how to play tennis, do you? Fine. Why should you be any different from the other 212 million Americans clogging up the courts?

Tennis is easy, cheap and relatively painless, unless you can jump only halfway over the net. Now watch closely and, before you can say, "Jimmy loves Chris" (a double meaning we shall get to under "Scoring"), you, too, can be a big man in court.

The Name—"Tennis" comes from the French term, "Tenez!" which means, "Attention!" A lot of tennis terms come from the French. So does a lot of highly refined heroin.

The Racket—Right off, learn that it is a "racquet," not a "racket." Do not make a joke about "Tennis isn't my racquet." This line was first uttered during the reign of Henry VII when the King of Castile played the Marquis of Dorset. The king, who used a racquet, conceded 15 to the marquis, who played with only his hand. The king won the set, the marquis uttered the remark, and promptly lost his head.

The Net—The net is put up to keep your opponent from kneeing you in the groin. Do not say, "This game is a net loss." (For details, read "The Premature Death of the Duke of Dorset, 1620–1640.")

The Court—The court is 27 feet wide and 78 feet long, which is just the right size to make sure your shots don't fit inside.

Singles—A lot of singles play tennis in hopes that they will soon be doubles. The term, "match point," thus takes on a new meaning.

Doubles—A lot of doubles play tennis, too. They usually end up as singles.

The Tennis Ball—It is usually held after a major tennis match so that everyone can get snockered and pour the punch bowl over the linesman.

Holding The Racquet—The racquet should be held at all times, particularly while playing; otherwise somebody will steal it. I recommend the Forehand Groundstroke Grip which will usually hold two racquets and a change of underwear.

Serving—Try not to serve if you can possibly help it. If all else fails, move to Canada.

Scoring—It goes 5 (or 15 if you've been to college), 30, 40 and then game. If no one scores at all, it's called "love," but then, a lot of things are called that, and most are forbidden, even to consenting adults.

Strategy—All right, now we get down to the meat of the matter. To start, you must psych out your opponent. This can be done by yelling, "Fore," just prior to each serve. If your opponent is serving, it works even better. Try to hit the ball where he is not. If you lose a point, cry. In doubles, I recommend the crosscourt return, followed by a recovery behind the baseline and towards the corner, then a volley to the right-rear corner and a final volley down his throat. But then, I also recommended Jake Jacobsen to John Connally.

Volley—This was mentioned earlier and should be explained. A volley is 1) hitting the ball before it touches the ground, 2) a rapid series of tennis strokes, or 3) help from several friends using M-1s.

Wimbledon—You will hear an occasional mention of "Wimbledon," usually mispronounced as "Wimbelton," since you're obviously in a pretty seedy tennis club. Wimbledon is an annual match held in England. It has a lot of prestige and very small monetary prizes, just the opposite of politics.

Deuce—This is when the score is all tied up and every shot counts, making for exuberant and often hotly contested points. Origin of the expression, "Deuces are wild."

Backhand—Hitting the ball with the back of your hand. This is frowned upon in some circles, but as the Marquis del Campo said in defeating the Count de Basie with a backhand to the left ear, "Points is where you find 'em."

Tennis Clothes—White clothes are usually required on tennis courts, so that the opposing player can't see the ball.

Healthy Exercise—Tennis is extremely healthy, if done in moderation. But do not overdo. For instance in the Paris Graun Pree (pronounced, "grand prix") in 1823, the Marquis de Theater played 46 sets against Emile Cortisone. The Marquis dropped dead of a heart attack while Emile passed away from a brain seizure, thus giving us the tennis expression, "Different strokes for different folks."

Luausy puns

Sheriff: Which way did the computer programmer go?
Rancher: He went data way.
There. That should set the pace for today's meeting. It is a front-end warning that punsters, troublemakers and preachers are among us, hatching stories which would cause the strongest to weep in anger. The above he-went-data-way offering is by someone named Scott L. Weeden of Houston, who also notes that once upon a time there were these two kingdoms which were at war. One of the kingdoms captured a count from the other kingdom and grilled him for information, but he refused to talk. So he was tortured. Still no information.
So they took him to the dungeon to be executed. The executioner was given the go-ahead and as the axe was descending, the count cried out: "Wait!" But it was too late.
Moral: Don't hatchet your counts before they chicken.
John A. Stoner of the University of Virginia Law School (yes, among our readers there is a Virginia) reports that there was a diplomat and his family who were invited to an authentic South Seas luau. All would have gone well except that the main dish was not the typical roast pig, but, instead, was roast-warrior-from-another-island.
The diplomat, being used to different people having different customs, was enjoying the feast, but his son refused to eat his meal or to have anything to do with the cannibals. A nasty international incident was avoided, however, when the diplomat took his offspring aside and explained: "One man's meat is another man's poi, son."
Every time I run some of these items, someone always comes out of the woodwork angrily to explain that such-and-such a story is not a pun at all, but is a spoonerism. In some cases this is true, but I keep sticking

to the Oxford English Dictionary, which gives as one definition of a pun, "a play on words." That would seem to cover most of these instances, and I really don't worry about those who overexamine and dissect humor. They probably jot down notes on the headboard while making love.

A lady sheep supported herself writing articles for literary magazines (if you buy this one so far, you'll buy anything). But she began experiencing an unusual problem: a few hours after writing the essays, the ink would turn invisible and all traces of her work would disappear. Finally, her neighbor, a retired Army officer, explained that he had been having trouble keeping his dentures white, but that a new denture powder had worked wonders and might just aid her, too, since nothing else was of any help.

She tried it and—oddly enough—it worked. The moral of this story is (ready?): What's good for the general's molar is good for the ewe's essay.

Under no circumstances is John Stoner to be allowed to get away with this. He is to be prosecuted and persecuted even unto the fifth and sixth generations.

Wait. Here's a final shot from Scott Weeden: Sign in a piano showroom: "Buy a piano now—only 10 Chopin days till Christmas."

I shall now rip off from *Centralities*, a newsletter from the Central Presbyterian Church, this historical note:

Alexander the Great first discovered that a piece of cloth soaked in a certain magic potion (later to be known as silver chloride) and spread out to dry in the sun became darker as the sun rose higher. Thus Alexander found that by noting the shade of the cloth he could tell the hour of the day. But he didn't want to keep running back to the spot to check the time all day, so he discovered that he could just tie the cloth around his forearm. A sort of early wrist watch, it was, which eventually became known as Alexander's rag time-band.

A DELICIOUS MOMENT

A Delicious Moment

There's a whiff in the air. No, just a sniff. Right there . . . no, it's gone. It was there for a moment, a delicious moment, and now it's gone. But it should be there on days like today.

This is spring, no matter what the calendar says. A spring day in Texas, when the air is pale blue and Saran Wrap clear. There is a breeze, but not a wind, just enough to shake the trees with their new buds peering out at their environment, wondering what hath God wrought. And on days like today, so many moons ago, I used to muck about the yard, doing whatever small boys did. There was the front yard, which looked out on other front yards up and down the street and always presented an unyielding scene of boredom.

The backyard was a maze of hedges and paths and sandpiles and driveways. And trees. And assorted brothers and sisters and friends running about on days like today. But wherever I was, whatever I was doing, every now and again, on days like today, I would stop. Stop still. Something was happening. I could smell it. I could almost hear it. I could *feel* it. The senses would perk and peak. The eyes would light up. The mouth would drool. For my grandmother, who lived next door to us, was in the kitchen. The stove was hot and she was cooking brownies.

Looking back it was obvious that I couldn't smell the mixings or the beating and melting. My senses were aroused only for the final act, as the oven was baking them and my grandmother was about to pull them out. I suspect that I was the alarm clock, the telltale sign that the brownies were ready, and that my grandmother waited for the proper sign to yank them from their incubator. She waited until she heard small footsteps up the driveway, the opening of the outside screen door, which always slammed shut with deafening violence. Then the three steps across the backporch, the opening of the kitchen door, and the expected, "Hi, Mamaw."

Certainly I didn't fool her for a second. It was not an innocent outpouring of a grandson's love. I didn't just chance by the kitchen to shower her with affection. No, I was not so much a spontaneous avalanche of tender charm as I was a hardened case of overt gluttony.

On days like today, I was never disappointed. I could be lying on my back in the grass, wondering why asps like hackberry trees. Or I could be dropping tennis balls at the top of the slide, so that—like a skijumper—the balls would whiz down the slide, hit the sandy rise at the bottom and leap up into the air, then fall down into varying pockets I had dug in the sandpile. I could be playing cowboys and cowboys—no one knew exactly how to be an Indian—or riding bikes, playing Kick the Can or Little White House Over the Hill. But the alarm would sound, and I would come, down the driveway, through the screen door, three jumps across the backporch and through the kitchen door. I was consistent in the extreme.

My job, at this point, was to look both excited and hungry. And I excelled. At the proper time, which was several years later, Mamaw would rise from her chair and wander over to the stove with glacial swiftness. She would look around and finally spot her hotpads, which were inevitably far across the kitchen. I would rush over and get them for her, thrust them into her hands, and stand by. The door of the stove would be opened, and out would come this pan, this large, flat pan. And there, spread from side to side, were the brownies. With nuts. Dark brown. Hot. But it wasn't the sight so much as the smell. It filled the universe with flavor.

Mamaw would set the pan down and select the proper knife. At this point I was ready for the slicing, and every single time she would explain that you had to wait for the brownies to cool. You can't slice brownies when they are hot. It has something to do with the consistency of the crust, I was told. But I knew, deep down, that the real reason was simply to torture small grandsons. So I would wait around the kitchen. Then, when I had paid for my real and imagined sins tenfold, she would slice them. And hand me one.

You cannot dream.

You cannot savor.

You cannot come with me on this trip.

For there is nothing to compare in any man's life with the taste of hot brownies from your grandmother's stove on a warm spring day in Texas.

She had a recipe, which I could give you, but I suspect that you would find it is no different from any other recipe you have for brownies. But you might lack the secret sauce, made from large appetites in small boys, heavily laced with mutual affection.

Years later, in the Marines I received a box from my grandmother. Inside was a headline clipped from *The Dallas Morning News* announcing that the Marines had landed in Lebanon. I had heard the rumor. Across the bottom she had written: "See, you always get the worst jobs." And under the headline were the most delicious brownies in the world. She had sent one son and three grandsons off to the Corps, and knew just what we needed—insults and praise.

In more recent times, my younger brother held an open house in Jakarta for his office, and had it all catered. His wife baked up a batch of Mamaw's brownies as an added attraction for all the bankers and oil ministers and generals and the like who frequent such free feeds. The Scotch and beer and peanuts and canapes and finger sandwiches went nicely enough, but the brownies were attacked by an international school of starving piranha. Small wonder, for there is nothing quite like those brownies.

And on fine spring afternoons in Texas, sometimes I think I can smell them again. Just a race down the driveway, through the screen door three jumps across the backporch and through the door into the kitchen. I can smell them on days like today.

Rich legacy

NORTH OF ROUND TOP—One of the nicest things about Texas is that it is so very rich. And, all in all, it is much better to be rich than not to be. Poverty is so tacky.

Now, by "rich" I don't mean that we all live up to the ideas somehow placed in the minds of non-Texans: that we ride our Caddies about the spread counting our oil wells before stepping into our Learjets for a quick lunch in Dallas. No, there are literally dozens of Texans who cannot do that, and you and I are among them.

Nor by "rich" do I mean that we do not have a lot of poor. According to federal standards, there are more poor people in Texas than in any other state. We have ghettos in Houston and barrios in Brownsville that would gag a maggot. No, we have millions of poor in Texas, and it is all the more our shame because the state has so much.

What I mean by "rich" is that we have an awful lot. And we didn't always. Take Houston, for instance. On October 25, 1837, the *Matagorda Bulletin* noted:

"Persons recently from Houston state that the city presents rather a gloomy appearance and worse in prospect. At the time our informant left, there was much sickness, principally fevers—of which there had been cases of yellow, congestive, and bilious. Every place was said to be crowded, and little or nothing to eat."

To be sure, on Saturday night along Westheimer it is still crowded and difficult to get anything to eat, but the problem is born of too many people having too much, rather than not enough. As for the sickness, today they come from throughout the world to Houston, in hopes of finding a cure. All of this in 146 years. The Russians say they have people older than that.

By "rich" I mean the sights of Texas which we tend to take for granted and overlook. Like the sunsets on the road out from Austin toward Fredericksburg. The Staked Plains north of Lubbock, where the grain looks so thick and tall that you could almost walk across the tops of it without coming within three feet of the ground. Or lying under a pine tree in Memorial Park and watching the joggers pant by.

I mean a good Friday night bloodletting when two high school football teams from adjoining towns go at it, leaving tape and teeth in their wake. The Alamo at night and the Pecos High Bridge at dawn. The UT Tower, banging out the hours. The sticky smell of Port Arthur's refineries, which in no way can be called pleasant, but it's there, and it's as much a part of Texas as anything we've got.

By "rich" I mean the vast variety of people, which now makes us the third most populous state in the Union—the advantages about which I am still ambivalent. It is absolutely impossible to point at one person and say with any accuracy, "He looks like a Texan." If he is an Anglo, what about the one-quarter of Texas which is black or brown? If he's in cowboy boots, what about the lumberjacks, roughnecks, short-order cooks and those who have no shoes at all? If she's from Flatonia, she's probably Czech, so what about the Germans in Waelder, the Chicanos in Crystal City and the masses of us who are crossbreeds?

I think most of us are turned off by the boasting, boorish professional Texans, with their tub-thumping, chest-beating bravado. They are an outrage to our senses and an insult to our truths. We can stand on what we've got without exaggerating. For we are rich—rich in the sense that we've got a lot.

There are the usual things we point to: the Astrodome and the LBJ Space Center and the oil and cattle and beaches. But there's also the drowsiness of Sanderson, the loneliness of Bandera County and the vast stretches north of Amarillo where nothing has ever disturbed the red dirt. There is the intense look of a Dallas lawyer, the easy pace of a Bolivar bartender, and the look on the face of the Texas Highway Patrolman walking up to your car. It is the most dangerous time for a law officer— you know all about him and he knows nothing about you. But he's holding a pencil, not a gun.

By "rich" I mean our history. No other state, perhaps with the exceptions of Massachusetts and Virginia, can match the history of Texas with our parade of scoundrels and nice guys, double dealings and single shots, bad times and good. Everyone knows about the Pilgrims' Thanksgiving, but don't forget the spring of 1843, when the Caddoes, Wacoes, Toncyes, Kickapoos, Delawares and Addarkoes gathered at Washington-on-the-Brazos with the Great White Father, Sam Houston (who wore a brilliant red silk robe, a gift from the Sultan of Turkey). And don't forget about the feast that followed.

By "rich" I mean not only the large cities which are getting fatter, but also the small towns, and the huge, sprawling under-populated land that seems to go on forever. Where nothing ever happens, because that's the way they want it. Oh, we have more than our share of con artists, braggarts, thieves, drunks and hypocrites. We have dust storms and mosquitos and car wrecks and crooked politicians and third-rate culture. We always have and we always will.

However, by some twist of fate and a lot of hard work by those who came this way before us, we also have more goodies than virtually any other place on God's earth. We can't take credit for it, so there's no point in puffed-up pride and hats and horns, but it is worth a bit of appreciation.

Back in 1836, an officer with Santa Anna, Captain José Enrique de la Peña, noted the land over which he was chasing Houston's little army, and wrote: "When Texas is populated and governed by good laws, it will be one of the most enviable places in the world, in which it doubtless will play a brilliant role."

That kind of rich.

Death on No. 9

Ah, there you are. Pull up a packing crate and hang on, because we're off on another train trip, the anniversary of blood and thunder, high adventure and sneaky dealings. (We only go on the more interesting trips, as you may have noticed.)

This is the mail and baggage car of Train Number A of the Southern Pacific, then the Galveston, Harrisburg and San Antonio heading west out of Del Rio. It's a cool and moonless night, a bit after midnight on March 13, 1912. Number 9 was delayed in Del Rio, so Engineer D. E. Grosh and Fireman M. M. Holmes up in the engine are trying to make up for lost time. We thunder through the night over gawdawful country, dry and mountainous. The Rio is just to the south and beyond is Mexico, abounding with bandits and revolutionaries.

Number 9 moves through Langtry, Pumpville and over Meyer Canyon, named for the army general who lost most of his supplies in the canyon during a gully washer. Through Malvado, which means "curse word" or "very wicked" in Spanish, and justifiably so. Canyons, mountains, desert. A mean place, this is. We stop for water at Dryden, elevation 2106 feet, then move on.

Here in the mail car, David A. Trousdale, an express messenger for Wells, Fargo & Co., looks out the door, then slams it shut as the train begins chugging harder up a grade. Trousdale sits down at his desk to shuffle through some papers. He is a slightly built fellow, 35 years old, 5'7", a Tennessee farm boy who once worked as a barber in the Texas State Hospital in Austin. By the light of the coal oil lamp, he starts writing as his helper, named Reagan, stacks some packages for Sanderson.

The train begins slowing down and finally stops a mile before Baxter's

Curve, named for an engineer who was killed here in a derailment. Like I said, this is a mean place. Trousdale dosen't pay much attention until the porter calls for him to come to the door.

Trousdale slowly gets up, somewhat annoyed, and slides open the car door. There he is greeted by the nose of a 401 Model Winchester, and finds himself squarely in the middle of one of the last, and most violent, train robberies in Texas history: the Holdup at Baxter's Curve.

It is a professional job, done by some old pros. One is Ben Kilpatrick, AKA Gil Fitzpatrick and "Partner," the last survivor of the notorious Hole-in-the-Wall Gang. Rather slight and balding, he is wearing a dark suit, black overcoat, several pistols and six sticks of dynamite.

The other fellow is larger and needs a shave. He is Frank Hobek, AKA, "Old Hobek" and Ed Walsh, originally from Minnesota. Hobek is heavy-set and—behind the mask—looks rather like Ernest Borgnine. He's all decked out in gray pants, and a black shirt with white buttons running up the front, two .45-caliber Colt revolvers, a Winchester rifle and a pint of nitroglycerine. Just a couple of good ol' boys dressed fit to kill.

They boarded back at the waterstop at Dryden, sneaking on after the train had started up. They climbed over the tender and onto the locomotive, shouting to the startled engineer and fireman: "Do as you're told and you won't get hurt!" They planned to stop the train at Baxter's Curve where a third bandit—unknown to this day—is to be waiting with three saddle horses and a pack horse, complete with a canvas cover containing large pockets for the loot.

Trousdale dosen't know any of this, nor does he particularly care. A quiet man by nature, his only brush with excitement has been playing semi-pro ball for Hutto, Texas. "Fall out!" Hobek commands Trousdale, who obeys and is quickly searched for weapons. Smoothly, professionally, the bandits gather up the crew, including Henry Erkel, the conductor, then uncouple the passenger cars from the front mail and baggage car.

The conductor and porter are ordered back to the passenger cars with the subtle advice: "Poke your heads out of those cars and you'll get them blown off." That seems to suffice. Everyone else is loaded up and the front part of the train rumbles down the line about a mile to the dreaded Baxter's Curve, where it stops. Trousdale, Reagan and the mail clerk are ordered into the mail car by Hobek while Kilpatrick remains up front with the engineer and fireman.

Poking and pushing Trousdale with his Winchester, Hobek commands that he open the safe. "I got him to take two packages," Trousdale recalls in his report. "One valued at $2 and the other at $37. After he looked over the car, he said he would go through and get what Uncle Sam had." Hobek begins ripping open mail pouches, packages, bags, emptying them into a larger sack.

"We'll go back and see what the passengers have," says Hobek from behind his mask. "Then we'll take you across the river with us." Trousdale knows what that means: a hostage to keep the posse at bay until they cross into Mexico, then a bullet in the back. It's a tradition around here.

"Have it your way," he replies. "I'm not getting fighting wages." But he is thinking.

"Dad was always a quiet fellow, never showed his emotions," says his son, W. N. Trousdale, a staff auditor for the Southern Pacific in Houston. "He probably would have gone along until they started bullying him. Dad didn't like to be pushed around."

They start marching toward the door, passing by an ice barrel full of oysters (yes, oysters). Here on the top of the barrel is an ice maul, a heavy hammer used for cracking blocks of ice. Trousdale picks it up and hides it. Suddenly he points to the stack of packages destined for Sanderson. "That one there is worth more than all you've gotten so far," Trousdale says helpfully. Hobek's eyes light up. He leans the rifle against his leg and bends over to pick up the package.

Wham! Trousdale slams the ice maul down on the bandit's head. Again! Again! "I knocked his brains out with the third blow," Trousdale reports to his superintendent later.

He grabs the two pistols and gives them to Reagan and the mail clerk. He takes the Winchester, then all three retreat to the end of the car, dousing the lights as they go. That way the only light comes from the door leading to the front and the locomotive. "I waited something like two hours for the second man to come back. He did not show up for some time and I fired a shot through the top of the car."

Quiet. Nothing. Then there is noise at the door. A voice: "Frank? Frank?" Silence. "Frank? Anything wrong?" Silence. The door opens, but Trousdale can't see if anyone has come in. Five minutes go by in the darkened baggage car. Suddenly a head peers around a crate, but before Trousdale can do anything, it disappears. The second time the face peers out, it is closer.

Trousdale gets off one shot. The last member of the Hole-in-the-Wall gang topples forward, shot one and a half inches above the left eye. The Holdup at Baxter's Curve is over.

Between Wells, Fargo, the Southern Pacific and Congress, Trousdale gets $2,500 in reward money and a gold watch. As for the passengers, they take up a collection and present Trousdale with an engraved badge showing that he is an official hero.

"My father never had the nerve to wear it as a badge, so he had it made into the watch fob to go with the watch," says W. N. Trousdale, looking at the inscription. "He never considered himself a hero. He just didn't like to be pushed around."

Shady's shots

THE PARKING LOT – "Just leave it right there, Mister. I'll take it on in," says the parking lot attendant as he takes my place behind the wheel. "Flaps down, power on, wheels up, stand by."

"Wait a minute!" I shout. "I'll park it myself. I should never trust my car to a parking attendant wearing leather helmet, goggles and a white silk scarf."

"When you've got it, flaunt it," he says testily.

"Hey, I know you," I say. "You're Rep. Shady, my state legislator and parking lot attendant. Are you out on bail?"

"Don't get funny with me, Constituent," he snaps. "You may have the upper hand right now, but you'll get yours. You can't fool all the politicians all the time."

"What are you talking about, Rep. Shady?"

"You know perfectly well what I'm talking about. I'm talking about Proposition 13. You'll rue the day it came about."

"Actually, I think it's a great idea. People are being taxed to death by their governments. Proposition 13 was simply a direct way of telling lawmakers what we've tried to tell them for years: We want less government and less taxes. There really is no great surprise in all of this. It's like the old joke about hitting mules over the head with a two-by-four. First, you've got to get their attention."

"With no firemen, no policemen, no paved streets and no garbage collection, see if you still think it's a great idea, and don't come crawling to me, pleading to triple your taxes."

"Now hold on, Rep. Shady," I say. "No one wants to cut the salaries or numbers of police, firemen and the like."

"That's what you'll get. I'm asking the governor to call a special session of the Legislature so that I can introduce a bill cutting back on all essential services."

"Rep. Shady, you miss the point. For example, a special session of the Legislature would cost a lot of money. It's things like that which people want to stop."

"But that's an important function. I get mileage and per diem cash allotment and a staff allowance, and there's those great parties the lobbyists throw, and there's practically no work to do."

"If Texas does get a Proposition 13," I say, "then expenses might have to be cut, but why don't you cut them in areas like your own salary? Or cut down on your mailing expenses? How about a few less staff members?"

"Those are too important to cut. Nope, we're gonna get 'em where it hurts. No more roads, no more DPS, open the prisons and close the schools. That'll show 'em."

"You are behaving like a spoiled brat, Rep. Shady. You are against Proposition 13 and when you get overruled by the people you're supposed to be serving, then you overreact and try to hurt the public. You don't want to cut the budget, you want revenge."

"I've been talking to other elected officials, and they feel the same way," Shady says.

"That is not only immature, that's silly and spiteful," I say.

"You get what you pay for, Constituent."

"Wrong, Rep. Shady. We're not getting what we pay for. If you and your colleagues really want to carry out the will of the people, start cutting back on programs we don't want and can't afford. Stop flying to London with your wives and staff members to pick up a copy of the Magna Carta. Stop taking junkets at the taxpayers' expense, voting yourself pay raises, fringe benefits, pensions and football. tickets."

"How else are you going to attract good people to government service?"

"Rep. Shady, with all due respect, a lot of good people stay away from government service because some creeps give it a bad name."

He scowls. "You probably would be against my plan to cut lunch money to widows and orphans."

"Yes, but I would go along with abolishing a bunch of government programs which cost a lot of money and don't do anything but keep a lot of bureaucrats employed in tasks no one ever heard of."

"Constituent, you forget that every one of those bureaucrats is a voter. On the other hand, the people leading a tax revolt are really not that numerous. I don't think they've started much by this."

"I don't know, Shady. They started something once before."

"What was that?"

"The United States."

His little hate list

The American political system reached a new level with the announcement that the White House actually kept a hate list of its enemies. Shades of *1984*.

When news of the list was divulged by John Dean (leading it to be called, of course, the Dean's List), the White House acknowledged that it did, indeed, exist, but was kept only for social purposes. The administration did not want the wrong type showing up at Presidential functions.

This made sense, needless to say. The present administration couldn't be too careful what with all that talk about buggings, burglaries and blackmail running amok. Why lands sakes, Dr. DeBakey might turn up right there in the East Room, rubbing elbows with decent, God-fearing folks.

Still, if it's good enough for our leaders, it's good enough for us, as the Germans used to say. So, I feel it is my patriotic duty to draw up my own list, and keep a close eye on my neighbors, too. Strictly for social purposes, you understand. Please toss this in your sociable paper shredder when you're through.

First on any list must be people who call up on the phone and say: "Bet you don't know who this is?"

A close second is the person who sends you a Christmas card signed simply, "Pete."

Trucks which thunder down the freeway with a load of uncovered sand which sprays those of us behind, thus creating a free freeway sandblast which works wonders on a new paint job. A must for my black list.

Bob Haldeman on general principles and a total lack thereof.

Motorcyclists who roar up and down hill and dale right outside my window on weekend mornings. This particular entry on my list may be scratched shortly—once I get a rope strung between two trees about neck high.

Churches which quietly fold up their downtown domain and retreat to the affluent suburbs to run up a multi-million-dollar-complex where they can preach the need for charity and social consciousness.

Motorists who drive at 45 miles an hour in the passing lane.

Television news shows that divide their 30 minutes equally among news, sports and weather, thus giving World War III the same play as a low pressure area over Toronto.

People who say, "At this point in time" when they mean "now."

Fat girls in bare midriffs.

Women who dress like a serf, cuss like a knight and still expect to be treated like a princess.

Whoever thought up that buzzer that keeps going until I put on my seat belt, close the door, empty the ashtray, say my prayers and start my car.

My Marine drill instructor.

Whoever thought up my Marine drill instructor.

Downtown overhead walkways that block out the sun, keep in the fumes and interfere with what little bit of nature that creeps into downtown Houston.

The City Council for allowing all of the above.

Plastic flowers.

Rock groups that turn up the volume on their electronic machinery to disguise the fact that they are tone deaf.

Jeb Magruder (see: "Haldeman").

Alarm clocks.

People who tear pictures out of books.

Letters that begin: "Dear Occupant, This is a personal invitation to you. . . ."

Monday mornings.

A dollar twenty-nine for ground round.

People who toss beer cans out of cars.

Beer cans which toss people out of cars.

Return envelopes which have a metered stamp so that I can't soak it off and use it.

People sitting right behind me who have read the book and keep explaining every scene in the movie.

People who ask them to.

Government officials who forget that they are employed by the people.

People who let them forget.

People who tell other people that they cannot pay a ridiculous amount of money to go behind a locked door to watch a boring porno movie, and then require that the police—who might have other things to investigate (murder, arson, riots)—enforce their self-appointed guardianship.

Whoever decided that cuffs on men's trousers were out, then waited until we all bought cuffless trousers before telling us that cuffs were back in.

The inventor of the head cold.

And finally on my hate list is a group of bright, buttoned-down, ivy-covered young men with boyish charm and winning smiles—and their leaders—who kept telling us that long-haired hippies were about to topple the government. Then they systematically corrupted our government, rewarded their friends and punished their enemies, and brought us to This Point In Time where we have hate lists. They go to the head of the crass.

The Rose saga

We have assorted places around the state named for Texas heroes of the Alamo: Travis County, the city of Bowie, Crockett State Park and so on. But we have nothing named for Moses Rose.

For one thing, there would be a problem of just what to call the namesake. This Rose was known by many other names: Moses Rose, Louis Rose, Lewis Rose and once was listed as Stephen Rose. Mrs. Dickinson, a survivor of the Alamo, recalled in 1876: "His name to the best of my recollection was Ross."

The second reason we have never put his name on any place of honor is that Rose is the one who got away, the only man in the Alamo who fled. He went over the wall and out of the picture. Indeed, for some time there was the definite possibility that Rose never existed, or had made up the whole thing. Perhaps he was only the Anastasia of the Alamo.

For years afterwards, few believed his story; serious historians ignored both him and his version of those final days in the Alamo. Most especially, they disregarded his statement that Travis took out his sword and drew a line in the dust, asking all who wanted to stay to cross the line.

He was listed as killed in the Alamo as late as 1860. His name was carved on at least two monuments. To further confuse the story, there was another Rose in the Alamo, J. M. Rose, nephew of President James Madison. In one history book, Moses Rose's story is listed under: *Some Old Errors*. "Rose has been forgotten, will continue to be forgotten," J. Frank Dobie once wrote. He was the man who never was.

Then, in 1939, R. B. Blake—who had been interested in the mystery— was poking through the faded records in the Nacogdoches County Court-house and kept coming upon land claims filed by the next-of-kin of the Alamo's defenders, seeking land grants. The question asked by the County Board of Land Commissioners was: How can you prove Charles Haskell (or David Wilson or Marcus Sewell) was really at the Alamo? In six different cases they brought out the one who got away, the local butcher, Moses Rose. And each time, Rose proved conclusively that he had been there.

So it appeared that the oft-stated claim, "Thermopylae had her message of defeat, the Alamo had none," was not totally accurate. But his cowardice is our credit, since it gives us a bit more information on the last desperate days of the Alamo.

For this reason, let's take a look at Moses Rose, who survived the Alamo, but—in one of history's little ironies—died an agonizing death because of it.

He was a Frenchman. Born in France about 1785. He joined Napoleon's army and fought all the way to Moscow, then survived the freezing retreat through the Russian winter. He may have fought with Napoleon in Italy, or simply served with many who did. In any event, he knew all about the Italian campaigns.

No one knows if Rose was at Waterloo, but after the fall it is assumed that he joined a band of refugees under General Lallemand and came to America.

He split from the group, which was headed to a settlement on the Trinity River, and went instead to Louisiana. In 1826, Haden Edwards recruited men for the ill-fated Freedonian Rebellion in Texas, and Rose apparently signed up. He arrived in Nacogdoches in 1826—a swarthy soldier of fortune, whose Spanish was better than his English.

The Freedonian Rebellion died but Rose, as always, survived. He remained in the Nacogdoches area, working in sawmills. In 1832, he joined the American side in the Battle of Nacogdoches, and his stock with the townspeople went up considerably. He got a job as a messenger between Nacogdoches and Nachitoches, La., and became paymaster for a cargo company. So, he must have been considered trustworthy.

A local judge, John M. Dor, issued a Certificate of Character for Rose on Aug. 25, 1835, stating: "I, the undersigned, certify that the citizen, Louis Rose is a man of very good morality, habits and industry, a lover of the constitution and laws of the country and of the Christian religion."

This might have been stretching it a bit. In one week Rose ran up a bill at the company store for three purchases of whiskey, including one for a full gallon.

In the fall of '35, war was in the air again. Thomas Rusk raised a company of troops and marched off to San Antonio to fight the Mexicans.

Rose didn't go, but his old soldiering instincts were aroused. On Oct. 7, 1835, he borrowed all he could from Vicente Cordova, pledging his personal belongings as collateral. One month later, Cordova sold off the belongings at an auction.

Rose also sold off his ranch west of the Angelina River, and—with horse, blanket and weaponry—he left Nacogdoches about Halloween of 1835, heading off to war. He was 50 years old, unmarried, so illiterate that he signed his documents with a mark, but the bugles were blowing and the drums were beating.

In addition, he had a friend in San Antonio, name of Jim Bowie.

The Texans chased General Cos and the Mexican Army out of San Antonio, and the tedium of garrison duty set in. Many troops left for home, but Rose stayed around. He and Bowie and the rest eventually retreated to the Alamo, set up shop, and waited for help to arrive. You will be surprised to learn that it never did. Rose was certainly surprised.

At the time, the spring of 1836, the Alamo was not in downtown San Antonio. It wasn't even on the edge. The town then covered about one-half of a peninsula in the river, quite a distance away. The area in between was covered with thick mesquite and—for a few days—most of the Mexican Army.

A Texian soldier named W. P. Zuber, whose family knew Rose, spent a large portion of his life writing about Rose, and defending his version of the Alamo from detractors, both foreign and domestic. This is the way Zuber recalls Rose's story of the time before the fall:

"During the last five days and nights of his stay, the enemy bombarded the fort almost incessantly, and several times advanced to the wall, and the men within were so constantly engaged that they ate and slept only at short intervals, while one body of the enemy was retiring to be relieved by another; yet they had not sustained a single loss.

"About two hours after sunset, on the third day of March, 1836, the bombardment suddenly ceased, and the enemy withdrew an unusual distance. Taking advantage of that opportunity, Colonel Travis paraded all of his effective men in a single file, and taking his position in front of the center, he stood for some moments apparently speechless from emotion. Then, nerving himself for the occasion, he addressed them substantially as follows."

What followed was a dramatic, beautiful speech. But it may have never happened. We don't know. Zuber says that Rose repeated the speech, verbatim, to Zuber's parents within weeks afterward. Historians note that Rose was illiterate and could speak only broken English. Zuber counters that this is not a weakness, but a strength: Like a blind person who relies on sound, an illiterate person relies on memory. Zuber's mother, years later, sided with her son: That's the way Rose repeated it to me, she said, and in no way could he have made it up.

We'll never know for sure, but it's still a resounding declaration of a commander facing his troops with a simple choice: Stay and buy time and die, or leave and live. "My choice is to stay in this fort and die for my country, fighting as long as breath shall remain in my body. This I will do, even if you leave me alone. Do as you think best. . . ."

It was at this point that Zuber recounted Rose's most dramatic moment: "Colonel Travis then drew his sword and with its point, traced a line upon the ground extending from the right to the left of the file. Then, resuming his position in front of the center, he said, 'I now want every man who is determined to stay here and die with me to come across the line. Who will be the first? March!' "

This tale did not come out until 1873, when Zuber told it. He was doubted then and he's doubted now. It's a helluva good story, and if it's not true, it should be. Walter Lord, in *A Time to Stand*, quotes J. K. Beretta: "Is there any proof that Travis *didn't* draw the line? If not, then let us believe it."

So, all crossed. Even Rose's good friend, Jim Bowie, dying on a cot, asked his troops to lift him over. All crossed, that is, but one. Moses Rose sank to the ground, and covered his face. No one said a word, most were headed back to their places on the walls. Then it hit him. He was dark, he spoke fluent Spanish, maybe—just maybe—he could get through.

Rose looked up and there was his old friend, Jim Bowie, speaking with Davy Crockett. Bowie turned and looked at the one man on the other side of the line. "You seem not to be willing to die with us, Rose," said Bowie.

"No," Rose answered. "I am not prepared to die and shall not do so if I can avoid it."

Then Crockett spoke up. "You may as well conclude to die with us, old man, for escape is impossible."

"I have often done worse than to climb that wall," said Rose, in what must go down as one of the most telling statements in our history.

Some versions say he jumped up at that moment and climbed the wall. Others say he waited until night. One story has Crockett helping him out a window. In any event, he grabbed his knapsack filled with his clothes, and got to the edge. He threw the bag out first, and it spilled open, the clothes landing in a pool of blood. He paused for a moment, then jumped.

Thus Rose—at the age of 51—leaped into history of a sort. He gathered up his clothes, and made his way past the carnage of the Texas sharpshooters. He did not head east immediately, but went into San Antonio, which was deserted. He turned down the river and when he had gone about a quarter of a mile along the riverbank, he heard a noise. It was the roar of a cannon, which continued to roll across the Texas prairie until, at dawn on March 6th, Rose heard no more cannon. It was over.

His trip on foot took him past deserted farms and ranches. The Runaway Scrape had left the land empty. He couldn't swim, so he hung onto logs to get across rivers. His legs became covered with thorns which dug into his flesh and caused him to limp and cry with pain. He eventually made his way to the Zuber place in Grimes County. The Zubers had already seen a copy of the *Telegraph and Texas Register* which listed Rose as killed in the Alamo. "My God, Rose," the senior Zuber cried, "Is this you or is it your ghost?"

"This is Rose, and not his ghost," Rose replied.

The Zubers fixed up the legs, and Rose rested there for some weeks, going over every detail of the battle, and Travis' speech, real or imagined. A maid washed out the Mexican blood from Rose's bag of clothes.

Well, I'm running out of space, so suffice to say that Rose returned to Nacogdoches, neither a villain nor a hero, although once in court he was referred to as "Luesa Rose," the feminine form of Louis, used apparently as an insult to his courage. He became a butcher, got in a few fights with customers. ("If you come in here complaining again, I'll cut you half in two.") He testified often in land deed transactions for the next-of-kin of the Alamo defenders, but he never got a bounty or veteran's land from Texas. He eventually moved to Logansport, La.

There he died about 1850 at age 65. His last years were a time in great pain because of his legs. Wounds from the cactus thorns he picked up during his flight from the Alamo never healed, and he became bedridden, suffering terrible agony. In his last years, Moses Rose was often asked why he fled the Alamo, why he alone, out of all who were there, had been the only one to leave.

His answer was always the same: "By God, I wasn't ready to die."

Cooking lesson

PARIS—"The first thing to do is wash your hands," says Michael Marolleau through an interpreter.

I nod in total agreement, for it is evident that Marolleau—the super chef here at this Left Bank cooking school—is not one to mince words. And now the class begins its lesson for the day. The soup is *Potage Germiny*, made from sorrel leaves. Then comes *Mullet en Papillote*, a fish seasoned with mushrooms and wrapped in a paper bag. Finally, the biggie—Puff Pastry. As I have had considerable experience in eating, doing it almost daily, I am one of the lucky few assigned to handle this final, and most demanding, course.

"You must work it in as quickly as you can," says Chef Marolleau, mixing the flour and water. "American flour is quite different from our flour." He does not explain just which is better, but I have a feeling that I already know. The chef works quickly and dexterously with flying fingers. He kneads the dough, pounds it, flips it and adds a chunk of butter, kneads it some more, then tosses the glob into a plastic bag which he puts in the refrigerator. "Now it's your turn," he says, passing the rolling pin on with the finesse of a relay racer.

All around me in this chromium classroom are other gourmets who have flocked here to La Varenne, Ecole de Cuisine, which is supposedly the hottest thing going in gastronomical warfare. Craig Claiborne raves about it in *The New York Times*. And *Time* magazine calls it a "challenge to Cordon Bleu," the 80-year-old standard of status. Julia Child, James Beard and Simone Beck ("Simca") are among the sponsors. Everybody who is anybody wants in.

Big deal. But now they come to the acid test. Can La Varenne teach me to make Puff Pastry? Me, who thought you preheated the oven to boil water? Who thought that Chicken Teriyaki was the sole survivor of a kamikaze squadron? We shall see, for it is my time on the marble slab. Yes, to knead dough properly one must use a marble slab or at least a board. I mean, a true chef would no more pound out the dough on Formica than Patty Hearst would be elected Miss Congeniality.

Pound, pound. Knead, knead. "Work together with the fingertips," says the lesson sheet, which is quickly becoming illegible under a layer of flour and butter. Add a little water. My partner, who has obviously been in a kitchen before, takes over and the flour flies. We now have this unseemly glob which is called the *detrempe*—a French word meaning "unseemly glob." We put it in a bag and plop it in the refrigerator for 15 minutes.

Meanwhile, other students are working with the easy courses, the fish and the soup. Child's play, to be sure. Our waiting period is now over and we take the *detrempe* out and begin beating it with a rolling pin.

Chef Marolleau comes over, eyes the fight carefully, and declares: "Never use a dirty rolling pin." We clean it off and continue beating and rolling. "Roll it out to a rectangle 5–6 inches wide and 14–15 inches long," says the lesson sheet, and we act accordingly.

Anne Willan, an Englishwoman and school director, comes by, looks at my *detrempe*, sighs and walks on. Obviously she knows an expert when she sees one. Now we have got the hang of the thing. I roll, flip, roll some more, then stuff it in the plastic bag for more resting in the refrigerator. This Puff Pastry will no doubt set records in cooking circles and will cement—perhaps a bad choice of words—the Franco-American alliance. Already I can tell by Chef Marolleau's expression that this is one Puff Pastry he will never forget.

To be honest, I should note that all is not well—I am having trouble getting my corners square each time I roll out my 5-by-15-inch slab. Pulling and tugging are allowed, but, while I don't want to start rumors, Madam M — at the next slab is *cutting* her corners square! Honest. Would I lie about Puff Pastry? Perhaps I should saunter up to Chef Marolleau and fink. Certainly he would want to know. Then again, Madam M — would probably be sauteed and fried in a deep fat fryer at 450 degrees for 38 minutes, which would hamper my train of thought and possibly even hurt the Puff Pastry. No, the price is too high. I say nothing.

Now we come to the final round of pounding and rolling. It has taken me most of the morning to make this one dish. At this rate I shall eat once every four days. No wonder Chef Marolleau looks so trim. We put it in the plastic bag one more time to get cool, then turn to the final exam: lunch. We must eat our efforts. Chairs are brought and set up around the table and each team proudly brings out its pop quiz.

The *Potage Germiny* is fine. I'd give it a B+ or maybe an A– if I get through without running into any tough sorrel stems. Nothing ruins my lunch like a tough sorrel stem. Now the *Mullet en Papillote* which, as I mentioned, is cooked in a paper bag. Chef Marolleau deftly explains how to open the bag without burning the fingers—an old French trick. An A for the mullet makers. That out of the way, we come to the piece de resistance, my famed Puff Pastry, crown jewel in a tiara of also-rans.

"Beautiful!"

"Delicious!"

"*Fantastique!*"

Chef Marolleau smiles modestly. "It is nothing," he says. Gad! Humiliation! It appears that we are eating *his* Puff Pastry, not mine. Okay, his is all right, if you like that sort of thing. Mine, on the other hand, is to become a cornerstone for the new Puff Pastry Wing. Until then, it will double as a marble slab.

Faucet fuzz

THE FRONT YARD – Odd. Someone has left the hose sprawled across the driveway. If I back the car over it, that will be the 13th time I've had to change hose nozzles this year. I'll just. . . .

"Hold it! Make one move and I get another notch."

"What?" I say.

"Caught you wet-handed, eh?" says this voice from behind me as the cold, round muzzle of a gun is poked between my shoulder blades.

"Who *is* that?" I demand.

"Bovine," says the voice. "Water Watch Division. We're also known as the Tap Dancers."

"Bovine," I sigh, "it's me. Your favorite pinko commie-symp. Now put down that gun." I turn around to see a dejected Officer Bovine holstering his weapon.

"So it's you again, civilian," he says. "And just when I thought I'd caught a live one."

"Bovine, what are you doing, pulling a pistol on me?"

"Nothing to worry about, civilian. It's a water gun. Rather appropriate, don't you think?"

"I don't understand," I say.

"So what else is new? I'm now attached to the Water Watch Division. And no jokes about being 'the head drip of the faucet fuzz.' I've heard that a million times."

"Good grief, Officer Bovine," I say. "I didn't know the Police Department was really serious about the water rules. You mean they've switched all the officers to enforcing the mayor's rules?"

"Not all."

"How many are on the job?"

"Oh, a few."

"How many in the Water Watch Division?"

"You're looking at it."

"Wait a minute. You mean you are the only policeman on this assignment?"

"I'm used to it. Remember when I was the Homicide Division, moonlighting as the Vice Squad? We're still a little shorthanded."

"How's this job going?"

"Not too good. All I've got to show for this week is sunstroke. Almost caught a car washer, but he was already out on shock probation and the judge said another arrest would undermine the guy's self-confidence."

"How do you go about your duties?"

"Simple. After my regular daily tour as the Burglary and Theft Division, I go out and check for violators of the water rules. I look for clues like green yards, clean cars, weak Scotches. Actually, anyone who doesn't brad on his stamps is a suspect."

"Sounds tough, Bovine. But you don't need to worry about us. We've been doing our part. We vacuum our windows. I sand my face each morning, and we only water our grass when we're supposed to. For this house it's between 4:12 and 4:15 a.m. on alternate Christmases unless there's a full moon. Then I can clean my goldfish bowl or make Kool-Aid if I haven't sweated in the past week. And I recycle my bath water."

"How's that?" Bovine asks.

"Well, first the entire family uses just one tub of water. Then we use that water to wash the dishes, then the clothes. Next we make coffee out of it and finally we use it in the car radiator. After that, we burn it."

Bovine flips out his pad. "You have an EPA permit to burn water?"

"Do I need one?"

"I'll let you off this time with just a warning, if you'll sign this petition for police raises," he says, busily filling out a form.

"Thanks."

"Don't mention it," he says, ripping off the warning and handing it to me. "Well, I'd better get. I still haven't covered inside the Loop today."

"Frankly, Officer Bovine," I say, "it seems to me that you've got an impossible task."

"Oh, it could be worse. My last assignment was to arrest speeders on the West Loop at 5 p.m. Before that, I was assigned to the honor guard at the Vault of the Unknown TV Cable Franchise Owners."

"Before you go, Bovine, can I get you something? Would you like a glass of instant iced tea to chew?"

"No, thanks. Got to be on my way," he says, picking up his oars.

"Watch out you don't slip while getting into the boat," I say.

"Yeah," says Bovine. "Somebody really ought to do something about these water main breaks."

Loanly efforts

It started out simple enough. I needed some money. Just, you know, money. For this and that. So I went to the bank. The bankers said they couldn't give me any money, but they could loan me some. The prime interest rate was 15 percent, which sounded all right, since I didn't plan on paying back anyway.

"What corporation are you?" the bankers asked.

"Do I look like a corporation?" I replied. "I'm a person."

"Then you can't have a loan at 15 percent. That's our prime rate, reserved for our best corporate customers. Fill out these forms and come back in a month to talk to our loan officer, who will turn you down."

"Why can't you turn me down?" I asked.

"Sorry, that's the job of the loan officer," they said.

So I left the bank. Next I went to several friends, who had been having the same problem I had, but they had solved it by getting money from the government. That was a good idea, so I went to see my congressman. One of his aides explained that the congressman was fact-finding in France just then, but when he got back he'd help me get some money. So I went to my senator. He was attending a NATO meeting in Rome, but his staff assured me that he'd get some money for me when he got back.

The Small Business Administration said it had lots of money, but since I wasn't a small business, I couldn't qualify. The Defense Department said it had billions of dollars for research and development, but I didn't qualify because I wasn't a big business. I soaked my living room to qualify for a flood loan, but was rejected because I wasn't a federally declared disaster area.

Blight. Yes, that's it. My St. Augustine was dying so clearly I was a farmer who was the victim of crop failure. The Federal Crop Failure Agency said that if I were really a farmer I would have dug up the West Mall of the Capitol last winter with my John Deere. No deal. OSHA had grants to help make my factory safe, but I didn't have a factory. I applied for a grant to build an unsafe factory, but was turned down by the EPA because my environmental impact statement was written on both sides of the paper.

If there was a medallion by my front door, the government would give me money to maintain a historical site. But the medallion cost $350, and if I had $350 I wouldn't be looking for money, now would I? Energy is all the rage. I could put up a windmill or solar panels and qualify for an energy-saving loan, which wouldn't have to be repaid until after the next election. It sounded like a good idea, but I couldn't afford the wind and the sun. Disguised as New York City, I went to HUD and almost got a $2.3 billion allotment until my mask fell into a potted aspidistra.

"What you need," said a fellow at the State Department, "is to create a job, then fill it. Like Bob Krueger did." So I created the position of Ambassador to Baytown and asked for $60,000 a year plus allowance. Unfortunately, Bob Gammage was already in line for the slot.

HEW offered to pay me if I had VD, an illegal abortion or prickly heat. I didn't. I joined the boat people, NOW and Veterans Who Want Money. I was keel-hauled by the boat people. NOW threw me out, not only because I wasn't a woman, but also because I was a sexist. The veterans were all over at the Officers Club and wouldn't come out until after happy hour.

An acquaintance of mine came by the house driving a new car. "Uncle

Sam bought it for me," he explained. "Just deduct it from your taxes. In my case, I'm a doctor. I need the car for housecalls."

"But you operate on gallbladders," I said. "You've never made a housecall in your life."

"Tell it to the tax man," he said, backing over my EEOC grant application. I did, when asking for a new car. The tax man tossed me out of his office.

There was a lot of money if I was an illegal alien, but I couldn't convince the Border Patrol that I shouldn't be here. There were funds for old folks to buy heating oil for the winter. But I didn't qualify, both because I wasn't old and because my house didn't burn oil.

"Impact educational funds," the sign said. I went in and nearly got a lot of money until they discovered that I was already educated. They ripped up my student loan application, my research grant for study of the effects of impact grants on education, and my third grade report card. I was getting desperate. I went to the Social Security office, looking for money. They said I was in arrears on my Social Security payments and took my watch.

I tried everything. But I wasn't an alcoholic, narcotics addict, a persecuted minority in a secessionist state, reformed oil man, an American Indian, former resident of Eniwetok or defecting KGB agent.

"You really need a lawyer," a friend told me. He was just back from a round-the-world trip looking into dry holes. He likes working for the Department of Energy.

So I hired a lawyer and we sued because I wasn't getting any money which violated my rights as an American citizen. The government countersued, charging me with harassment and damage to a pot of aspidistra. The entire matter came to court and the judge was really quite lenient. I'll get out in 1984 and be eligible for a federal rehabilitation allotment.

Right as rain

THE YARD – Gad, it's hot. Just standing out here under the trees, I am wilting. The sun is cracking my driveway and scorching my grass. Only mad dogs and Englishmen would get out in this midday. . . .

"Taxi! I say, taxi!"

A voice from somewhere. Ah, yes, across the street, there's a fellow out on the curb trying to hail a cab. In this neighborhood? That can mean only one thing..Add to mad dogs and Englishmen, my New York neighbor, Ulysses S. Sherman. I shall go over and once again explain that you can't get a taxi in Houston like you can in New York.

"Hi, Mr. Sherman," I say.

He looks around, one hand trying to shade off the sun. He's wearing a pith helmet and safari suit complete with Bermuda shorts. He squints in my direction. "Eh? Is that you, Reb? Get up here on the curb or you're likely to get run over."

"Mr. Sherman, there hasn't been a car on this street all afternoon. Running Rats Acres isn't like Fifth Avenue."

"Don't remind me. I've just been up for a visit to the Big Apple, you know," Mr. Sherman says. "Thought I'd died and gone to heaven. Ah, the traffic, the noise, the crime, the heat and humidity. Fantastic."

"You don't have to go to New York for that, Mr. Sherman. We've got it right here in Houston."

He snorts. "You call this traffic?" He gestures at our empty street.

"No, our neighborhood is a bit sleepy. But the West Loop at late afternoon. The Gulf Freeway on a foggy morn."

"Bush league," Mr. Sherman says. "I'll bet your subways don't even shut down during transit strikes."

"Houston has never had a subway strike, Mr. Sherman. You're right as rain."

"Rain," he repeats, squinting up at the sky. "I thought Houston was supposed to have a lot of rain. What a laugh. A heavy dew would cause everyone to line up two by two."

"We are behind in our rainfall this year," I agree.

Mr. Sherman wipes his sweating forehead. "Why, oh why, did I let the company transfer me to the gawdforsaken spot? I should be getting hardship pay. And the drums, always the drums."

"I think that's your air conditioning unit, Mr. Sherman. It needs some work."

"It doesn't need work, Reb. It needs a rest."

"The weather has been pretty awful this summer, Mr. Sherman. I can't argue that. But this is not the norm. Usually we have pretty good weather for a town this size."

"You could have fooled me, Reb. Yesterday, it got so hot that I had to put coolant in my thermometer."

"That's hot."

"I never had my hair sweat before."

"Yep, Mr. Sherman, it's hot."

"My icemaker needs a pacemaker."

"Cheer up. August is almost over and then comes September."

"Really? You people use the same calendar? What happens in September?"

"Mostly just hurricanes."

Mr. Sherman fans himself with last week's *Times*. "I don't know if I can hold out. It's so hot that I can't even use my swimming pool any more."

"What happened?"

"I took the Nestea plunge and got third-degree burns."

"Gee, that *is* hot."

"When I was back in New York last month and read in the paper that Houston was 106, I thought maybe that was the total IQ score. Little did I realize it was the temperature."

"You'll get more used to it as you go along, Mr. Sherman."

"Not me. I'm not made for this weather, Reb. The natives know how to handle it, but I need to stay cool. Even cold. I turned the air conditioning down so low that, everytime I open the front door, the light goes on."

"That should make you more comfortable, Mr. Sherman. You see, in Houston in the summer you've got to stay out of the heat. That's why we've got shopping malls and indoor jogging tracks and the Astrodome, where it's always 72 degrees. You can watch the Astros and the Hurricane and the Oilers in comfort."

"Ah," he says brightly. "That reminds me. I haven't heard from the New York headquarters on my latest proposal."

"What's that, Mr. Sherman?"

"I highly recommended that we sponsor the Goodyear blimp telecasts at the Oiler home games."

They also served – 1973

It is good to have them back, our POWs who have been languishing in Communist cells. Some of them have been there for years, suffering humiliation and frustration and total, relentless boredom.

They have all been closed-mouthed about much of their experiences for fear of jeopardizing those still awaiting release, so it may be some time before we learn how really rough it was.

They have been welcomed back to their homeland in a proper fashion. No one should begrudge them the red carpet treatment, the parades, the warm and sincere welcome their government, their leaders and colleagues, and their countrymen have given them.

No doubt part of the reason for the effusive homecoming is simply that this has been a war without many heroes. America likes heroes, be they in baseball or battle, yet this seamy, unpopular war gave us very few. So now that the ball is over, we are grasping for reasons to hold a parade, and it has fallen to the returning POWs to be the object of worship.

No doubt they deserve it. Thus far the record indicates that our POWs conducted themselves with poise and pride under horrendous conditions. No turncoats, no propaganda broadcasts, no ratting on their buddies.

They certainly rate our thanks and esteem.

But they were mostly military men, career officers who were well trained, well paid; volunteers who knew the score before they suited up. They entered the way on their terms and played the game according to the rules. And they accept their situation with grim determination—you notice that none deplanes with whining complaints, righteous indignation or excuses.

Yet without pulling them down, it seems a shame that we cannot elevate our esteem for the others, those who trudged back—not to brass bands and red carpets—but to hospitals and barracks and a jobless future. It is not mutually exclusive to hail the pilots who returned from the Hanoi Hilton and the grunts who sweated it out in some forgotten swamp.

For the vast majority of those who bore the burden in Vietnam marched off to war only because their leaders wanted them to. Once again, old men decided that it was a good idea for young men to fight each other. We hear a lot about those who rushed to Canada or Sweden, who burned their draft cards and turned their backs, and the debate now raging is whether we should grant them amnesty.

We love to get off on tangents while ignoring the million-plus men who quietly did their job. Where, for instance, were the generals and admirals when the stretchers arrived at Brooke and Bethesda with the human debris of a misadventure? Where were the TV cameras and reporters when the pine boxes were lowered into America? How many parades were held for those who managed to live to fight another day? Where, pray tell, was our concern for them then?

Obviously we couldn't hold a million parades to honor a million men, but did we hold even one? No. We pretended that the war halfway across the world never really happened, and these returning servicemen were some sort of non-persons.

Perhaps it is because the war itself became so unpopular that anyone who had anything to do with it somehow was caught up in collective guilt. They got their hands dirty carrying out our national garbage and had to re-enter our house through the back door. It is like holding a doctor responsible for saving the life of a Mafia chieftain or declaring a lawyer guilty for successfully defending a known murderer. The taint is transferable.

It is hard to say whether it is because of or despite this national isolation that the Viet vets have kept such a low profile. No bonus marches, no political pressure groups, no public weeping and self-pity. Even the traditional veterans' groups report that the Viet vets are slow to join up. These young men have silently slipped back into a society which seems embarrassed by their mere presence. They remind us of our mistakes, like a bastard son at a family reunion.

They accept this role with a shrug and a smile. If that's the way we want them to act, then they will. Even out of uniform, they are good troopers who obey orders. Our will be done, in America as it was in Vietnam.

Again, this is not meant to demean the well-deserved attention and adulation we are now giving our returning POWs. A salute to the silent olive-drab majority is not a thumbs-down to the pilots. But in our haste to find and honor heroes, we seem to be running roughshod over those million men who were ordered off in the best years of their lives to do a dirty job.

And now they are back among us quietly pursuing their private lives much as they did before it all began, non-persons who fought in a non-war. No parades, no TV cameras, no hats and horns. They are only the troublesome reminders of some years which most of the world would like to forget.

So when we all rush out to the airport to wave and cheer and feel good that the POWs are home and patriotism has awakened after years in hibernation, we might pause for a moment and remember that when Johnny came marching home, no one showed up at the bus depot to meet him.

Filthy words

The U.S. Supreme Court has ruled that the Federal Communications Commission may ban seven "filthy" words from the airwaves. In a 5-to-4 decision, the justices upheld the FCC ban on these words during hours when children are likely to be listening.

The minority dissented loudly, two justices declaring that words "the court and the commission find so unpalatable may be the stuff of everyday conversations in some, if not many, of the innumerable subcultures."

All of this is very interesting, to be sure, but the obviously unanswered question is: *Which* seven filthy words? I mean, you could sit down with a nun and in 10 seconds come up with scores of words someone might find filthy. Our language is rich with trashy nouns and verbs, turgid with functions and parts and acts which add spice to an otherwise vanilla vocabulary. To think that only seven of them are too strong for our children's shell-like ears clearly means that the others are at least acceptable to the U.S. Supreme Court, not to mention some, if not many, of the innumerable subcultures.

These seven deadly words must be strong stuff indeed, for in no news story have I seen them listed. (Needless to say, in light of the high court's ruling, we won't hear the forbidden words being ticked off over the air, so we must depend upon the printed medium to carry the word, however filthy it might be.)

Without official supervision, each one of us is free to draw up our own list of words so heinous, so awful, so appalling, that they—like some virulent bacteria—must be kept under lock and key to prevent contamination, if not the plague itself.

I have given the list a lot of thought and believe that I am now on the high court's wavelength. First and certainly foremost, the judges must have been thinking of the word *source*. How many times on TV news shows have we seen the network reporter, wearing a trench coat with the collar up, standing in front of the White House with the south portico all aglow, use the word *source*? It comes at us in all its sordid, filthy forms: "an official source," "a highly placed source," "a White House source." The reporter would be more accurate by declaring authoritatively: "somebody said." More accurate, and unemployed.

A second entry, certain to be on the justices' list, is *constipation*. Right in the middle of an opera, earthquake or assassination, we all pause for a moment to consider the heartbreak of constipation. A visitor to this small planet, with only television as his source (forgive me) of information, would think that the average American family awakens each morning to ponder the pitfalls of constipation. If that word is not on the court's list of prohibited prose, it simply shows that the U.S. Supreme Court is a subculture unto itself.

Since we are not allowed to see the actual list, we are told only that these are "words" and naturally enough think of single words. But I would bet there are some members of the Gang of Seven which are not words, but terms. Yes, two, three, even five words, neatly tied together to curdle our tastebuds. If this is the case, then high on the list must be *20 percent chance of precipitation*.

Whether we are in a monsoon or a drought, we have a "20 percent chance of precipitation." It is a copout, neatly designed to cover any eventuality. You get rain or you don't get rain, and you can't blame the weather forecaster either way. You simply fell into the 20 or the 80 percent. I agree with the judges. There is no place in our society for such trash.

A word which started out in proper company, but which quickly sank to degeneracy though overuse, is *incredible*. It used to be a fine, card-carrying member of the English language, running about with *fantastic*, *wonderful* and *terrific*. But the world suddenly discovered *incredible*, and attached it to every bath soap, rug sale and record of Elvis' 432 greatest hits. It began to get shopworn, dowdy, even seedy. Today, *incredible* hangs around the airwaves, bumming recognition from every passing product. I would hope that it has made the judges' bottom seven. A mercy killing, if nothing else.

Another word which began life well enough, but has fallen on hard times is *we*. Not in every instance, of course, but only when used by sports reporters. "Well, folks, *we* almost pulled it out in the bottom of the ninth." "*We* play Green Bay next Sunday, and you remember how cold *we* got there last winter."

It rather makes me wonder who's paying the reporter, the station or the franchise. If the court could be selective in exactly how words are used, rather than a blanket condemnation, then the sportscasters' *we* belongs on the list.

I toyed with putting *Mini-Cam* and *Instant News* on the list, but these are fad words which should soon pass on. Here is one which is a sure-fire entry: *union demands*. "Federal mediators say that the union demands in a new contract etc. etc." Why is it that only unions demand? What does management do, whimper?

A great deal of thought went into this last filthy entry which is to be banned from the airwaves. For a while, I considered *The Newlywed Game*, which is about as trashy as they come. But it paled in comparison to this, which grates on my soul and sends me fleeing from the room: *We'll be right back after this word*. Not only is it false advertising—when was the last time you heard a single *word* from the sponsor?—but surely ranks even above the incredible 20 percent chance of constipation. At least, that's what sources say.

Conned again

Gad. I have just been conned again. No, maybe that is too strong a statement. I have just *let* myself get conned again. I could see it coming. I knew exactly what was happening, so I can't plead ignorance, or stupidity or that he came up on my blind side. After all this time, in these matters I don't have a blind side.

But it happened. He came to me with a request, a proposition, a thing to do. And I didn't want to do it. I didn't have the time, nor energy, nor ability, nor that much interest. So when he said would I do it I said no. A simple no. But a simple no is not enough anymore. He said that I should do it.

And I said no.

He said that if I had a flake of self-respect and decency I would do it. And I said no.

He said that he didn't want to ask me to do it. He had begged others to ask me. He had pleaded with them but they had made him do it. And now he was asking me to do it.

And I said no.

Well, to make a long story short, I finally agreed to do it. I had said no and no and finally I said yes. I said yes simply so he would go away and leave me alone with all the things I needed to do. It was an expedient way to end the torment and pressure and trouble.

So I said yes.

But now comes the real problem. The moment I said yes, I regretted it. I wished I had not said yes. But I said yes to something down the road. Things down the road will somehow take care of themselves. Life will simplify and ease and become quiet, so agreeing to something today that won't happen until down the road is not so bad, because things will be easier and I will have time to do all the things that I don't have time to do today.

Ha. They never do. But I felt guilty. Yes, that's it. He made me feel guilty. He found that I would say no to a straight-forward approach to do something I didn't want to do, so he hit my Achilles heel. He made me feel guilty. and that is the quickest way to make me do something. Make me feel guilty and I'll do anything. So he made me feel very guilty — guilty enough so that I agreed to do something I didn't want to do.

That seems like dirty pool to me. Dirty pool. Sneaking up on me by making me feel guilty. But he didn't sneak. I saw him coming and still I felt guilty. The problem with agreeing to do something you don't want to do is that, after you have agreed, you get mad. No, not mad at the person who made you feel guilty enough to do it, but mad at yourself. I am mad at myself. I should not have agreed. I should not have felt guilty. A grown man getting conned by that ancient device.

I am told that an entire book has been written about how to say no without feeling guilty. I am told that it's called "How to Say 'No' Without Feeling Guilty." I haven't read it, but I could have written it. Even so, I would not have taken my own advice. It is one thing to say no. It is quite another to say no without feeling guilty.

OK, we can analyze it. We can sit down and draw neat little diagrams between the conner, the conee, the guilty and the guilt. It makes pretty diagrams and leads to all sorts of in-depth discussions. But it doesn't work. When the phone rings and someone says that I should do something because it is my patriotic duty and God is watching and little orphans will starve in the snow if I don't, I do.

Guilt is the ticket. You can move mountains, cause brave men to cry and heros to run in fear by using guilt. It is stronger than dirt. More powerful than a locomotive. Guilt can accomplish anything. Anything, that is, but happy acceptance. Oh, I'll do it, but I won't be happy about it. Of course, he doesn't care if I'm happy. He has accomplished his goal, which was to make me say yes. I said yes and his own guilt is gone. I will be where I am supposed to be when I am supposed to be and his guilt will be gone. He won. I lost.

Actually, this whole thing is silly. I should not feel guilty. I should not be mad at him or at myself. Down the road things will ease up and smooth out. It will all be OK. Still, after thinking it over very thoroughly, I hope his soul rots in a vat of lye.

Why Go Texan?

Last week on the West Loop, a car in front of me, with Michigan license plates, was stopped in the heavy traffic. The driver—clearly a new arrival—leaned out the window and asked directions from the driver in the car next to him. That driver shook his head, indicating that he didn't know either. The second car had Pennsylvania plates.

We are now, and always have been, a place of newcomers. And for them this is a particularly difficult time, since today is Go Texan Day, the day when dentists and stockbrokers dress up like drovers and ramrods. Newcomers to Texas often find it hard to understand, and even funny, corny, phony, perhaps. They raise a very good question: Why?

Well, first of all we Go Texan for the same reason people in New Orleans dress up for Mardi Gras and New Yorkers turn out in Times Square on New Year's Eve and Parisians go wild on Armistice Day: It's fun. Secondly, and more importantly, the day is a good time to remind ourselves that we didn't invent Texas, we only inherited it. The good things we've got going here were created by others who paid dearly for them.

If February 27 is Go Texan Day, it also marks the fifth day of the Siege of the Alamo. That Feb. 27 was cold and blustery in the fortress, a day of growing concern that help was not on the way. Col. William Travis needed to know the situation, but faced a tough choice over whom to send. He had already dispatched his childhood friend, James Bonham, who slipped through the Mexican army to seek help. After that first trip out of the Alamo to safety, Bonham had announced that he was going back to the mission. Others protested that he was headed to certain death, but the 28-year-old lawyer had responded: "I must get back to Travis." And Bonham had returned to join the fight.

Now, on that Feb. 27, 1836, Travis had to ask his friend once more to risk his life. This time the dangers were all the more, as the size and strength of the surrounding Mexican army had grown. Still, he asked and Bonham accepted. It was a difficult choice, but not surprising. The two had been children together in South Carolina and had gone to the same school. When Travis' family moved away, the young men had kept in correspondence. They looked so much alike that many thought they were brothers—each was taller than 6 feet; they were handsome woman-chasers and rebellious. (Bonham, along with his entire senior class at South Carolina College, had been expelled for rebelling against the rules and bad food.)

Travis, who had arrived here three years before Bonham, had written his old friend: "Stirring times afoot here; come out to Texas and take a hand in affairs." Bonham had come and had immediately found a home. "His influence in the army is great," Sam Houston wrote, "more so than some who would be generals."

On that fifth day of siege, Travis didn't need a general, just a man who could be trusted. His troops were getting edgy. "I'd rather go through these gates and shoot it out with the Mexicans beyond these walls," Davy Crockett said. "I hate to be hemmed in."

But it was Bonham, all alone, who departed. He rode out of the fort and once more through the encircling army to safety. He went to Goliad and Gonzales to tell what was happening back in the mission on the outskirts of San Antonio. He must have needed to ask directions, because Bonham, too, was a newcomer to Texas, having been here less than four months. Indeed, the only native-born Texans in the Alamo were Mexican-Texians. Everyone else was from somewhere else.

I suppose in this way, modern-day Houston has that in common with our past and our traditions, but not much more. Except our hats and boots, which is why we put them on to Go Texan. It reminds us of what happened and why, who did what and why. Much of it is incredible.

At 11 a.m. on March 3, the defenders inside the Alamo were startled by a commotion in the midst of the Mexican army. Jim Bonham was returning. He had approached the town with one or two companions who, upon checking out the situation, decided it was impossible to get through the army and into the Alamo. Only Bonham went. He wanted Travis to know the bad facts: There was no help on the way. It was to be surrender or die.

Bonham tied a white handkerchief to his hat, a prearranged signal so that he wouldn't be shot by his own men, and spurred his white horse, which by then was dark with sweat. He bent low, and moved out at a gallop. The startled Mexican soldiers and sentries reacted too late as the lone rider flew past. "I will make my report to Travis," he had said, "or die in the attempt." He dashed through the south gate and into the fortress to stand alongside his friends in certain death. Three days later, as the Alamo fell, Travis slumped over a cannon, shot through the forehead. A few minutes later, Bonham fell dead, too, slumped over another cannon.

We cannot duplicate their feats. No one has asked us to, and I'm not so sure today there are many who would respond in the same way, or die in the attempt. But we can, and do, remember the Alamo, the men and women inside, those who could easily have stayed outside, and a lot more. We remember them on days such as today when we Go Texan. We put on our hats and boots and ride horses and wave flags to remind us that we are the recipients of something rather special in our minds, Texas. And when you start feeling the same way, no matter how long you've been here, then you—like Bonham and Travis and all the rest— have found a home.

Bull's Head pints

ASHBY-DE-LA-ZOUCH, ENGLAND—It is 5 o'clock on a damp and gray afternoon and the local watering hole, The Bull's Head, opens for business. This pub has been here since the early 1600s and was serving drinks to Cromwell's troops as they laid siege to Castle Ashby up on the hill.

In 1649 they blew up the castle, leaving the shell that stands there today, roofless and ruined—another fitting monument to the family's fortune. But here in The Bull's Head, the peasantry is coming in for a snort after a hard day of singing hey-nonny-nonny in the master's fields, or whatever it is they do in this village of 7,000.

The innkeeper, Jake Drury, stands behind the bar as the first customer arrives. He is Ivan Dutton, a surveyor for the Coal Board.

Dutton: "Most of the people of Ashby live and are employed right around here, although some commute to Birmingham. Not all are miners."

Drury: "No. Some of 'em work."

Dutton (raising his glass): "To the miner. The best friend this country's got, particularly since the mines were nationalized."

Drury (pouring himself a pint): "Communized, you mean."

Several other customers come in, including Jacques Harel, the French teacher at the local boarding school. The conversation turns to the referendum on the Common Market.

Dutton: "The Americans want us in, and I think we should do what they want in this case. I mean, we can't take their protection an' help all the time and then not take their advice."

Harel: "But I dunno if we want you in our Common Market."

Drury: "Damn right, because then it wouldn't be *your* Common Market."

Dutton: "The French. What can you expect from a bloody Frenchman, anyway? But the Americans—they keep backing Israel, when they should be backing the Wogs."

Drury: "We call a 'Wog' anyone who's south of Calais."

Harel: "What's the matter with Calais?"

217

Dutton: "But economically we're bound to them."

This seems to put a cloud of gloom over the entire gang at The Bull's Head, Jacques Harel included. In comes another customer. It's Ian Smith, a local businessman.

Dutton: "Smith's a Scot."

Smith: "I'm only a missionary down here to the heathen."

Drury: "We'd a-eaten 'im a long time ago, but he's too tough."

Smith (grabbing a pint of beer from Drury): "All Scots are tough. We have to be."

Mary, the pub's waitress, appears. She's Irish. The Bull's Head is beginning to look like a U.N. Security Council meeting. The conversation turns to Parliament.

Smith: "Our MP is a surgeon who drives a Bentley. He's a Laborite."

Drury: "A bloody leftist, you mean."

Smith (continuing undisturbed): "He was in a helicopter crash just recently."

Dutton: "Pity. Pity it didn't fall a bit harder."

More pints are lifted, more world issues are solved. Finally The Bull's Head Debating Society turns to local history.

Drury: "We've got Coleourton Hall here. Byron lived there when he wrote. And Wordsworth laid out the garden. Now it's a den of bloody idleness."

Dutton: "It's the local headquarters of the Coal Board. Jake doesn't like the Coal Board. He's a Conservative, which is why this place is half empty."

Smith: "A bomb once fell on Ashby. One bomb in the whole war."

Dutton: "Aye. The pilot got lost and thought we were Coventry. The bomb blew up a field. Some tomatoes were our only war casualty. We also serve."

Drury: "William Joyce's family came from here. Some of them still live here. You may have remembered Joyce. He was Lord Haw-Haw during the war. We hanged him afterwards."

Dutton: "Ah, that reminds me of the Earl of Ferrars."

There is a general nodding of knowing heads around the pub. A pint is raised to the Earl of Ferrars.

Drury: "His Lordship woke up one night—back in the 1700s, it was— and found the butler coming out of Lady Ferrars' bedroom, so he shot him. He was tried and convicted—the first time a peer was ever convicted of murdering a commoner."

Dutton: "He went to his execution in a coach pulled by six white horses, and His Lordship wore a white velvet suit. He was hanged by a silken rope."

Smith: "Aye. They do things in style in Ashby-de-la-Zouch."

Doing the "Polyester Joe"

THE FRONT YARD—"Taxi! I say, taxi!"

Now who could that be, calling for a taxi out here in Running Rats Acres? Oh, jeez. Who else? Standing across the street, waving his *Wall Street Journal*, is my New York neighbor, Ulysses S. Sherman. "Mr. Sherman," I say, walking over to him. "I've told you before, you can't flag a taxi here on the curb like you could back in Manhattan."

He turns slowly and looks at me carefully. "Have we been introduced?"

"Of course."

"Don't tell me. At the club? I've got it. You summer at Southampton, right?"

"No, but I Tuesdayed at Friday's. Does that count?"

He looks at me closer. "Oh, it's you, Billy Bob. Or Jimmy Ralph or whatever. Is the corn frittering and the lightning whitening?"

"I don't think so."

"Then shouldn't you be out lynching the minority of your choice?"

"Mr. Sherman, how long have you been in Houston?"

"Eons, it seems. I was the first missionary to the savages since John McMullen. To think that my own company would transfer me here when I could have had Bangladesh."

"I know it's been a real strain on you, putting up with our strange ways."

"Strange ways? Pickup trucks, gun racks, longnecks, the Polyester Joe."

"That's 'Cotton-eyed.'"

"If you people only spoke English it would make things a lot easier. Anyway, I have tried to learn your ways, I really have. I went to Brooks Bros. and ordered a leisure suit with white belt and white shoes. I put an *I Feel Affection for You Azure* sticker on my car."

"You bought a car, Mr. Sherman? But you told me that you didn't need one in Manhattan, so you wouldn't need one here."

"My mistake."

"Now you're learning."

"My mistake was in buying the car, Reb. I was going to the Galleria and traffic was terrible. The manners were worse. Don't you people know how to drive? So, as I was going down the median . . ."

"You were on the grass?"

"Surely you don't expect me to wait in line with the natives, do you? I was going along when this fellow orders me to pull over. Do you know that even your motorcycle gangs are armed?"

"Mr. Sherman, that was a Houston policeman."

"You're kidding. A policeman? He wasn't carrying a picket sign."

"Our police don't do that. They earn money the old fashioned way."

"You make them earn it, all right. I mean, you people don't even have uniform license plates. Red plates and blue plates. Some read, 'Land of Lincoln,' others read, 'Great Lakes State.' Can't you Texans get together on something that simple?"

"Mr. Sherman, those were out-of-state plates. We have lots of them."

He looks shocked. "Out of state? So that's it. There's hope for Texas after all. Help is on the way."

"Yessir. We're putting up a big welcome monument at the Houston Turning Basin. It's a statue of Miss Libertarian. In her raised hand she's holding a rolled up Want Ads section. And there's an inscription at the bottom: 'Give me your jobless, your hopeless wanderers of union halls, your poor, your overpriced former employees of shut down businesses.' It is really a touching welcome."

He peers at me, worried. "Are they coming?"

"Yessir. You are standing in the fastest growing city, county and metropolitan area in America. Between 1970 and 1980 Houston grew by the size of St. Louis. The county grew by the size of San Francisco. There are now more people in the city of Houston than in Alaska and Hawaii put together."

"Are they finding jobs?"

"They used to. In the '70s, the Houston area created more new jobs, that's *new* jobs, than all the jobs there are in Austin and San Antonio put together. The problem is that we can't create new jobs as fast as the unemployed come here. If we could put a wall around Houston, our unemployment rate would be zero and the rest of the nation's would jump. We just can't keep up with the demand from the rest of America."

He suddenly brightens up. "Now I've got it. Weren't you at the coming out party for Bunny Baker at Martha's Vineyard?"

"Nosir, but I did go to a drying out party for LeRoy Baker in Jed John's backyard."

"Gad, the third world is alive and well in Houston," he sighs. "Well, I can't wait here all day. Suppose there's a taxi strike, too. Not to worry. I can still get to work."

"How's that, Mr. Sherman?"

He holds out his hand and smiles cunningly. "Subway tokens."

Whittling at Texas

As any schoolboy knows, Texas still has the right to divide itself into two, three, four or five separate states. It's not the sort of thing you bring up during a bank run, but it is a tale filled with greedy statesmen, conniving politicians, international meddlers and other fictional creatures.

Let's begin at the beginning, for a change. When the U.S. and the Republic of Texas were dickering over annexation in the 1840s, there was a notable lack of enthusiasm east of the Sabine. After all, most Texans had been run out of the U.S. in the first place, so why get them back? Thus the annexation treaty failed to pass the U.S. Senate in June of 1844.

The departing U.S. president, John Tyler, was worried because Mexico still cast covetous eyes on the Republic. And if Britain's plans had come about, there would have been seven flags over Texas. So Tyler came up with another plan—instead of a treaty, how about a joint resolution, which would require fewer votes of approval? It was drawn up with several changes aimed at sweetening the pot for both the slave and anti-slave forces. One of the changes was Point Three:

"New States of convenient size, not exceeding four in number, in addition to said State of Texas, and having sufficient population, may hereafter, by the consent of said State, be formed out of the territory thereof, which shall be entitled to admission under the provisions of the Federal Constitution. . . ."

The article went on to say that any state formed south of the Missouri Compromise line could come into the Union as either a slave or free state, and anything north had to come in as a free state. The resolution passed the House 118 to 101, and finally slipped through the Senate 27 to 25. A single senator switching his vote would have killed it.

Rumor has it that Texas did join the Union, although there are those even today who doubt it, or regret it. And, again as all the schoolboys know, Texas sold off about one-third of its western lands to the U.S. This act not only fattened the state's depleted coffers, but solved the free-state slave-state question, since the new northern border became 36 degrees 30 minutes north latitude, which happened to be the same as the Missouri Compromise line. A fantastic coincidence.

Ah, but the ink was hardly dry on the resolution before various schemes were hatched by—can you believe?—Texas politicians. In 1847, Congressman Isaac Van Zandt ran for governor on a platform of splitting up Texas. Unfortunately, Congressman Van Zandt took his campaign to Houston, where he promptly contacted yellow fever and died. So much for that effort.

Three years later, Sen. Henry Stuart Foote of Mississippi got into the act with a plan to create the State of San Jacinto out of everything in Texas east of the Brazos River. That would, among other things, have separated A&M from the Chicken Ranch, but no one else liked it, and the plan died.

In 1852, yet another scheme was hatched, this one in Austin. There would be two states, see, East Texas and West Texas. Some of the legislators liked this, since one of them could be governor, a couple more could be senators, and all the rest could be congressmen and land com-missioners and the like. But public sentiment prevailed, and this plan was killed, 33 to 15.

Now we come to the Reconstruction Era, when Texas was privileged to draw on out-of-state consultants: the Carpetbaggers. They came up with the best plan of all. The Constitutional Convention of 1866 drew up the sovereign State of East Texas—the 38 counties east of the Trinity River. Everybody who wants to be a congressman, raise your hand.

Then there would be the State of Texas, stretching out to the Pecos River. Now comes the best part of all, gang. We sell to the U.S. all of Texas west of Midland. And the money would go, uh, well, wherever money goes in Austin. Chuckle-chuckle.

Alas, that idea didn't even get to a vote. But it did put ideas into the mind of a former governor, Elisha M. Pease, who sprang them on the next constitutional convention, in 1868. He wanted to sell West Texas instead of dividing it. But other delegates had other plans. Then there was the State of Lincoln, and the State of Jefferson. The prohibitionists had a plan. So did John Nance Garner. And there was the near-secession over Aggieland West.

Under the Congressional Plan, there would be three not-so-lone star states: Texas, East Texas and South Texas. Another delegate, William Wallace Mills of El Paso, who was once arrested as a Union spy, sug-gested that all of West Texas be sold to the U.S. That idea was defeated by the narrow count of 38 to 32.

Meanwhile (still with us?), one A. J. Hamilton, who was twice appointed governor of Texas and was twice defeated by the voters, came up with his own plan. We divide Texas into three parts, OK? The Brazos River will be the border between East and West Texas, and a third state will be carved out of Texas north of Waco. That way three of us can be governor, and six can be senators and . . .

Wait a minute. Here comes another delegate, James P. Newcomb, a Canadian-born journalist whose pro-Union paper in San Antonio was so beloved that his readers wrecked it. His plan is to split the state at the Colorado River. Sigh. All of this was too much for the delegates, most of whom had trouble finding the spittoon, and the whole thing died in the convention.

Ah, but it was born again in Washington, with the Colorado River as the dividing line and everything south and west of there to be the State of Lincoln. It didn't get out of committee, which must have pleased Lincoln. Now it is Feb. 25, 1870, and Congress gets the Howard Bill, with a new twist. Texas would be readmitted to the Union only after slicing off everything east of the San Antonio River and west of the Colorado.

And here's the twist: the two newly created chunks of land would become U.S. territories. The eastern part— virtually everything east of San Antone—would be Jefferson, requiring a new name for Houston's NFL team. The western part would be Matagorda.

Meanwhile, busy little beavers back in Austin came up with this one—a four-way split. No one liked that idea, either. So things drifted along until 1907, when a totally new plan was presented to Congress: Texas would create four legislatures (good Lord!), all under one governor, and Texas would get eight U.S. senators. Two years later, there was a good fight over prohibition in Texas, and some sectors wanted to split. (Wet Texas, Dry Texas, I suppose.)

West Texas began growing, but couldn't get added representation in Austin and Washington, and the idea of splitting off came up again in 1914. This time the State of Jefferson would be created out of four state senate districts in the west but only six senators supported the plan. Incidentally, you can read all about this in *The Handbook of Texas* if you wish.

Now it is 1921, and the governor vetoes a bill to create another A&M, this one in West Texas, and the people out there are irate. There is another groundswell for secession, but once again it all dies down, although the Son of Carpetbagger is ready to help. Then came the final push for divorce, Texas style. In the 1930s, John Nance Garner decided that it was just too hard for a politician to campaign all over Texas, so he suggested we go the full route—five states: North, East, South, West and Central Texas. Ten U.S. Senators. Garner's plan, like all the rest, met with instant apathy.

Thus, we have the union of the state. Until now, that is. Yes, indeed, it's time for our latest contest: The Size of Texas Contest. Come forth with the best division of Texas, up to five, and win John Nance Garner, or something. Remember, if it includes land north of the 36th latitude, it will have to enter the Union as a Free State. Get busy.

December bride

DALLAS—The family gathers and stands out here on the front porch. And spreads down the steps. And across the lawn like a poised, foolish, happy tide.

Brothers and sisters ànd sons-in-law and daughters-in-law and a gaggle of grandchildren running about and grinning fiercely. Mostly Southern Presbyterians, with a smattering of Roman Catholics and not a few outright agnostics, mixed with some timid atheists. Teetotalers, social drinkers and unsociable drunks. Democrats, Republicans, carpetbaggers and unreconstructed Confederates. White knights and black sheep. Trespassers and those who have trespassed against us.

This is all my family, minus a younger brother who lives with his family in Jakarta, Indonesia, for some obscure reason that probably has something to do with the rebellion in Timor. We are an odd lot, we are, an organization of individualists.

"I can't see her."

"I don't see her, either."

"Where is she?"

Someone peers through the window and back into the house. Nothing. Not a sign. We all stand around, wondering what has happened. Has she given us the slip? Has she sneaked out a side door, leaving us all out here, holding handfuls of rice in our sodden grasp? No, she has never disappointed us before, and shall not now, in her moment of departure.

"I've seen her come out this door a million times," says a sister from California. "She's come here to let us in and let us out. She's come out this door to our weddings. And to a funeral. I've seen her come out of this door a million times."

And so we stand about, waiting for our mother on this, her wedding day.

Going to your mother's wedding is an odd experience, but one which I heartily recommend. Chances are that most people do not get to attend the marriage of their parents, which is a shame. How much fun I would have had seeing my mother and my father get married. It would have been one of those occasions treasured through the years. But, social norms being what they are, our parents' marriage is one of the major events we must miss.

So it is that I am not able to compare, but I do know that this wedding is an absolute delight. My mother, the SMU beauty, the mother, the widow for these many years, marrying an old family friend.

"I first met her in 1929," the groom recalled a bit earlier at the reception. "She was at SMU then, before she met your father. Or maybe about the same time. That was 46 years ago."

We also serve who only stand and wait. More rice is passed around. Suddenly, up pop two strangers, nice fellows but obviously strangers. Ah, a brother comes out to meet them. One of the strangers is from Stockholm, the other from Rome. They seem to work for the brother, who is in computers or software. Then again, they may have something to do with the rebellion in Timor. One never knows.

In any event, they get handfuls of rice and wait by the door. This is the same door that I used to come up to late at night, after the curfew.

And then I would find, as usual, that the door was locked, so I would have to ring the doorbell, then bang the large knocker several times to attract attention. That, of course, was part of the master plan – to attract attention to the fact that I was coming in late. And my mother would come down the front steps to let me in, noticing on the huge grandfather clock in the hall exactly what time it was. She never said a word about my tardiness. She didn't have to.

We stand around and wait. Several grandchildren are busy out at the curb, using a can of shaving cream on the groom's car. "Just married," it says across one window. "Love birds," across another. Assorted goop covers much of the remaining glass. Two grandsons are busy at the back bumper. They are carefully tying a string to the license plate. At the end of the string are two crushed beer cans, and the prospect of their grand-mother and her brand-new husband clattering down the street with beer cans on their bumper is already sending them into gales of muffled laughter. A policeman in his squad car has come by once, carefully eyeing the wayward grandsons and wanting to know if they are tampering with the license plates. They explained the situation and noticed for the first time in their young lives that police, too, have a sense of humor.

"I can't see her."

"Why's she taking so long?"

The groom's daughters and their families are also standing about, waiting with handfuls of rice. We wait by the front door, the same door through which the bride sent one brother and three sons off to the Marines. The same door through which scampered sons and daughters, and sons of daughters, and daughters of sons. The same door where we have put up Christmas decorations, Halloween decorations, funny signs and black bows.

There is a mail slot in the door, and over the decades the mailman has stuffed in such an assortment – valentines and IOUs and Vietnam scrawlings and notes from all over, letting the mother know that her children are alive and well and love her. And the messages went out from here, too, telling the children that they are missed.

"I see her! Here she comes."

There is scampering on the porch, there is excitement in the air, there is rice in the hand. The door opens, and out they come, the bride leading the way.

"She looks like an angel," squeals a granddaughter. And the grand-daughter is inarguably correct. Up go the cheers, up goes the rice, up go the huzzahs and hoorays and spirits. And through it all rush the newlyweds through the door and down the steps and across the lawn to the car, which rattles off down the street to the tune of banging beer cans.

Theme restaurants

Having had a rather close brush in my efforts to achieve new financing for the DeLorean Motor Co., I sought out a better way to become wealthy and powerful enough to keep with my friends in oil and medicine.

"You need to open a restaurant in Houston," a Tanglewood neuropsychiatrist said, calling from his weekend villa outside Nice.

"But I've already tried that," I replied. "Lost my apron strings."

"You were in too early," explained a drilling executive from his condo in Aspen. "The smart money is getting in now."

So I took my life savings and opened up a small cafe in the Heights called Just Good Food. It went bankrupt.

"Of couse it did," I was told. "A plain vanilla cafe never works. You've got to have a theme."

So I opened up a Lebanese restaurant called A Bit of Beirut. The next week I was shelled by the kosher delicatessen across the street. Fortunately, waiters from the French and Italian restaurants up the block ran out and put a stop to the fighting and owners of the American hamburger joint next door agreed to pay for the damages since it was all their fault.

"You need to get the commuter crowd," I was told. "Everyone in Houston lives in his car." I leased 200 feet of land in the middle of the Southwest Freeway and opened a drive-in called the Happy Median. Three days later an 18-wheeler came through and flattened the place.

"What's the biggest minority in Houston?" a pipeline official visiting Moscow wrote back. "Yankees, of course. You need to open a place for them to eat, where they'll feel at home."

Soon The Yankee Doodle was ready. I built it in a lean-to under the Milam Street bridge, decorated the walls with pictures of Tip O'Neill and served only Boston clam chowder on Michigan black plates. However, when my imported waiters from Ohio kept demanding higher and higher wages until I was bankrupt, I closed. And when the waiters saw the size of their state unemployment checks, they sued Texas for breach of promised land.

"It's not Yankees who are the largest minority in Houston," said a Shell janitor, as we watched his crew get the catamaran ready at the Galveston Yacht Club. "It's Aggies."

Of course. That's when I opened Reveille's Rejects, featuring Ags and bacon. I called my menu a John Deere Letter on College Stationery. My first customer chased me out of the place with his sword.

"Your overhead is too much," said an Exxon trainee from his car phone. "You've got to keep it low. Find a cheaper operation. Oh, excuse me for a moment. Turn here, Charles."

By the end of the week I got 13 brand-new Grumman buses for $45 and created my theme restaurant, the MTA. But customers soon complained that the service was too slow, the waiters were rude and the air conditioning didn't work. I hired a new maitre d' from Atlanta who suggested service could be improved if we built an upper deck. I thought a basement room would be better, but he convinced me that an upper floor was quicker and cheaper. So I built the addition on the top of the buses. Everyone then complained about the noise and vibration, and I went bankrupt again.

"I'm told there isn't a decent gay bar in Houston," a podiatrist told me as we watched his racehorse work out. "You could make a fortune."

The clear answer was my next endeavor, Mister Macho, in Montrose. Within a week I was raided by Marvin Zindler, who found mold on my quiche. My attempt to lure the kinky crowd to the S&M, featuring whipped cream and leather steaks, was hit by the vice squad.

"Turkey Delight," was a catchy name for my drumstick-and-dressing restaurant. It lasted until some Armenian terrorists blew up the chef. Later they apologized for the mistake and offered to rub out an enemy of my choice.

"It's the fast pace of Houston," said a psychiatrist over lunch at the River Oaks Country Club. "People want to relax while they eat."

The obvious answer was my cafe on Fannin, Little Bit of Boredom, featuring dull food and a constant update of the NFL players strike, as read by an air traffic controller. When the cashier dozed off, a sleepwalker in a ski mask took everything.

"Look," a urologist carefully explained while overseeing his ranch near San Felipe (the street, not the town), "what everyone wants today is to feel safe. People are afraid of crime. You've got a ready-made clientele."

Within days my new venture, The Cop Shop ("Take a Truncheon to Luncheon") was ready. I dressed all my waiters in long-sleeved shirts and ties, although they objected bitterly. Soon their union threatened to strike if I didn't allow them to drive their food carts home from work. When the union went on the 6 o'clock news to complain that their jobs at my restaurant didn't allow them sufficient time for their moonlighting, I closed.

Well, that is about how it went. My favorite, the Pun Palace, with lettuce pray and take-it-on-the-lamb, finders kippers and Bullwinkle mousse, was labeled "pukelear warfare" by a food critic. I opened the Houston Lunch & Plates, called it HL&P. Between the time you ordered your food and the time it was served, the price had doubled. And I tried the William Wayne Hall of Justice: No matter what you ordered, the waiter overturned it. Everyone had to eat at separate tables, and the bus boys were just that: boys bused in from across town. When the customers ruled that my cooking was cruel and unusual punishment, I quit for good.

The other day I ran into a couple of friends, a geologist and a proctologist, who suggested I should go into something different if I really wanted to make a fortune. They recommended oil or medicine.

Pun regicide

Fidel Castro was highly enamored of the poultry industry, one Bertrand Moser informs us. In fact, Castro even built a highway which could be used only by chickens. The highway, of course, was a red island road.

Yes, it is time once again to commit regicide against the King's English. From Texas A&M, Les Palmer tell us that a hamburger franchise chain is trying to capitalize on the election of Jimmy Carter. In its Georgia outlets, the chain is test-marketing a burger that consists of a meat pattie and a glob of peanut butter. It's called a Cracker Jack.

In the spirit of equal time, Allan E. Turner of Austin says he was on his way to a UT football game recently, but first dropped by the alumni center across from Memorial Stadium for a cocktail party. A freshman there got so thoroughly drunk that he ripped off his clothes, then collapsed in the doorway. As the alumni left for the game, they had to step over the naked young man, and some men began dropping their neckties in strategic places to cover him. He briefly woke up and asked what was happening. "Relax, boy," said one alum, "the ties of exes are upon you."

"Did you know," ask Carole and Howard Marmell of Houston, as if I didn't, "that the man who wrote the 'Star Spangled Banner' later went into a life of crime? To escape he traveled to the sparsely settled interior of the U.S. where no one could find him. He ended up living in Kansas, scot free.

"One of the problems of the Viking spacecraft," they continue in total disregard for their personal safety, "was with the Mars' mangled scanner. Then there was Jack Paar, who brought some hides home from Africa. Paar called a leathermaker to come to his house to fix up the skins. When the leathermaker arrived, he was wearing yards of cheap jewelry, thus making him the Paars' bangled tanner."

Mrs. R. L. Noark of Hitchcock recalls this oldie: An ailing tribal chief was told to chew a long strip of leather to cure him of his sickness. He swallowed the whole thing, but felt no better. Turning to the medicine man, the chief said, "The thong is ended but the malady lingers on."

We have the story of the pleasant receptionist who asked Howard Boland how he liked her new dentures. Boland peeked inside, then asked, "What's plates like you doing in a nice girl like this?"

When a deer hunter served guests at his hunting lodge a roast cut from his eight-point trophy, one guest remarked that the venison might taste even better if it were more skillfully sliced. The host disagreed, saying: "You can't judge a buck by its carver."

That comes here from Frederick W. Harbaugh of Nassau Bay. The man obviously has a lot of free time on his hands, for he also sent in this story. A visitor to the Siberian prison camps asked why the cleverest prisoners were so roughly handled by the guards. He also had another question: Why did the prison chef hang the camp's yak jerky outside in the cold? The commandant explained: "Canny are mauled, but chews are frozen."

A final effort from Harbaugh, who will then be sent to Tehran to demonstrate against Pappy Bond. It seems that a farmer whose crops were being ravaged by mice instructed his children to fight the scourge till the crisis was past. The following Saturday the farmer looked out the window and saw his oldest son who, instead of capturing mice, was walking his strawberry mare around the corral. This sent the farmer into a tirade, as he angrily shouted to his son: "A strolling roan gathers no mouse!"

Two Eskimos sitting in a kayak were cold, so they lit a fire in the craft and it promptly sank, thus proving that you can't have your kayak and heat it, too.

Finally, I leave you with this bit of wisdom. Last Saturday, Texas A&M celebrated receiving the one-millionth book for its library. A rare book it is, costing $3,500, a gift from Mrs. M. F. (Chan) Driscoll. What's the title? You'd never guess. It's *Prose and Poetry of the Live Stock Industry of the United States.* I'll hum a few bars.

HE HAD TRIED TO SMILE

He Had Tried to Smile

TEXAS CHILDREN'S HOSPITAL—This is the hardest part of all. Waiting. Just sitting around and waiting. There is not a single thing you can do. Nothing. Just wait.

Hospital waiting rooms should be some sort of decompression chamber—a place where you might sit down and ease up, following a hectic race, high tensions, probing doctors, worried parents. Yes, it should be a place for the calm after the storm, after its occupants have passed the baton off to the pros, who are even now wrist-deep in your eldest son.

But it is not. This is not a cooling-off place nor a stairstep down from Adrenalin Suite. Quite the contrary. For tensions rise in a hospital waiting room as each person here waits for the doctor and The Look. You know exactly what I mean. It is the way the doctor sets his face after coming out of the operating room but before saying a word. It is The Look. It says a thousand things before he opens his mouth.

There is no code, no unique and technical knowledge needed. I seriously doubt if they are taught how to give The Look in medical school, or even know they are giving it. For it is not medical, but human. A frown. A stern, set jaw which means that there is bad news ahead. Things did not go as they should have gone. Or maybe they only went as expected, and no one could change them.

Doctors are forced to come into the waiting room and give this look occasionally, for they are not miracle workers, just people trying to do something for someone. Perhaps we put too much faith in pilots, judges and surgeons. Perhaps we elevate them in our own minds to lofty heights that belong to no mere human. Like it or not, planes do crash.

I am not looking for this look. No, I am waiting for the other one. The smile. The beam. The Look that is a mixture of pleasure for the patient and simple self-pride in a job well done. That is The Look I am waiting for. Certainly that is the one I will get. Certainly.

The room is gaily painted and nearly empty. There is a family down at the other end. The father passes by and I speak to him. He stretches his palms out and says, "I no speak English," in an accent that could be anything from Croatian to Californian.

Silence. A TV set perches on a wall, but it is off and no one makes any attempt to turn it on. More silence. We also serve. Suddenly another couple comes in. He is a big, open-faced fellow, an agrarian type. He spots the TV set, goes up and turns it on, flipping around till he settles on a baseball game. Then he takes his place.

There is a noise coming down the hall and instinctively everyone in the room looks up. But it is only a nurse, who walks past the waiting room and on down the hall, not knowing how her mere passing-by had riveted attention to that doorway, which now yawns vacant. The baseball game drones on and the afternoon settles in to stay. The past hour has taken only 10 minutes.

When I last saw him, he was lying flat on his back on a bed with large wheels. The bed was being pushed down the hall by a covey of doctors, all dressed in flowing blue-green gowns, caps, masks, from their heads to their shoes, shuffling down the hall like Benedictine monks heading off for evening vespers.

Lying there on that bed, he had tried to smile, but it just didn't bloom. To a 10-year-old, a stomach ache usually has something to do with too much junk consumed at a circus or rodeo, and nothing whatsoever to do with an appendix, whatever that is.

There is, of course, absolutely nothing to worry about, I keep telling myself, but whoever could sell that line to anyone in this room is a real miracle worker. It is, indeed, something to worry about, and no one can convince me any differently. The TV set continues to grind out the game, inning by suffocating inning.

What other parents have waited in this very room? Wrestling with their mental might-have-beens? Car wrecks, open bottles, closed freezers, the thousand and one things that always happen to other people's children. And The Look, what kind was it? Did their doctors come down that hall and around that corner and peer at them, jaw set and stern? Did the plane crash?

There are more footsteps coming down the hall, but by now everyone is so mentally wiped out that the expectancy is not here, only dull wonderment. Shuffle-shuffle. Around the corner come two doctors, the monks are back from vespers, and one of them is mine.

I look at him. He looks at me. He smiles.

At earth's end

STRAITS OF MAGELLAN—The very word "Chile," means "end of the Earth." And this is the end of the end, here on the southern tip. Right now is the height of summer, but the weather is rotten most of the time. This evening is damp and gusty. The sun is still up and won't set until about 10:30 p.m. It will rise six hours later. In the winter, night lasts from about 4:30 p.m. until 8 the next morning.

"These are the only three girls we'll meet tonight," says Capt. Luke Brouwer, as we push through the cold, gray waters. He motions to low-lying mounds on the horizon: the islands of Isabel, Marta and Magdalena.

The supply boat, Smit-Lloyd 52, chugs along slowly as Capt. Brouwer, a pipe-smoking Dutchman, and his first mate keep checking the charts, various scopes and dials, and the horizon. It is tricky going in the straits, and always has been.

Ferdinand Magellan, or Hernando de Magallanes (mah-ha-LANE-ess) as locals call him, was the first person known to have sailed through here. That was in 1520, when he was coming down the Atlantic side of South America. Before finding the strait, Magellan came upon a huge Indian wearing skin moccasins stuffed with straw for warmth. The fellow's feet seemed so large that Magellan called him "Big Foot," or Patagon, and called this part of the world "Patagonia." Today in the main square in the city of Punta Arenas, the only city on the straits, there is a large statue of Magellan, with Patagon sitting below him. It is considered good luck to kiss Patagon's big feet, which are rubbed bright by countless believers.

It was the spring, the middle of October, four and a half centuries ago, that Magellan led his four ships through here, and nothing has changed, for there is not a sign of civilization, not a light from shore in the gray muck. Not another ship. Not another soul. It is, indeed, the end of the Earth. Capt. Brouwer puffs slightly on his pipe, peers down into the scope of the radar screen, then shows me the outlines of islands on both sides. We thread through as rain begins to fall. The seas are not particularly rough, certainly not so bad as I had imagined, but they are cold, 34 to 36 degrees, and a man can survive only about seven minutes in the water.

The Smit-Lloyd 52 chugs along smoothly. It was built in Australia four years ago and since then has served in Australia, Singapore, the Philippines, the Red Sea and Africa. It's been in these waters a year and a half. The crew is usually seven men, but this trip there are four Dutch and four Chileans working on board. Capt. Brouwer works 12 weeks on, seven weeks off. But he gets comp time off for weekends and holidays. "So, five months total each year I'm off," he says. "I like it because when I'm home, I'm home. In Rotterdam, I don't work."

He wanders back to the charts. "We take bearings here and here and here," he says, pointing to three spots on the map with his pipe. "This is two miles wrong. Not the islands, not the signals. It's this bloody piece of paper that's wrong."

This is a bad place for unreliable charts, or anything else which isn't exact. On shore not far from here is an old double sidepaddle ship, the Olympia. It was being towed through, going from the Mississippi to San Francisco to be a gambling ship. A storm hit, and today the Olympia sits on the shore, a huge hulk, its metal paddles and boiler works rusting. In this treeless part of the world, most of the wood was stripped long ago. The bell is over at a sheep ranch. One story has it that the Olympia was filled with Yugoslav immigrants when it was beached.

The first steamship to make regular runs in the straits was the Amadeo, built in 1892. In Punta Arenas is a photograph of it, under full steam. In 1932 the Amadeo was beached in a storm, and you can still see its remains over there on the rocky shore. It takes two pilots to get large ships through the straits, one to work while the other rests. In 1960 the lone pilot on the Grace Line ship, Santa Leonora, dozed off after 20 hours on watch. Today the Santa Leonora rusts in the straits, overturned. "Then there's the Metula," says the first mate brightly. "Three years ago she ran aground at Bajo Satelite. She was a Shell tanker, 209,000 tons. They finally pulled her off."

The rain is falling harder now, and the skies are dark. Down below, some crewmembers are watching the evening news, sponsored by Chevrolet.

On shore, an American helicopter pilot, Bob Holly, told me, "On our wind gauge we've registered 90 miles an hour. Fifty to 60 is not that unusual." A British navy map of 1870 warns: "In proceeding to the Pacific, ships should not attempt to clear the Strait in one day from Point Gallant . . . as the west and southwest gales come up very suddenly and without warning, it is impossible to run back and find an anchorage during dark nights. These remarks apply more especially to Winter navigation." From Magellan's wooden ships to Bob Holly's SA-365 Dauphin helicopter to this 4,000-horsepower ocean-going tug, the weather remains a common enemy. As I said, nothing's changed.

A spread of lights marks the industrial complex of Cape Gregorio. We pass the spot, then return to the empty end of the Earth. The beach marking the southern terminus of the American continent is rocky. Large, water-smooth boulders line the sea side of the beach, then the rocks become smaller but no less smooth. There aren't many shells. The sand is dark gray and black. Hard-packed sand hills rise up maybe 40 feet along here. At the top is wind-stunted thistle, plus calafate and mata verde. Rabbits and assorted birds live there, plus sheep, cattle and nandu (there's a tilde over the first n, so it's pronounced yan-doo), an ostrich-like bird which runs in groups and won't pose for my camera.

I go below for a meal and some sleep. The motors of the boat plug along, heading us east toward the Atlantic. The entire strait is actually a big V. This side, the eastern leg, is not very deep—it can be dangerously shallow—and the land is flat. The western half is deeper, with high mountains on the sides. It took Magellan more than a month to go through his straits, and he never returned. But he left his name here, and named a lot more. Like the land to the south, Tierra del Fuego, land of fire, so called because of the Indians' campfires he could spot. Today, this is still the land of fire, but the blazes have moved to the north side, where natural gas is flared off.

At 3:30 I am shaken awake by a horrible noise as the anchors are dropped and the crew springs into action. Going on deck, the scene is like one from a science fiction show: Towering hundreds of feet above me, bathed in floodlight, is the Diamond M Nugget. The crew straps a greasy lifejacket to me, tosses my bag onto a flimsy device, and I am told to hang on the outside. It seems as though I should be on the inside of the contraption, where it's safer. A crewmember gives the word and a crane yanks me up into the night. Now I am being swung maybe 150 feet above the ocean, in a driving rain, while thinking that I should be selling shoes in Amarillo.

It's funny to remember that Magellan came through here looking for new trade routes. Thousands of 49ers passed by on their way to the gold fields of California. The whalers, the explorers, the Spanish galleons, all came and went, not realizing that they were passing *over* the biggest prize of all. Oil.

How to make a million

THE STREET CORNER—"Ssssst," a voice says from behind me.
"Take my wallet, but don't hurt me," I reply.
"I don't want your wallet."
"My watch? OK, here it is."
"Not your watch, either, laddie-boy. Just your signature."
Eh? I know that voice and I recognize that smoke from a two-for-a-quarter cigar. "Is that you?" I ask, turning around to see my old acquaintance, Heinrich Armtwister, lobbyist extraordinary.

"Just sign right here, laddie-boy," he says, thrusting a paper toward me with one hand and deftly taking the borrowed bank pen from my shirt pocket. "I'm going to make you a star. You can thank me later."

"Hold on, Mr. Armtwister. Are you still president of the I Go Tojo Fan Club?"

"Uh, no. The Justice Department failed to see the humor in that particular pursuit. I'm into something much better now."

"I know. I got your mailout about 'Make Big Bucks on Braniff Stock.'"

Armtwister folds up his papers and puts my pen in his pocket. "All right, turn down the chance to make a fortune in your spare time, at home."

"Doing what?"

"Oh, so now you're interested. Make money the old-fashioned way. Writing books."

"Come on, Mr. Armtwister. Publishers don't grab people off street corners to write books."

"You haven't been to a bookstore lately, have you? Look what's selling. You, too, can crank out books like that on your coffee break."

"What's selling?"

"Diet books. I want you to write *Dr. Armtwister's Fig and Fudge Diet*."

"Wait a minute. You're not a doctor."

"Of course I am. Here's my certificate. Doctor of Theology from the Lazarus T. Leviticus School of Religion and Bait Camp. You can't write a diet book without having a 'Dr.' in front of your name. Doesn't make any difference what kind of doctor you are."

" *'Fig and Fudge'*? Come on."

"OK, I've got others. *The Eat All of Anything You Want Anytime You Wish Diet Book*."

"How can you lose weight doing that?"

"You work out the details, laddie-boy. That's in the contract. Here's another: *The Dr. Armtwister Thin Is In Diet Book With Illustrated . . .*"

"No thanks. I really don't think I could write a diet book."

"No problem. You can write a kiss-and-tell book."

"Huh?"

"Those are always big sellers. Someone exposes someone else as the beast the public never knew. Look at *Mommie Dearest*. Bing Crosby's kids just did a beautiful scalping job on him. And look at what Peter Sellers' son did in *P.S. I Love You*. All you have to do is just wait for someone to die so he can't defend himself, then write things you'd never be brave enough to write when he was alive. But, remember, it can't be flattering or no one will believe it. Readers *want* to believe that well-known people are really rotten underneath. It supports their own inadequacies."

"I don't know anyone famous and rotten who isn't already known to the public as famous and rotten."

"No problem, laddie-boy. You can write a how-to book."

"You mean how to paint a chair or build a summer home?"

"Good grief, no. Those went out long ago. Get with it. Today's big-selling how-to books tell you how to make a fortune or be irresistible to women."

"I always thought if you accomplished the first, the second followed automatically."

"Not necessarily. Here's a sure-fire best seller: *How To Corner the Diamond Market With $500*."

"That's ridiculous, Mr. Armtwister."

"You think it's too dull? OK. *How To Corner the Diamond Market With $500 While Making Love to Beautiful Women*."

"Mr. Armtwister, that's terrible."

"With a subtitle: *And Lose 30 Pounds.*"

"Oh, come on."

"I'm not through. *As You Meet Chester A. Arthur—The Man, the Monster.*"

"That's as bad as *Lincoln's Doctor's Dog.* Mr. Armtwister, count me out. I'm not interested."

"All right, you've forced me to let you write my biggie, laddie-boy. Get a numbered bank account in Zurich to handle the world-wide syndication, plus serialization, Book of the Month Club and TV rights."

"What is it?"

"*Dr. Armtwister's How to Write a Diet Book.* Here. I'll even loan you my pen to start work. Got it from a bank."

Texas was just a Hoosier away from independence

Let us now consider the curious case of one Henry Shoemaker, a farm-hand from Smithfield Township, DeKalb County, Indiana. His is a fairly well-known story in parts of the Hoosier State where it affected people, but Shoemaker had an even greater impact on you, and you don't even know it. So keep reading. For help in this matter, I am grateful to James Gilreath of the Library of Congress in Washington and Helen S. Morrison of the Indiana Commission on Public Records, both of whom waded through musty archives to find answers to my inquiries.

Our story begins dully enough on the first Monday of August 1842, in Indiana, where elections were held for local offices. In addition, reapportionment had given the adjoining counties of DeKalb and Steuben a single representative to the Indiana House of Representatives. The two candidates were Enos Beall, a Whig, and Madison Marsh, a Democrat. On election day, Henry Shoemaker, a farmhand, remembered that he had met Marsh during the campaign and had promised to vote for him, so Shoemaker saddled up a horse and rode 12 miles to Kendallville, arriving at the polling place late in the afternoon.

"When he applied to vote," the Indiana Committee of Elections later reported, "the inspector handed him a sheet of tickets, but as all of them contained the name of Enos Beall for Representative, he enquired for 'another kind,' and the inspector handed him a sheet of tickets with the name of Madison Marsh for Representative, that he then enquired of the same inspector if he 'had scissors or a knife to cut them with,' and the latter handed him a penknife."

Not wishing to vote the straight party ticket of either Whigs or Democrats, Shoemaker proceeded, quite literally, to split his ballot. As the voting officials looked on, Shoemaker cut out the name of Marsh from one ballot along with the others he wanted, then cut other names from the second sheet. He handed the clippings to the inspector—four separate pieces of paper, three small sheets inside a larger one. The inspector accepted them and put them in the ballot box. Shoemaker hung around the voting site for an hour or more, but no one said anything about his unusual ballot. Later, however, when the tabulation began, the voting officials threw out Shoemaker's ballot.

On the next Sunday, the sheriffs of the two counties met at the Steuben County courthouse to compare the certificates for the election for representative. The final results were 360 votes for Marsh and 360 votes for Beall. A tie. The sheriffs then "by casting lots," chose Beall as the winner. Marsh immediately appealed to the Committee on Elections, which held extensive hearings on the matter.

The committee found that in Smithfield township, only 16 votes were cast for representative, all of them for either Marsh or Beall; that there was only one person named Henry Shoemaker in the township and he was a qualified voter; that he had voted "openly and with no appearance of concealment or subterfuge" and had not tried to vote twice; and that the inspector had accepted Shoemaker's ballot and had put it in the box; and "we have the uncontradicted oath of Henry Shoemaker, that he did intend to vote for Madison Marsh for the office of Representative." Also, the committee noted that it was the inspector's knife which was used in the surgery.

"In summing up the whole matter, your committee find that Madison Marsh has received a majority of the legal votes, if they had all been counted, and the voice of the ballot box had been properly regarded, and that he is therefore entitled to the contested seat." The Indiana House agreed, and Marsh—a Democrat—took his seat in the state Legislature.

Now we move to the next step. Prior to the 17th Amendment, U.S. senators were chosen by state legislatures. In 1842–43, the candidates for the U.S. Senate seat from Indiana were Oliver H. Smith, the Whig senator who was up for re-election, and the Democratic candidate, Gen. Tilghman A. Howard. Both were well-known and competent men. The only question was which one would get the nod.

The Indiana Senate joined the House and on the first ballot, to everyone's surprise, neither got the majority: Howard 74, Smith 72, and Edward A. Hannegan, a darkhorse, got three. Marsh voted for his fellow Democrat, Howard. On the next ballot, Smith received 75 votes, one shy of the 76 needed for a majority. If Shoemaker's vote had been rejected and neither Beall nor Marsh had been declared the winner, Smith's 75 votes would have been the majority and he would have been returned to the Senate.

By the time a fifth ballot was taken, the legislators were growing restless. There was still no majority, so they knocked off for lunch, agreeing to meet again at 2 p.m. that day. After lunch the Senate heard a bill letting Richard Palmer build a mill-dam across the White River (it was referred to the Judiciary Committee), then went over to the House to resume the selection of a U.S. senator. It was immediately clear that some politicking had been under way during lunch, because on the sixth ballot Smith got 69 votes. Howard got one vote. Joseph G. Marshall—a new name—got four. And Edward A. Hannegan got 76, making him the new senator from Indiana. Hannegan's winning vote was supplied by Madison Marsh.

Four years later, in 1846, the U.S. Senate was bitterly divided over whether to declare war on Mexico. A caucus of the Democratic senators, which comprised the majority in the Senate, was called to determine which way they would vote. But even the Democrats couldn't agree. The vote in the caucus was a tie. Then it was determined that one senator was not present: Edward Hannegan of Indiana. He was sent for and promptly voted "aye" for war. It broke the tie, fixed the Democrats' position and war was declared.

That is how Henry Shoemaker is best remembered in Indiana, yet there is one other point to be made. The war with Mexico was touched off by the U.S. annexation of Texas one year earlier. John Tyler was president at that time, having taken office upon the death of William Henry Harrison. That left the vice presidency empty.

The move to annex Texas had failed as a treaty, which needed a two-thirds vote in the Senate, so Tyler tried again—this time as a simple resolution, which needed only a majority. It passed, 27 to 25. A one-vote change by a supporter of annexation would have resulted in a 26-26 tie and, there being no vice president to break the deadlock, annexation would have failed and Texas would have remained independent. For the record, Indiana Sen. Albert White voted against annexation. Sen. Hannegan voted for it. Curse you, Henry Shoemaker!

Streaking rules

The newest phenomenon on college campus today is, of course, streaking. In case you are just back from Skylab III, streaking is a game whereby the participant takes off his or her clothes (in this game it's easy to determine which) and races across a crowded area.

The playing field may be the campus, a student dorm (of the opposite sex, naturally), sporting event or alumni clambake. The idea is to surprise and shock the onlookers, be they school administrators, campus police, or your fiancee's parents who show up unexpectedly.

Officialdom does not like streaking. Deans look askance at it, which is hard to do while staring in wonder. Some campus police have responded with record speed to reports that feminine fig leaves are falling in the halls of ivy. Meanwhile, the FBI in its typical dour fashion warns darkly, "A streaker could never be hired by an outfit like ours." And no wonder— where would you pin the badge?

The problem with such epidermal epics is that streaking is still an outlaw sport. It is not yet sanctioned by the NCAA. Coaches do not connive and falsify to get streakers on athletic scholarships. Streakers cannot get their high school grades lost, their college transcripts altered, their parents flown down in alumni Learjets to look over the campus and play golf with the college president.

Streakers cannot get their university to give them free room, board, tuition, laundry and phony summer jobs. They cannot go first in registration lines so that they can enroll in soft courses. They cannot attend college for four years, stay scholastically eligible, and still be semi-literate.

Again, the reason is simply that streaking is not yet an official sport. If any streaker, dodging and waving his way across the campus at breakneck speed, did the same thing in uniform carrying a piece of inflated leather under one arm, he would be hailed as a great young man, an inspiration to the youth of America and be drafted for a quarter-million dollars. Then he would get paid enormous amounts by Gillette to take it all off.

Amateurism has no place on the American college campus, so we must remedy the streakers' plight immediately and make all the nudes fit to sprint. We must set up rules, schedule contests, scalp tickets, and delay the televised strip-off until after the last commercial from Joe Namath and his magical popcorn machine. Streaking must be big business to be respectable. Let's have some rules.

Rule I: Streakers shall be on their toes during the high hurdles.

Rule II: In cross-country streaking, coed teams must finish the race in three days or less.

Rule III: Howard Cosell will be allowed to cover streaking only if he is in uniform.

Rule IV: Don Meredith will not be allowed to insult Howard's uniform.

Rule V: Halftime shows will be encouraged, but marching bands shall be extremely judicious in both their formations and songs. Strictly prohibited are such numbers as "Hey, Look Me Over," "Funny Face," "Close to You" and "Why Can't a Woman Be More Like a Man?"

Rule VI: Under no circumstances will the Rice MOB be allowed to comment about the Aggie streaking team.

Rule VII: The Longhorn Band will be allowed to play "The Eyes of Texas Are Upon You" only if the crowd quits snickering.

Rule VIII: Relay races shall be allowed only if the utmost care is taken in passing the baton.

Rule IX: As with school songs, some consideration must be given to choosing names for college streaking teams. The Baylor Bares is allowed on grounds of school tradition, ditto for the Arkansas Pig Skins and the Kansas U. Jaybirds. Still under advisement are the University of Perth Day Suits and the Montreal Expos.

Rule X: Ski masks are not allowed unless the streaker looks better wearing one. Tennis shoes (known in the trade as streaker's sneakers) are allowed only if the thermometer is below 32 degrees or if the meet is held at the A&M experimental farm.

Rule XI: Each contest shall be controlled by officials. Infraction of rules includes obscene tattoos, tossing carpet tacks in your wake or wearing tear-away skin. Penalties range up to and including sliding down a holly bush.

Rule XII: The winner is the streaker who crosses the finish line without contracting double pneumonia. The loser is the streaker who runs clear across campus buck nude and no one notices.

There you have it, rules for bringing streaking up to the professional level of other college athletics. Show me a school with a good streaking team and I'll show you a fine student body.

Icy beaches

THE BEACH—All the summer vacation houses are empty up and down the line, since no sane person would come to the beach in winter.

Chuckle-chuckle. Little do they know what they are missing. For the beach in winter is as good as, if not better than, the beach in summer. First of all, it is empty. No neighbors are around, and that pleases me immensely. I can see no reason to pack up, leave Houston, spend good vacation time and hard-earned money to join everyone I just left in some other place. If I want to see people, I can hang around the West Loop any afternoon.

No, there are times when people get to me. Too many other humans, crowding around, taking up valuable space, intruding into my bubble. Every now and again everyone needs to get away from everyone else. So the beach in winter is the perfect place. No people. You walk along the beach as the cold wind cuts into your innards, and sleet bangs away at your face, and water splashes into your shoes, and you are cold. And miserable. And frostbit. But you are alone, and it is a small price to pay for the pleasure.

Another thing. It is quiet. Do your realize how rarely you actually hear no other human sounds? Not often. I recommend silence at least once a year. Silence in that there is an absence of human-made sounds. There is still the wind. And the waves cascading and churning and generally swirling about. And the sea gulls. Nice sounds, natural sounds.

The weather is another factor. Unlike in the summer, during the winter, the worse the weather is, the better. You come here knowing that it will be cold and rotten, and if it is not, then there is acute disappointment. I always bring my oldest sweaters, my grubbiest tennis shoes, my most dilapidated jackets. If the sun shines brightly, all is lost.

But this year the weather cooperates. It is lousy. So, I stay indoors, snuggled up against a crackling wood fire. I wear a glass of brandy and a red nose and puff on a cigar continuously. At close hand is a good book, and in the background is soft music. Hee-hee. Outside, 'tis not fit for man nor beast. The wind howls, the rain splatters on the windows. The fog creeps in and swiftly surrounds the beach so that the offshore rigs are totally veiled. The moon is only a bright haze. The outside lights down the way are dull glows, rather than their usual pinpricks of beams.

Snug in this cocoon, let it snow, let it rain, let the elements do their worst. I and my little family are safe. Yes, my little family. This is becoming an annual outing, or inning, I suppose. We come down here, just us, and get re-acquainted. Soon, to be sure, the little ones will want to bring along their friends. Then, in a few years, members of the opposite sex. And eventually, steady dates, then fiancees, and—after being newlyweds who would just as soon come down here by themselves—they will bring along their sniveling little brats who will cry all night and sleep all day.

But for now, it is just us. My wife, my children, my dog, and me. If you are getting the idea that your children share only your last name and your roof, I recommend a week at the beach in winter. It will quickly show you why you don't want to know them any better.

It is dusk now, and time for my daily pre-news stroll. I have this habit of keeping up with my world, and even at the beach I need a general knowledge of the day's events. So I skillfully time my day: Up at 10 sharp. Coffee, a brief foray to get the morning paper, then games with the kids. A bit of shell collecting, since beachcombing in the winter is so much better than in the summer. Lunch, snooze, some reading, and—if I have worked it right—it should be about 4:45. Perfect. In the winter, the sun is beginning to drop rapidly right about 4:45.

So, I bundle up, two or three sweaters, and take a dusk stroll on the beach, with or without the rest of the clan. A stroll along the beach snaps you out of your doldrums, plucks you from the ennui, makes the blood circulate and the senses perk. Coming back up the beach, frozen solid, I spot the fire in the darkened beach house up the dunes.

That and frostbite quicken my pace. So I return to my nest. If all has gone well, there is just enough time to:

Unpeel my many layers of clothes.

Crank up the tube.

Make sure that the world is surviving without my leadership.

After this half-hour rendezvous with the outside, off goes the TV and it is time to battle with more important matters than presidential trips to India. Such as: How long can you eat left-over Christmas turkey?

Darkness is the best for the beach in winter. The fire becomes even redder. The crackle of the burning wood is even more pronounced. And the contrast of the snug beach house with the foggy mess outside is all the greater. The satisfaction of being warm and mellow when all about you there is wind and rain and fog and avalanches and a pestilence of locusts gives you an ego trip. You are above mere typhoons.

And now it is late evening. The only noises are the howling of wind, the splatter of rain drops, and the crackle of the fire. I am now into the fifth chapter of a good book and the second half of a good fifth. We have played TV tennis, hunted for shells, argued about who hit who first, discussed the intricacies of the wishbone over the veer, and the relative merits of skateboards. Everyone is asleep except me.

The beach in winter—I recommend it heartily.

Plots thicken

To: Director,
Central Intelligence Agency
Langley, Va.

From: Felix T. Mildew
Agent-in-Charge

Subject: Operation Ozzie

As per your instructions, I have done a thorough investigation into recent charges by British author Michael Eddowes that the man buried in a Fort Worth cemetery is not Lee Harvey Oswald but is, in fact, a Soviet agent who was substituted for Oswald by the KGB.

First, I determined that a great number of people are buried in Fort Worth. Eventually I narrowed my quarry down to a gravesite with a tombstone reading: "Edgar J. Cumquat." This name, I had reason to believe, was often used by Oswald as a cover. More investigation revealed that—if Oswald and Cumquat are one and the same—he has an excellent alibi as he died in 1948. My search then went to Dallas, where I viewed the famous Zapruder film, surveyed the grassy knoll and used computer analysis to determine the actual direction of the motorcade. Next I interviewed eyewitnesses, reviewed reports from the Dallas Police Department and checked out several books from the Dallas Schoolbook Depository.

My investigation led me to conclude that Oswald was really Oswald but that John Kennedy was a Soviet agent. Further investigation turned up another possibility: Kennedy was actually speaking to a Rotary Club in Bangor, Maine, that day. The man in the car was a KGB substitute, one Edgar J. Cumquat.

All of this, I'll admit, is explosive stuff. But I submit to you the following unexplained circumstances:

Lee Harvey Oswald lived in Dallas.

Previously, he had lived in the Soviet Union.

The KGB also lives in the Soviet Union.

Lord Mountbatten, who also once visited the Soviet Union, had trouble spelling IRA.

The IRA, the KGB *and* the CIA all have three letters.

Now, chief, comes the clincher: Jim Bishop and Abraham Lincoln both knew men named Johnson.

At this point I turned to the next part of Eddowes' theory: that the real Lee Harvey Oswald was rubbed out in Russia by the KGB. I checked the obit pages in *Pravda* from 1957 to 1960 and found no mention of any such death, thus proving the ridiculousness of such a theory. Just to make sure, I wrote the KGB asking for any information on this matter.

A prompt reply was forthcoming—actually I got the reply before I mailed the letter, which makes me wonder if my cover has been blown—and I was assured that Lee Harvey Oswald (known to the KGB as "Bull's Eye") only visited Russia briefly while escorting Margaret Trudeau to an orgy. I would go into further detail, but you can read all about it in Mark Lane's recent book, *Jack Ruby Is Alive and Well in Spandau Prison*, which he plans to turn into a Broadway musical.

(Incidentally, chief, I would like to ask you to nudge the Disbursement Section a bit. My expense account is extremely low, due mainly to the cost of gathering information from the Dallas Cowboy cheerleaders. Also, my cover as a fabulously wealthy Texas oilman is running a great deal more than expected, particularly after hosting the Texas-OU game.)

In summation, I have determined that Michael Eddowes is partially correct, The KGB did pull a switch, but this was done while you were a Soviet agent working for the Warren Commission and before you defected from the Bolshoi. It also proves that Anastasia was not a Romanov.

While working on this case, I was absolutely appalled at the number of crackpot theories and paranoid rumors going around. In addition, I can't count all of the quick-buck artists trying to make money on every conceivable aspect. I discussed the problem for some time with my agent, who suggested we contact the William Morris Agency. This I shall do and will embark next week on a 34-city lecture tour just to set the record straight. In addition, several publishers are interested in my rough draft.

Yr. Ob't Sr'vt
Felix T. Mildew
Agent-in-Charge

Giving eternity the slip

THE FREEWAY—Ah, the open road. More or less. Houston's freeways are not so much open as they are ajar.

I am whipping along at about 50 in the middle of the afternoon, surrounded by my fellow motorists, most of whom are obeying the law and just trying to avoid higher insurance rates.

There is a large flatbed truck up ahead with a piece of earthmoving equipment on it—one of those big bulldozers or scrapers or whatever. Everytime the flatbed hits a bump—which is often enough on our freeways—large chunks of dirt jar loose from the bulldozer or whatever and come merrily bouncing my way. I am being sprayed with clods.

Now I am behind a car, between two others and just ahead of a fourth. Snug in my surroundings, I come up and over a rise and down the other side. Suddenly the car in front of me twists sharply to the left, nearly sideswipes the van in that lane, but straightens out just in time and continues on.

The view from here is clear. Up ahead, perhaps 100 feet — it's impossible to say exactly how far anything is on a freeway in heavy traffic—is a large something. I can't tell what right now. It's there, in my lane, right in the middle of my lane.

A box. Yes, it's a box. Since it is rapidly coming into view, I can see clearer and clearer what it is. A large cardboard carton, a packing box. That heavy brown cardboard which all items over 10 pounds always come in. The box is about 4 feet high, 4 feet wide and maybe 6 to 10 feet long. It is not exactly rectangular, since each end seems to be heavily lined with additional cardboard, probably to soften the crunch in handling. How much will it soften my crunch?

I can't see any metal bands around it, those tight, black bands which are impossible to cut except with the pruning clippers. No colored stickers attached to it with shipping orders and obscure messages to handlers. The big box is still sealed. Whatever's in it is still in it.

At this point, you may be wondering just how it is that I know so much about a container in a moment. It's not the kind of thing I—or you—see each day, especially in the midst of a freeway.

I shall tell you why I know so much about this box. It's because I am studying it in blind panic. It is branded on my eyeballs. It may well be the very last thing I shall see on this earth. Eons hence, while singing from a cloud, or stoking a furnace, some fellow worker will glance over at me and ask: "How did you get here Mac?" And I want to give him exact details. Why not? We won't be in any hurry to go anywhere.

So it is that few things in my life are so noticeable as this box, which is in effect heading my way at about 50 miles an hour.

As I get closer, I can see in blue lettering along the side: "Whirlpool." Ah, so that's the story.

But it really won't be much of a story. I mean, there I am with witches burned at the stake, cowboys scalped by Geronimo, babes snuffed out in a *pogrom*, and when it comes time to tell my tale, as every eye around the campfire turns toward me, I'll have to say: "In the spring of 1979, I slammed into a Whirlpool water heater."

Sigh. There will be snickers. Probably outright guffaws from submarine commanders, tightrope walkers, from traitors to the cause and virgins to the end. And the conversation will quickly move on to the effects of gamma rays on those heading our way.

"Whirlpool." Shall I mutter it in my last moments, like "Rosebud"? It is coming on fast. I try to veer to the righthand lane, but a car there does not see the danger and won't let me in. No wonder. I have only just now seen the barrier myself. To the left then. A car refuses to surrender. It's one-on-one now.

There is no point in hitting the brakes, I would simply skid all over the freeway and, even if I could avoid the box, I would only slam into another car. Then—this is silly, I'll admit—I honk. I lean on my horn in livid frustration, as though the box up there has only been dozing and will suddenly prick up its ears, hear my plea and wander off. I honk in anger and outright hate. If the person who put that box there and is about to make my family fatherless was standing alongside his temporarily misplaced mountain, I would run right over him with glee.

Ahead, I can see a pickup truck pulled over on the shoulder and the driver is getting out. In the back of the pickup truck is a tall brown box, with extra cardboard on the ends to prevent damage.

At the last possible moment I veer to the left. The driver over there is not pleased, but I really don't care about his or her state of mind at this moment. It is a case of either making a fellow motorist slightly angry for a few minutes, or really ticking me off for eternity.

I sneak past, not 2 inches to spare. The motorist on my left is most upset, probably having never seen the huge box. To the right, on its side, the Whirlpool. A water heater, maybe. An oven or refrigerator. A washer or dryer or dishwasher. I came within an instant of getting pre-heated or agitated. In any case, I would have been permanently pressed.

As I squeak by, over on the shoulder of the road the pickup truck driver is counting his big, brown cardboard boxes. He seems to be missing one.

I suppose I could have twisted my story a bit, and told the crowd around the campfire that I met my untimely end at a Whirlpool. Sounds rather dramatic, don't you think?

Ranger life

COMPANY A—In 1896, a rowdy crowd of visitors showed up in Langtry, Texas, for the prize fight between Bob Fitzsimmons and Pete Maher. They poured into the Jersey Lily where one waiter, a Chinese fellow, tried desperately, and unsuccessfully, to serve everyone.

The crowd grew impatient and one patron picked up a pepper sauce caster to toss at the waiter. The patron was Bat Masterson, one of the most renowned gunfighters in the West. Just as Masterson was about to let fly, a small fellow sitting nearby said, "Don't do that." Masterson stopped and looked over at the intruder. It was Capt. Bill McDonald of the Texas Rangers.

"Maybe you'd like to take it up," said Masterson evenly.

Capt. McDonald smiled. "I done took it up," he said.

Masterson lived for another 35 years, possibly because he decided not to throw a pepper sauce caster in a saloon in Langtry, Texas.

Today, 94 men done took it up—94 Texas Rangers scattered across the state but neatly packaged in the six regions of the Department of Public Safety, of which they are a part. Each region has a Ranger company with a captain in command, a sergeant to assist (there are no lieutenants in the Rangers) and some privates. Houston is one of the six regional headquarters, with Company A, Texas Rangers—a 16-man outfit (there are no women in the Rangers, either) covering 30 counties in southeast Texas, stretching from Matagorda County in the south, up around the Gulf to Louisiana and north to Nacogdoches.

"This is by far the most heavily populated Ranger region in Texas," says Sgt. Grady Sessums, the second-in-command.

"Three men handle Harris and Galveston Counties. The others in the company live and work elsewhere in the region, but we all come under Capt. Pete Rogers. He's the boss and we do what he says.

"Our basic job is to assist local law officers when they ask. We do not go into a case unless asked. The only exception is when the governor orders us in—when there has been a total breakdown in law. Houston is a large city and has a large police and sheriff's department, but this is not typical. I came here from Del Rio and in two counties in my region they had only the sheriff, that's all. Not a single deputy. Not a single other law officer."

Being a Texas Ranger in the fifth largest city in America poses some problems, but not too many. "We get calls from other places, somebody from Houston did something and we need to check it out. Today, for instance, we received requests for help from Rangers in San Angelo, McAllen, Livingston and Liberty. And a woman called whose son had been killed in Palo Pinto County. She wanted to know what had happened and we found out for her."

Texas Rangers have never worn uniforms, but are supposed to dress according to the area they serve. In Houston this usually means a casual or semi-western outfit, complete with coat and tie. In other parts of Texas it can mean Levis and snap-button shirts. But all Rangers wear boots and large Western hats. And, of course, the star.

"They are carved from the old Mexican five-peso piece," says Sgt. Sessums, showing the back of the badge which is, indeed, a Mexican coin. "It's called a quentemoc. You see, in the early days Rangers were not issued badges, and those stationed along the border began carving their own. The piece is 92.5 percent pure silver and is rather soft. We still wear the same kind, round with a star in the middle. A Ranger captain's badge is gold and is carved from the old 50-peso piece.

"It used to be that when you joined the Rangers you were asked only three questions," says Sgt. Sessums. " 'Can you shoot? Can you ride? Do you have a horse?' Later they started getting picky and asked about the condition of the horse.

"Today, we have a long waiting list to get into the Texas Rangers and are very choosey. You have to meet all the requirements of the DPS. You must have 60 hours or more of college. You have to be between 30 and 50 years old and have at least eight years of law enforcement experience. I came to the Rangers from the Highway Patrol and so do most of the new men, but we don't have many vacancies because no one leaves."

Once in the Rangers, the recruit goes to school, then goes back to school again. Sgt. Sessums estimates he has 1,800 classroom hours in criminal investigative work. Privates are paid $1,104 a month. Later, there is longevity pay, now increased to $4 per month for each year in the service up to 25 years. Since they don't have uniforms, each Ranger, regardless of rank, gets an annual clothing allowance of $500.

They are issued an unmarked car without official license plates (Sgt. Sessums' 1974 Plymouth has 51,000 miles on it) and a small armory: a Smith & Wesson .357 combat magnum pistol, a 30-06 semi-automatic rifle and a 12 gauge shotgun for riot duty. Many Rangers prefer to carry their own weapons, which is perfectly all right with the DPS except that the weapon must be a .38 caliber or better and the Ranger must be able to qualify with it on the shooting range.

"Rangers are no longer required to have a horse," Sgt. Sessums explains, "but they must have access to a horse. I have been in Houston only since June, so I'm a-fixing to get access to a horse. Capt. Rogers' orders."

Do we still need the Texas Rangers?

"Do you still need the Houston Police Department, since the Sheriff's Department covers the entire county?" fires back the sergeant. "Every bit of work we do would have to be done by some other law enforcement agency if we didn't do it. And in rural areas, there just isn't anyone else.

"We have been upholding the law in Texas since 1823. We're the oldest law organization of its kind in the world, and when a Texas Ranger goes out of state on a job, people know him, they know about him. They know and respect the Rangers. To be a Texas Ranger is to be there. It's not a stepping-stone."

They done took it up, Bat.

Going home

DALLAS—Cars go by outside every now and again, and quite a few honk their horns.

The reason they are blasting away the quietness of this street corner is that the drivers see a sign—a long, bright sign, along a wall. It bespeaks of my brothers' total lack of taste and tact in telling the world that our mother is 70 and everyone should honk.

Inside the house—the one I was born in, raised in, and am now standing in—my mother is crying. She is not one to cry. Texas ladies do not cry. They laugh, they charm, they can whine and come on with pouts and promises and perseverance, but generally speaking, they do not cry.

But my mother is crying a lady-like cry. The reason is the appearance of all her children together. Truly, this would generate a good sob among most law enforcement agencies, not to mention assorted lawyers, accountants and obscure parliaments.

But her cry is one of joy, since she has not seen the entire gathering of the clan in 12 years, since my father died. Oh, to be sure, we dutifully report in, singularly and constantly: A brother in Dallas, me in Houston, a sister, captured at Stanford and sentenced to life with a Californian, and a brother who dwells somewhere in Indonesia until the heat dies down.

The entire mob is here today, with various offspring, in-laws, my stepfather and, lest we forget, the Sewing Bee. It is hard to explain the Sewing Bee. It is a group of a dozen ladies who have been meeting regularly for 47 years. They began as a bridge club, but children kept appearing at unscheduled times, and the members decided it was better to give up the bridge and stick to their knitting.

I can remember as a lad coming home from school to be met by this same motherly mafia. I would sit down on the rug by my mother's chair and read my Dick and Jane as the gang dissected humanity. In later years they gave up the facade of knitting altogether, and simply met to gossip and decide such matters as who was to be the next mayor of Dallas and the heir apparent to the Dalai Lama. When the Sewing Bee meets, the Security Council listens.

The doorbell rings and three small girls come in. They had been riding by on their bikes and had seen the sign. My mother had taught them in the first grade, and it seemed natural enough that they should join the festivities, too.

It is now the next day. The birthday party is over, officially. Today I am lounging around the family dwelling. A few years ago the house became the residence of a brother, which is the only way we could get Mother out. The place was eating her alive, but she wouldn't leave. So a brother moved in and that seemed to make it all right. When this house leaves the family, the British leave Gibraltar.

Anyway, I am soaking in his pool and drinking his beer—the computer business must be fantastic—and getting to love my loved ones. It is a beautiful, golden day. All of Dallas is ablaze in color. The azaleas, snug in their winter outfits only a week before, are splashing over the Texas prairie. The radio tells of partly cloudy skies, but as I bob about the backyard, there is not a cloud in sight.

There is, however, a bit of smoke, a hint of Havana in the air. It's because I brought with me a box of excellent cigars, an unexpected gift from my wife. When one leaves Houston for the outback, one must be prepared with adequate provisions. My brothers attack the cigars like a school of starving piranha.

At a table nearby is my mother, holding court. We report in, one by one. Name, rank and children number. An update on every cavity, each report card. Grandchildren come by to receive an overabundance of love and affection. My mother, who raised us with a smile and a switch, does not show a hint of her old self in dealing with my little creeps. They are darlings. I am an ogre. How dare I swat them? Funny, I could swear this is the same woman who chased me around this very back yard one afternoon after my totally reasonable tantrum at a clothing store. Who wants to try on short pants?

Do you ever have a really good day? When things go right and all is well? This is one of those days. It is a Sunday, a beautiful, bright and warm Sunday. Relatives come and go, sit and talk, smile and laugh. God threw a party and invited me.

252

And now it is coming to an end. The parade of relations is over, the sun is setting and the moon is rising right on cue. We retire to Mexican food at a local Mexican restaurant. The hostess takes one look at our gang and shunts us to a corner. Mother is getting cold and has been provided a jacket by an offspring. We march in and spread out over a long table.

Enchiladas, beer, margaritas, tamales, nachos, crisp and soft tortillas. We eat and drink and are merry. And down at the end of the table, at the *head* of the table—of course—is my mother. She is very tired. It's been an unexpectedly long weekend.

Finally it is all over—the meal is over, the weekend is over. There was a big crowd here when we first arrived, but they are all gone, every one. Either we took longer to eat than the rest, or ran them off.

The waiter comes with the check, looks around, and presents it to my mother. And why not? He has easily surveyed the situation: A long table full of sons and daughters, children and grandchildren, presided over by a happy 70-year-old, white-haired woman in a red-and-gold United States Marine Corps jacket.

KAKL News segues from Connie Cleavage to Mae West

THE TUBE—And now, hahaha, KAKL-TV, Channel Four in Houston, presents Four-Play News.

> *Hahaha!*
> *Four-Play News!*
> *Four-Play News!*
> *Blood and guts and sex and booze.*
> *Turn on the set,*
> *Turn off your brain!*
> *With teeth and hair,*
> *We make it plain*
> *On Four-Play Neeews!*
> *Hahaha!*

Now, to drop you into a safe harbor away from the storms of reality, here's everybody's favorite anchorman, Den-ny DEN-tures!

Thank you. Yes, it's time once again for more punchy comments, lots of jokes and happy talk, some irrelevant ingredients and—who knows?—maybe even some news. Speaking of cooking, what's on the front burner tonight, Consumer Affairs Reporter Connie Cleavage?

Thank you, Denny, particularly for just once introducing me as the consumer affairs reporter without some dumb joke about having affairs with consumers. If I hear that tired line once more . . .

Speaking of tired, Connie, how was your date last night? Got any instant replays? Hahaha.

Watch it, Buster. You're out of your league.

That reminds me, Connie, tonight we also have super fan Homer Fields, who gives us the day-by-day play-by-play. Right, Homer? Hahaha.

Right you are, Denny. Right off the bat, Astros' right-fielder Lefty Wright was caught sniffing the air over Beaumont. We'll have an interview with Lefty later in the show along with highlights of the Dan Pastorini Self-Destruction Derby.

"Derby" brings up the subject of hats, Homer. Among those who wear several hats is President Reagan, who today started some kind of war, I think. Maybe in Central America. We've got some film. And, while on the subject of film, what's developing in the weather picture? Here's our own high-pressure area, Rainer Shine.

Thanks, Denny. On Four-Play WeatherWatch tonight, I've got some great satellite shots of Argentina.

Uh, Rainer, what's that got to do with Houston?

Nothing, but the Four-Play WeatherWatch CloudCam is still broken. How long can I keep saying, "There's no clouds anywhere"? They send that dingbat Homer Fields to the winter Olympics, but they're too cheap to get the CloudCam fixed.

"Fix" brings to mind the Southwest Conference, eh, Homer?

Fix is right, Denny. Which is why I'm dressed up in a tomato suit tonight.

I was going to ask about that.

A rotten tomato to the Southwest Conference, Denny, for allowing coeds to go out before thousands of fans and parade around in those teeny-weeny majorette costumes. I wish they'd fix that because it's indecent. We'll have lots of film to show what I mean later on the show. God doesn't like sin. Abner McCall sits up there at Baylor and won't let *Playboy* in, but does he do anything about what's happening right out there on the 50 yard line?

Uh, Homer. Abner McCall has retired.

Who asked you, Connie? Go back to your Shake 'N Bake.

OK, Homer. You're gonna get . . .

Shake 'N Bake brings us to California, where later on the show tonight we'll have a report about an earthquake that seems to have devastated San Francisco. Or maybe it's Santa Clara. While on the subject of Santas, little Tommy Smedly is going to have an early Christmas this year because . . .

Uh, excuse me a moment, Denny.

Yes, Connie?

Well, I can't help but notice that tonight you are linking everything together. Like when Homer was talking about Dan Pastorini and you blended that into Central America. You somehow linked fixing a camera with the Southwest Conference.

You didn't see the memo, Connie?

What memo?

From the ratings consultant. He suggested that, besides lots of happy talk and meaningless chatter, we should easily slide from one subject to the next so it won't jolt the viewer. Hahaha. It's called *segue*. It's French and rhymes with me-too.

See-goo? Denny, you've got the brains of a retarded rock. It's pronounced saygway. From a West African word, Say-hay.

And speaking of West, Rainer, in West Virginia today a coal mine collapsed leaving 128 dead and . . .

See? There you go again. What the heck does an African dialect have to do with a coal mine?

Look, Rainer, we paid this consultant a grand a day for his advice, and the boss says we'd better use it.

A grand a day! And I can't even get the Four-Play CloudCam fixed for a lousy $34.76 plus labor.

Meanwhile, Labor Secretary Donovan declared that unemployment figures . . .

Come on, Denny. Good Lord.

Elsewhere in religious news, the Vatican today . . .

Denny, look, this is so stilted. I mean, one thing has nothing to do with the next. It's corny.

Corny? In Iowa, farmers are . . .

Denny, I've found it. Segue is pronounced seg-way. It comes from the Latin for . . .

Latin was spoken by the Romans, who also named the month of June. Which comes after May. In Hollywood, where Mae West once worked, Oscar nominees today . . .

> *Hahaha!*
> *Got the blues? What's to lose?*
> *Get some rest*
> *With Four-Play Neeews!*
> *Hahaha!*

Ghastly ghost

THE BED—Eh? What is that noise coming out of the pits of eternity? It is a short "woof." Then another, "woof." It is the family dog, waking me up so that I will let him outside. Why is he doing this to me in the early dawn? It's not even noon yet.

I stagger to the door and let the dog out, then grope my way to the kitchen, where the coffee pot is located. The coffee is cold, which means the coil is burned up. A glance out my rear window reveals that my garbage cans, all of them, have been turned over in the garage and their contents scattered all over the driveway and the yard. Since this very same scattering happened only the day before, I know whose dog it is. I shall buzz up the forthcoming next-of-kin and deliver my final warning. I lift the receiver from the phone's cradle and am greeted with a horrible noise, a piercing electronic scream. The phone is on the blink again.

I have been awake for four minutes and have already witnessed enough disasters for a week. This can only mean one thing. "All right," I yell. "Where are you?" Silence.

"Come out here this minute!" I yell. The only sound is the drip of a faucet accompanying the crash of a picture frame hitting the floor. Suddenly a gray figure appears in the air, sitting on the kitchen counter. It's him. My house ghost, Lawrence of Suburbia.

When things go wrong, when disaster hits, when the bells won't ring and the pongs won't ping and the warranty expires the day before, when the paint peels and the toaster blows in rapid succession, it always means the same thing. Lawrence is back in town.

He is sitting there smiling sheepishly, wearing his I-Brake-for-Chinch-Bugs button pinned to his Houston Apollos T-shirt. "I'm back," he says brightly.

A wave of depression hits me. I sink into a chair. "Why me, oh, Lord? Why me?"

"Just your lucky day," says Lawrence above the crack-boom-pop of the transformer blowing up on the utility pole outside.

"My wife's car is in the shop again," I say. "That's the second time in two weeks. The kids' Atari set is so screwed up that the gunfighter shoots himself. They just got it for Christmas."

"Have you paid for it yet?" he asks.

"Last week."

"Good. I hate to get ahead of myself."

"Why do you haunt me?" I say testily.

He shrugs. "Somebody's got to do it."

"The stereo is back in the shop for the third time. My wristwatch is back at the jeweler's. Fifth time. And look at the kitchen floor. Saltillo tile. Do you know how much that *cost*? And it looks terrible. I mean, it's awful."

"Say, I'm hungry. What's to eat?" says Lawrence. He jumps off the counter and opens the refrigerator as the light goes out. "Yeah, it's always good to be home. I've been busy, you know."

"Doing what?"

"I headed up the Carter re-election campaign. Then I went to work for Ted Kennedy."

"As a campaign adviser?"

"No. Marriage counselor."

"What else have you been up to?" I ask with little interest.

"Oh, just the usual. I was Alexander Haig's adviser on human rights. I handed out television cable franchises for Houston. And I was in charge of the new format for Channel 2 news."

"You fiend."

"It was the least I could do, after getting Dan Patrick for Channel 11. Oh, here's my latest. I'm particularly proud of these." He holds a bumper sticker reading: "Ban the Bum."

"Ha!" I shout. "You're too late, Lawrence. Bum Phillips has already left Houston. He's gone to New Orleans."

"Dummy," he says. "These are *for* New Orleans. I call them 'Bum-per kick-ers.' Cute, huh?"

"Go away, Lawrence."

"I appreciate the hospitality, but I've got to leave. Have to walk my pet termite. Then I'm holding speeding classes for gravel trucks. And I've got the litter distributorship for Telephone Road."

"Drop around again next decade. Or later."

"Oh, I'll be back before then. I'm in charge of the MTA Appreciation Dinner. I hate crowds."

Plain English?

"I would make boys all learn English; and then I would let the clever ones learn Latin as an honor and Greek as a treat. But the only thing I would whip them for is not knowing English. I would whip them hard for that."

So said Winston Churchill, who was rather well known for his mastery of the English language and thus had an inside track. But he may have been a bit unfair, for of all languages around, certainly English is one of the hardest to learn.

Its grammar has been slapped together like reports from a legislative committee. Take, for instance, the ever-deadly split infinitive. H. W. Fowler, in his *Modern English Usage*, says: "The English-speaking world may be divided into (1) those who neither know nor care what a split infinitive is; (2) those who do not know, but care very much; (3) those who know and condemn; (4) those who know and approve; and (5) those who know and distinguish."

Those in the last category walk around saying "really to understand" rather than "to really understand" which is what most people would really understand. There are even those who furiously read newspapers and magazines in the hope they will find split infinitives and thus can dash off a letter to the culprits. A friend of mine received such an epistle and wrote back, "I promise to never do it again."

You also know about never ending a sentence with a preposition, of course. Never say: "What did you hit him with?" Not only might such a question be unhealthy, it would also be ungrammatical. As with split infinitives, there are those who get their jollies by running around catching prepositional endings.

No doubt you have heard the story of Churchill (again) spotting a note from an official of the Exchequer ordering his staff to stop ending sentences with prepositions. In the margin, Churchill wrote: "This is the type of arrant pedantry up with which I will not put." If you spot someone of this ilk, ask him: "What did you bring that book I do not wish to be read to out of up for?" Those five prepositions at the tail will drive him the wall to.

Then there is spelling. A terrible mess, to be sure. Is it axe or ax? Employee or employe? When is it capitol and when is it capital? How about when polish starts the sentence and suddenly becomes Polish right before your eyes? Threw and through, not to mention to and two, too.

When we need a word but don't have it, we steal. Thus we have flak (from the German Fliegerabwehrkanonen, of course), amok (Malay), kowtow (Mandarin Chinese), bayou (French) and troika (Russian). Sometimes, we just make them up: smog, superstar, freeway, rock (as in rock and roll), radar (like flak, it's an acronym for Radio Detecting And Ranging) and McCarthyism.

We have at least three from the Vietnam war—hooch, grunt and R&R—which are now in popular usage. Even our newly-found good friends, the Russians, are helping out. One of the departments of the First Chief Directorate of the KGB is the Disinformation Department. Its job is to put out slightly altered truths, half-truths or outright lies so as to confuse the opposition.

We have no such word as "disinformation" but it makes sense. If the First Chief Directorate isn't careful about security, we may just nip off with his word.

Of all the problems besetting us poor users of the King's English, prefixes and suffixes are among·the worst, tying with "to really understand" and "Polish." Inflammable and flammable mean the same thing, for some totally ridiculous reason. And if it is priceless, that should mean that it has no price whatsoever. But is it invaluable—without any value, either?

If you are bejeweled you are loaded down with jewels (and probably with debts, too) just as if you are bewitched you are loaded down with witchcraft. Ah, but if you are beheaded, you are just the opposite. You are unloaded. Therefore, you should be disheaded—you once had a head but do not have one anymore.

You can be uncouth, but can you be couth? If you are ruthless, can you be ruth? How about a couth ruth?

It may be an illicit deal, but if it isn't, can it be a licit transaction? If you are a judge, should you be uninterested or disinterested?

Discuss. Now there's one for you. Is the subject under discussion one without cuss? Or did it once have cuss and lost it (see: Disheaded)? How about uncontented as opposed to noncontented? Or even miscontented. Alas, we are none of the above, but are malcontented, which is much the same as discontented. If this doesn't make any sense, go ask Winston Churchill, then stand by for the beating of your life.

All of this may get you down a bit, so take heart in remembering that when the signers of the Declaration of Independence got together, we had probably the greatest gathering of minds at one time and one place in the western world. And they came up with "certain unalienable rights." The word is "inalienable" but who—on July 4th, 1776—was going to point out that they were violating the King's English?

Auto harping

THE FREEWAY—Stuck here, as usual. A long line of cars is ahead. In my rear-view mirror is the reflection of hundreds more. Squeezing me from both sides are others. On the radio is the news: Douglas Fraser of the United Auto Workers warns that Chrysler is about to collapse unless the federal government guarantees yet another loan, this one for $400 million. He explains that foreign competition is cutting the wheels out from under Detroit. So Chrysler gets the loan.

Now, I am sorry for the stockholders of Chrysler. I am even sorrier for the workers. The dealers, too. And their families and their customers and pets and potted plants. But I not sorry for the past Chrysler leadership, and I am not sorry for the U.S. auto business as a whole.

America had a virtual monopoly on automaking for decades—no, generations. If it moved with a motor, there was a good chance that it was built in Detroit. I remember seeing those old World War II films of wartime Tokyo, with Tojo riding in a Packard. So it was not a case of the U.S. standing at the bottom. We had the lead, and we let it slip away.

What went wrong? The energy crunch, I suppose, and higher interest rates and on and on, but it is not accurate to blame federal regulations for the problem, no matter how much we might like to make Washington the whipping boy. There is nothing wrong with getting Pintos off the streets if they explode when hit from behind. There is no fault in keeping our air fit to breathe by adding pollution equipment. And, tick off all the regulations and restrictions you wish, after all is said and done, other car manufacturers can meet these same requirements and still produce cars, and we can't. You ever go by the Port of Houston and see all those thousands of cars being off-loaded? Some businessman in Hamburg or Osaka can build a car, ship it halfway around the world, and still outsell a U.S.-made automobile.

U.S. auto management must take the blame for blinding itself to all warnings, to bankrupting multimillion-dollar firms. And the workers and their unions, who have priced themselves out of the international market while slapping together what is generally regarded these days as an inferior product, are not faultless.

Americans are car-crazy. We will spend far more than we should on cars. It doesn't take much to convince an American he needs a car. Nor, for years, did it take much to convince the rest of the world that they needed American cars. Yet by the millions we have switched. In front of me on the freeway is a Mazda. Beside me is a Toyota. And I am driving my '72 VW Beetle. I don't know about the others, but I suppose my case is typical enough. Back in '68 I needed a car and wanted something that got good gas mileage, even at those cheap rates. I wanted an American-made car but Detroit simply didn't build any small cars. So I bought the next best thing: an Opel. Built in Germany, but owned, sold and serviced by GM. An Opel.

I bought the car brand new and took exceedingly good care of it, and it was a piece of junk. After only about 35,000 miles I had to get rid of my Opel. Again I looked around for a small, cheap U.S. car. And, again, there wasn't one. So in '72 I bought this VW. It now has 72,937 miles and is still working like a Swiss watch. In that same time, my wife has gone through three or four products from Detroit. There is a lesson in there somewhere.

If Detroit has lost part of the U.S. market, it has totally surrendered abroad. In my assorted travels in other countries, spotting a Detroit-made car is like spotting an oxcart on Fannin. In Costa Rica, for example, the government decided that gasoline powered only cars while diesel powered farm tractors and trucks, more vital to the well-being of the nation. So a higher tax was levied on gasoline. Today it seems everyone in Costa Rica has switched to diesel-powered Toyota four-wheel-drive vehicles.

After the British occupation of Indonesia following World War II, all the traffic started driving on the left. But U.S.-made cars had their steering wheels on the wrong side and Detroit wasn't interested in whipping up any special orders. Along came the Japanese automakers. They'd sell cars with the steering wheels in the trunk, if that's what the customer wanted. As a result, today Japan has a death lock on Indonesian traffic. I dare say you could find similar stories in much of the world.

But here comes the kicker to all of this. Detroit cannot compete in its own back yard, so how does it fight back? By building a better mousetrap? By offering quality products at reasonable prices? By rolling up sleeves and, in the best tradition of the free enterprise system, giving this vast and waiting public what it wants? Not at all. The American automakers are competing by trying to get the U.S. government to limit foreign car imports. Fantastic. Why should I have to pay for Detroit's short-sightedness, even stupidity? If I want a well-made, inexpensive car, and my own carmakers can't or won't produce one, why should I be forced to buy it?

I am all for buying American, but I really can't see why—if a product gets too good and has too many customers—it should be excluded by law. I cannot see why I should have to pay more for a shoddily built product. Nor is it clear why I should have to suffer because overpaid executives in Detroit have mismanaged their companies and run them into the ground, then, while preaching free enterprise, race to the government to bail them out. As John Kennedy said about party loyalty, sometimes national loyalty demands too much.

Comic opera

Act I opens with Clemento sitting at his desk, counting his gold coins. He walks to the window and looks outside to see the jobless peasants hanging around the castle wall, and sings the joyful *Mia Sedco Bon Appetito*. Suddenly, in walks his heir apparent, Stracheotomy, who announces his intention of doing battle for the cause, singing *Gopo-Hopo*.

Clemento asks the musical question, *Que Lira por Theia and Mia?* Stracheotomy responds that there are plenty of campaign funds in the countryside if only they will join forces in raising them from the other nobles. Together they sing the touching duet, *Fatta Catta of That Strata*. Stracheotomy rushes out to do battle as Clemento ponders the future. He notes that he is a self-made king, having worked his way up to the top from his humble beginnings as the son of an oil baron, with his lament, *La Dia Mio Padre Oblagato Dismizzo l'Torpedo* (The Day My Father Had To Lay Off the Bodyguard).

At this point Stracheotomy rushes back in to say that when he was a boy, they lived on a farm that was so poor they couldn't raise their voices. "My room was so small, I had to go into the hall to change my mind," he sings. Clemento sings his warning that any more Henny Youngman jokes and it's no more truffles with the wine.

Together, they boldly proclaim their fear of losing, not only the election but their respective fortunes, in *Povertia Non por Mia*.

As the curtain descends on Act I, Clemento is left alone again to worry about his hold on the kingdom. Doubts set in and he asks, "Am I losing my grip?" (*"Que digitis arthritis?"*) He considers climbing to the top of his tax shelter and throwing himself out a loophole. He moans that there are rumors of another who seeks the leadership position. Some of the peasants have even been seen with "Clemento Finimento" bumper stickers on their ox carts. However, he reassures himself that the peasants still love him and are his best hope for a brighter tomorrow, singing, *Pesante, Honesto Manana* (Peons, the True Horizons)..

Act II opens with Clemento celebrating his certain re-election as king by partying with a group of Gopo friends at the Cafe Petro. The group sings the rousing march, *Tip-Toe della Condo* (Walk Softly and Carry a Country Club).

Suddenly, into the cafe walks an ambitious young lawyer and leader of the peasants, Marco Blanco. He announces to everyone that he will oust Clemento as king and take over in the name of all that is good, pure, beautiful and politically expedient. Clemento and his friends laugh mightily at the upstart Blanco, who responds with his aria, *Entra Audia, Bustante* (In Your Ear, Buster).

Clemento goes for Blanco but they are separated by Maria Como-d'America-Pascalli-Rizutto, chairperson of the League d'Votres Feminia, who suggests that both men put their case before the people with a duel—mudslinging at 20 paces. The two agree and leave, as Maria sings the haunting, *Que Era, Era?*

Seeking advice on how to woo the peasants, Blanco goes to another leader of the party, Guglielmo Posto, who explains that to run a race throughout the kingdom takes a huge amount of money. Blanco asks innocently if that doesn't mean only the rich can run for office. Posto replies with the most popular of all songs in the opera, *Maestro Vox Populi* (If You Want to Conduct Public Business, You've Got To Own an Orchestra).

Act III begins with the members of Gopo slyly telling the peasants that Blanco has a criminal record: 19 years earlier he had been arrested for riding while drinking. Also, they hint that he is tied to the criminal element in the countryside, singing, *Vino Gallo cum Carlos Marcello*.

Blanco angrily accuses Gopo of dirty politics and declares that he sticks to the issues of the campaign, such as Clemento's insensitivity, arrogance and ineptitude. He vows that he will win the duel because he is just a good ol' country boy and a man of the people. Blanco issues his statement simultaneously through 23 campaign headquarters, 12 TV commercials and 1,289 billboards, costing $3.4 million.

Dawn and time for the duel. Clemento's two seconds, Jacuzzi and Ferrari, remind Blanco that it is a fight to the finish. The referess, Maria Como-d'America-Pascalli-Rizutto, warns everyone that there are limits to the duel. Satire, misstatements of fact and outright lies are allowed, but, she sings, *Non Innuendo d'Homo*. Blanco says he would never do such a thing, but does charge that Clemento has the morals of a sewer rat.

With that, the duel begins. Clemento slings a quick string of accusations about Blanco's legal background with the highly hilarious *Scenario d'Chasseur d'Ambulance*. Blanco strikes back with his witty rhetorical question as to why Clemento put off building new dungeons until forced to do so by the courts (*Melody d'Felony*).

The two go at it and mud flies everywhere. The curtain goes down with the entire chorus of peasants and members of Gopo singing their poignant wail, *Este della Pits* (Out of 15 Million People in the Kingdom, Is This the Best We Can Do?).

Throwing the Book at them

This being Sunday, it is time to turn our thoughts to religion, which, in turn, brings us to Gus Mutscher's quote of the week: "God knows I am innocent."

Unfortunately, the jury roster for Taylor County is not that extensive, and a panel of mere mortals found him, State Rep. Tommy Shannon and aide S. Rush McGinty guilty of conspiring to render unto themselves what is Caesar's. Even so, Gus had a Biblical verse for the occasion, saying: "Matthew 5:44." (Pray for them which despitefully use you and persecute you.)

The jury, made up of current and former Sunday school teachers, fired back: "Exodus 21:24!" (Eye for eye, tooth for tooth, hand for hand, foot for foot.)

Now it is a lucky thing that the jurors softened later on, because if they had followed this eye-for-eye philosophy, they would have billed the defendants for the cost of their case, which dwarfs their bill from the FDIC. Luckily, you and I get to pick up the tab, which seems the least we can do.

Down, but not out, the defense said it was impossible to get a fair trial, declaring: "Joshua 6:27." (His fame was noised throughout all the country.)

The judge, however, thought differently: "Abilene is Exodus 3:8." (A land flowing with milk and honey.) "Ha," retorteth the defense, "it's more like Second Kings 18:32." (A land of corn and wine.) In any event, they finally got down to the case at hand. "Psalms 51:7," Gus whispered to his attorneys. (Wash me, and I shall be whiter than snow.)

"Proverbs 11:14," they replied confidently. (In the multitude of counselors there is safety.) The state opened up with its attack. "Sharp and Gus got along famously, and don't forget Amos 3:3." (Can two walk together, except they be agreed?) "Not to mention Proverbs 22:7." (The borrower is servant to the lender.)

Thus warmed up, the state bore in with Proverbs 28:20. (He that maketh haste to be rich shall not be innocent.)

That, as you can well imagine, set the courtroom to buzzing. Frank Sharp then took the stand to say quietly: "Proverbs 19:4." (Wealth maketh many friends.) And, of course, "Psalms 39:6." (He heapeth up riches, and knoweth not who shall gather them.)

"Get down to the nitty-gritty, Mr. Sharp," the state stormed.

"Genesis 13:8," he protested. (Let there be no strife, I pray thee, between me and thee.)

"Then what about the defendant?"

"Ah, yes, Mr. Mutscher. First Samuel 13:14." (A man after his own heart.) "But as I always told him, 'Gus, Proverbs 22:1.'" (A good name is rather to be chosen than great riches.) "And he would say, 'Mr. Sharp, Isaiah 1:18.'" (Come now, and let us reason together.) "But, I suppose, Matthew 7:8." (Every one that asketh receiveth; and he that seeketh findeth.)

"I see, and what happened then?"

"Well, I tried to stall him off, but he kept after me. He wanted this and that, I suppose Matthew 26:41." (The spirit indeed is willing, but the flesh is weak.)

"Thank you, Mr. Sharp, for your testimony. You have shown this court that First Timothy 6:10." (The love of money is the root of all evil.)

"I just try to do my civic duty. Do my part to build a better America. Oh, please don't forget my Matthew 26:15." (Thirty pieces of silver.)

"So, ladies and gentlemen of the jury, you can plainly see that John 8:32." (The truth shall make you free.)

"Ha," snorted the defense. "John 8:44." (There is no truth in him.) The defense sprang forward and hammered away with its own volley of verses. "John 7:24," one lawyer shouted, and the jury nodded in agreement. (Judge not according to the appearance.) "And, lest we forget, our client was a leader of men, a statesman in the purest sense. Indeed, John 5:35." (He was a burning and a shining light.)

The jury began to waver, it was clear that the state's case was in trouble. A defense attorney, with a jaundiced glance at the press table, slammed down his fist on the desk and proclaimed: "First Corinthians 15:33!" (Evil communications corrupt good manners.)

And that was that. The judge solomonly peered at the jury and advised them, "Galatians 6:7." (Whatsoever a man soweth, that shall he also reap.) "And, of course, First Timothy 1:8." (The law is good, if a man use it lawfully.) Then the panel disappeared behind locked doors to mull it all over.

"Second Samuel 1:25," sighed a reporter. (How the mighty have fallen.)

"Proverbs 7:22," nodded another in agreement. (As an ox goeth to the slaughter.)

As the hours wore on, the defendants grew restless. "Matthew 24:6," cried one of the three. (The end is not yet.)

"First Kings 18:21," shouted another toward the jury room. (How long halt yet between two opinions?)

"Now, now," said one of the defense attorneys. "Everything is going to be fine. Isaiah 1:18." (Though your sins be as scarlet, they shall be white as snow.)

It was at this moment that the jury room door swung open and the jurors filed back into their seats. "Luke 15:23," intoned the jury foreman. (Bring hither the fatted calf.)

"It looks bad," the defendants said to one another.

"What says the jury?" asked the judge.

"We say Daniel 5:27," thundered the foreman. (Thou art weighed in the balance and art found wanting.)

"Genesis 4:13," sighed one defendant. (My punishment is greater than I can bear.)

"What should I do?" he asked of his lawyer.

"Isaiah 26:20," he advised. (Hide thyself as it were a little moment, until the indignation be overpast.) Then, turning to the reporters, the lawyer fairly shouted: "Isaiah 53:7!" (He is brought as a lamb to the slaughter.) "But Second Samuel 1:20, if you please," he begged. (Tell it not in Gath, publish it not in the streets of Askelon.)

And that was the way it ended. However, the trial seems to have started something, as evident by these reactions sampled around the state:

"Job 19:20." (I am escaped with the skin of my teeth.)—Gov. Preston Smith.

"Psalms 75:6." (Promotion cometh neither from the east, nor from the west, nor from the south.)—Lt. Gov. Ben Barnes.

"Proverbs 22:28." (Remove not the ancient landmark.)—State Rep. Bill Heatly.

And finally, from a majority of the citizenry: "Isaiah 38:1." (Set thine house in order.)

Got a second?

Today we pay homage to all of those who never quite made it—like living at Number 9 Downing Street, or writing a book called "Gone With The Breeze."

Yes, for every winner there is a runner-up, someone or something which tried just as hard, but—because of a twist of fate or last-minute stumble—was robbed of the fame and fortune which went to the winner.

For instance, all the world watched as Neil Armstrong became the first man to step on the moon. His name shall live so long as men raise their glasses of Tang and deliver toasts in German. But what about the second man on the moon? How many people remember, even today, just a few short moments in history after it happened? Quick: Who was he? Edwin E. "Buzz" Aldrin. Throughout history, poor Aldrin will be brushed aside, simply because his one great step for mankind was the second step for man. So let's try to brush the cobwebs off these fine people who justly deserve our praise.

Every Texas student knows that Sam Houston was our first nationally elected president, but who was the second? (Stop at this point and write it down, before you get to the answer. No cheating.) OK, the second president of Texas was Mirabeau B. Lamar.

Speaking of presidents, George Washington was unanimously elected first president of the U.S. with 69 votes from the electors. But each elector had two votes—the runner-up would be vice president. Who came in second to Washington? John Adams, with 34 votes. Today no one goes around saying: "Adams—second in war, second in peace and second in the hearts of his countrymen."

Let's try sports.

Roger Maris hit 61 home runs in '61 and thus can claim being the home run king, although there shall always be an asterisk by his name because Maris played in more games for his record-breaking season than did the fellow whose record he broke. Who is now Number Two? An easy one. Babe Ruth, of course. But now we get down to the hard stuff. Ruth hit his 60 home runs in 1927, but who came in second that year? It was a tie between Frederick Williams of the Phillies and Lewis Wilson of the Cubs. They both hit 30 home runs, making '27 a very good year, except no one remembers it because Ruth's year was even better.

In the population category, what's the second largest city in the second largest state? Buffalo, New York. Now let's get a bit tougher. What's the second largest city (population) in the second largest state (area)? Dallas.

Quick. Who finished second in the Franco-Prussian War? Franco. But who was the runner-up in the French and Indian War? A tie between the French and the Indians.

Maybe business is your thing. According to *Fortune* magazine, General Motors is the largest corporation in the U.S., ranked by sales. Who is second to GM? Exxon, which, while only Number Two, still seems to be turning a buck.

What's the second biggest bank in Houston? Texas Bank of Commerce. But what's the second biggest in Texas? Republic National Bank of Dallas. On the other hand, the second biggest savings and loan association in Houston is Houston First Savings, which makes no sense whatsoever unless you consider that it couldn't be called Houston Second Savings.

Yes, the seconds, how they fly. KDKA in Pittsburgh was the second commercial radio station on the air: Nov. 2, 1920, following 8MK (now WWJ) in Detroit. Pecos is the second largest county in Texas, and this is completely overlooked by those who like to point out that the biggest county, Brewster, is the same size as Connecticut and Rhode Island. Harvard goes around noting that it's our first college, and poor William & Mary gets overlooked, even though it was actually mapped out 17 years before Harvard opened its doors. Nobody loves a runner-up.

Then there's Frank Luke. He shot down 18 airplanes and balloons in World War I, but Eddie Rickenbacker shot down 26 (22 planes, four balloons), so today no one remembers Frank Luke. Every history buff knows that the first atomic bomb used in warfare was dropped on Hiroshima from a B-29 called the Enola Gay. But what was the name of the plane which dropped the second bomb—the one on Nagasaki? No one knows. It was a modified B-29 called Bock's Car, piloted by Major Charles Sweeney.

But perhaps the most overlooked second place in history came at 8:46 a.m. on Saturday, May 21, 1932, at Londonderry, Ireland. See, you've already forgotten. That was when Amelia Earhart Putnam arrived after covering 2,026 miles in 14 hours and 56 minutes. Many had tried to be Numero Dos, and all had failed; most perished in the effort. We don't remember poor Amelia's successful effort. All we remember is that five years earlier, to the day, Charles Lindbergh was first.

Pot to spit in

THE PARKING LOT—"OK, back it up till you hear a crunch," says this voice from behind.

Eh? That seems a strange command.

"You want some new wheel covers? Well, almost new."

Very strange indeed. I turn to see who's doing the talking. Gad. Now I understand, it's Rep. Shady. "Why aren't you in Austin, looking after my welfare?" I demand.

He saunters over, hand outstretched. "I gotta work sometimes. Man does not live by lobbyist alone. That'll be two bucks in advance. For another buck I'll make sure Skylab doesn't hit it."

"Rep. Shady," I say. "You are a sleazy, unprincipled political hack."

"Somebody's got to do it," he says. "Besides, I've been working hard up in Austin."

"On what?"

"House Bill 852, that's what."

"OK, I give up," I say. "What's House Bill 852?"

"Probably the most important issue now before Texas government. Outside of finding more hangar space for Bob Bullock's air force, of course."

"All right! What is it?"

"House bill 852."

"You said that, Rep. Shady. What is House Bill 852? Does it stop the flow of illegal aliens into Texas? Solve the school tax crisis? Annex Louisiana?"

"None of the above," says Rep. Shady. "Not even close. I'll give you a hint. It has to do with transportation."

"OK," I say. "That's an easy one. House Bill 852 solves the energy crisis."

"Nope."

"Repeals the 55 mile an hour speed limit."

"Nope."

"Ah, it deals with Houston. It requires that the MTA buy buses large enough to push the cars of MTA officials."

Shady sighs. "You really are out of touch with the important matters before your legislature, aren't you?"

"I give up."

"House Bill 852 repeals the law requiring cuspidors in railway stations and on passenger trains."

"It *what?*"

"You heard me. It would repeal Rule 60, Article 4477 of the Revised Civil Statutes of Texas, 1925."

"Rep. Shady, I think you're putting me on."

He wanders over to a white and gold Continental. "Remember when all the doctors used to have a caduceus on their license plates?"

"I said I think you're putting me on. With all the important matters of state facing the legislature . . ."

"This is important. As a matter of fact, it's an emergency. When Rep. Bennie Bock II of New Braunfels filed the bill, he asked that it be treated as an emergency. Here, I've got a copy. It says: 'The importance of this legislation and the crowded condition of the calendars in both houses create an emergency and an imperative public necessity that the constitutional rule requiring . . .' "

"Shady, is Austin in the real world?"

" . . . requiring bills to be read on three several days in each house be suspended, etc. etc."

"Cuspidors are an emergency?"

"They are if you've got a mouth full of Red Man and there's not one around."

"I didn't know we had a law requiring cuspidors."

"Why not? It fits right in with all the others. Our state constitution allows the governor to call out the militia to protect the frontier from hostile Indians, and lets the legislature grant aid to disabled Confederate sailors."

"I see your point."

"Yep, now we won't even have a pot to spit in."

"What's the chance of the bill passing?"

"Not good. The cuspidor lobby is opposing it. Clements says he'll veto the bill if it does pass, because it's anti-business. The mop lobby likes it, but the train lobby is supporting House Speaker Clayton's bid for the governorship, which is tied to the building bloc's opposition to the oil and gas industry's bid for state education grants to support school decals from a participating dealer."

"And what do the people think?"

Rep. Shady looks puzzled. "The people? I dunno. No one has asked them. It's not an election year, y'know."

All quiet

THE HOME—There are many kinds of silences around. There is the brief moment of quiet when a car pulls into the drive way and, after hours of purring and puffing on the highway, a slight turn of the key brings the motor to a halt. There is the silence of a house after the door slams and the last guest has left a busy party. Between the chatter and music, and before the clatter of dirty dishes in the sink, there is that silence.

There is the quiet of a neighborhood at dawn, when a sole figure lurches out of the front door to pick up the morning newspaper, and pauses briefly to take in the total lack of noise in a usually noisy block. And there is the beautiful silence of a room when the television set is turned off in the midst of a used-car commercial. These are happy silences. Short slivers of solitude sandwiched.in between past and future periods of noise, and thus a quick refuge among the decibels.

But there is another kind of silence which is unwelcomed, which begins as a good thing and quickly turns into a growing monster, banging at the gates with muffled paws, and all the blaring radios in the castle cannot turn him away. It is the silence of absence. The quiet which seeps in because there is no parade of happy, familiar noises to keep it back. It is a home which has turned into only a house because the family has fled.

Every husband and father knows what I'm talking about. It is the period, usually in the summer, when the wife and children take off to visit grandmother or go to the beach or see friends in other cities. It takes weeks of planning and packing—the Normandy Invasion was less complicated. Then come the last frantic days of shopping (why is it that food bills skyrocket when the food is consumed in someone else's kitchen?) and doctor's appointments and car checkups and maps and sunglasses. Then the hour of departure—already eons behind schedule—comes in a final frenzy of chaos. Dogs, kids, lost shoes and strange pings under the hood.

Ah, then the pack is off, and no more welcome scene is there than that of the father waving to the overloaded station wagon waddling out the driveway and down the street. A burden is lifted. A cause is won. They're off, and an audible sigh can be heard throughout the block. The father trudges back to the house and is greeted by two sensations: absolute ruination of his once-neat home, and total silence.

But this is the welcome kind of quietness. The hurricane has passed and the calm after the storm is a good friend and true. At this point, the father and husband welcomes it. No crying, no dogs barking, no deluge of music pouring out of some transistor, no doors slamming and high-pitched, "Where's my sock?" The lack of dadgummits, dishwashers and decibels is solace to the weary. And the sole survivor is content.

But it is later, when he returns home in the evening from work, that it starts getting to him. Again, in the first few days it is welcomed. A slow, easy entrance, a drink or cold beer, a flop onto the couch and a few minutes to contemplate the day. A good time is had by all. But as the days go by, the returning king finds that he rambles around the castle deliberately humming, talking to himself, turning the stereo up just a bit louder, for the monster—the silence of absence—is crossing the moat. He does not admit it. He does not peer over the ramparts. But back there in the closets of his mind, he knows.

Some fathers go out to the movies. Some hit a restaurant. Some prowl Montrose or Dowling. Some do almost anything on the boys' night out, but there is still that moment when he must return. And no matter the hour, the quietness is there to greet him. Once again the battle is joined, as TV sets and radios and humming are poured into the fray. Then, at last, comes the final end of the day, when the house is dark and silent. Padding up and down the halls is a lonely, depressing job. There are no coughs, no snores, no rustle of covers from the rooms, no last wheeze of the dishwasher, no late calls about car pools and tennis.

My mother tells me that the worst part of her day used to be returning to the home once filled with a husband, four kids and two dogs, and making the daily discovery that she was there all alone. It happens to us all eventually, but the abrupt, overnight change from chaos to quietness is a heavy burden. If silence is golden, then the king in his castle is Midas, doomed by too much of a good thing.

Their final hour

AUSTIN—(If you already know how this all came out, keep it to yourself. In any event, no one will be admitted during the last two paragraphs.)

These are the last hours of the Texas Constitutional Convention—a gathering that asks the question: Where are you, Santa Anna, when we really need you? It has taken Texas 100 years and $4 million to get this far, but now the convention is bogged down and uptight over a number of relatively insignificant items, chiefly the "right-to-work" article.

"I believe we'll have to hold our nose and vote aye," says Rep. Joe Hubenak of Rosenberg, looking up at the clock. It is now 9:30, and Price Daniel Jr., president of the convention, has only until midnight to reach that magical number for approval of the charter—121 ayes. In the aisle, Mickey Leland and Walter Mengden, who are poles apart on political philosophy, discuss the latest proposal, Resolution 32. Neither persuades the other.

Daniel calls for a vote. A wild clamor to get to the voting buttons. The lights flash and the total pops up, like cherries on a slot machine. It is 112 to 66, a new high for approval.

"Lordy, nine more votes is all they need," says one of the 66.

Then Billy Williamson of Tyler votes aye, a major breakthrough from the right. Cheers from the 112 who are now 113. Only eight more are needed for passage. But eight is as good as a mile, and Resolution 32 fails. Bang! The gavel slams down.

Now the real work starts in little huddles on the floor, in the delegates' lounge, in the john. Backs are scratched, logs are rolled, deals are made among strange bedfellows. Four Houston Republicans, who have finally decided to back the charter, huddle together for self-protection. One has already received a call from a GOP biggie.

Ben Reyes of Houston shakes his head: "I spent last weekend talking to my constituents. They don't like the constitution." He'll vote against it.

"Are they pressuring you?" One delegate asks another.

"Only with my life," the other replies.

The clock on the chamber wall continues to move, and by now the gallery is packed. SRO. Reporters shuttle from the floor back to the teletypes, filing new stories. Sen. Bill Moore of Bryan explains his political philosophy in opposing the constitution: "I don't like Price Daniel."

Now it is 11:05 and Daniel is back on the podium, smiling slightly. "He's got the votes. You can tell. He's got the votes."

"Mr. Gammage has a motion," says Daniel, and the crowd is clearly startled. Gammage, a senator from Houston, has been an adamant opponent of any charter with a "right-to-work" clause. Now he bites the ·bullet.

Sen. Oscar Mauzy of Dallas speaks: "Some people are letting their ambitions get in the way of their principles." A few boos. "Now it is 11:09," Mauzy says, "And in 51 minutes we'll all turn into pumpkins, and there are those who say that wouldn't be so bad." He goes on to suggest that since politicians can't write a new constitution, it is time for the people to try. The gallery erupts in wild applause, and the delegates look disturbed.

It is 11:12 and there is a motion to reconsider Resolution 32. It fails to pass 120 to 59. Close but still no cigar.

"The chair recognizes Mr. Parker." Wild cheers from the 120. Carl Parker of Port Arthur, a chief contender for the speakership, begins to explain why he has decided to switch his vote. He chokes up.

"That's it," whispers a delegate. "That's 121."

A Parker supporter rises and waves good-by. "One of my former pledges has just left me," says Parker.

"You got some more," shouts a delegate.

"For those of you who think I've traded my vote for the speaker's chair," Parker says, almost in tears, then he stops, swallows, and says: "You can go to hell."

Now it is 11:25 and Ron Waters of Houston stands to say that he can understand a man changing his mind, even going back on his pledge, but he won't. "Let's vote and go home."

Gene Jones of Houston has strong labor support. He rises to speak for the charter. He sits down with shaky labor support for the future. Now it is 11:35 and Resolution 32 is up for adoption. The delegates rush once more to their buttons. The lights flash. "They got it now, they've got it," says a reporter. But the totals come to only 116 and 63. "Mr. Doran changes his vote," says Daniel, and cheers go up. That makes it 117 very strange bedfellows.

But now tempers are running high and time is running out. Doran can't change his vote under the rules, some are charging. Daniel says he can. "Mr. President," shouts an angry delegate into the microphone, "you are a liar!" A split second of stunned silence on the floor, then a chorus of boos. in the heat of battle, you never lose your cool.

"Mr. Williamson changes his vote." Now it is 118.

"This is unheard of in the annals of democracy," shouts a delegate.

"Does that mean you're a Republican?" asks another.

It is now 11:47. Shouts come down from the gallery. Price Daniel chews mints. No, he gulps mints. The delegates are surging toward the podium now, shouting and shoving. "I thought the Sharpstown fight was mean, but this . . ." The delegate does not finish.

"Is there a doctor in the house?" Daniel asks. Sen. "Doc" Blanchard, who has already suffered one heart attack, has been taken to the lounge. It is 11:50. Another delegate who had undergone open heart surgery is taken out. Now it is 11:53 and Daniel takes a slow drink of water, since there is no hemlock at the podium.

The TV cameras have opened up a barrage, the gallery is standing, and if there was a band on hand, it would be playing "Deguello." Where are the votes? Those three more votes? Are they coming? Daniel slams down his gavel at 11:59. "There being 118 ayes and 62 nos, Resolution 32 fails of adoption."

It is midnight.

Nothing but a beer joint

AUSTIN – "All right, little family," I say, guiding my flock along, "now you are in for a real thrill."

"I'm all touristed out," sighs my eldest.

Gad, the little creeps, they fail to appreciate true culture. All they do is gripe. Here we are in Austin, where I have brought them for a tour of the sights and perhaps to point them toward truth, beauty and an appointment to The University of Texas, but I'm not making much progress.

At the UT campus, they kept asking if that was the Charles Whitman Tower. At the LBJ Library, they wanted to know why there was practically no mention of the Vietnam War. At the Capitol, they just wanted to climb to the top of the top level in the Rotunda. So in desperation, I have brought them here. My ultimate weapon.

"What's this place, Daddy?"

"This is a Texas landmark, known to thousands of legislators and students alike as the true fount of inspiration and wisdom in the Southwest. It's called Scholz Garten."

"Daddy, this is nothing but a beer joint. Let's go."

"Swine before Pearl. Or Coors," I say, herding my reluctant mob to a back table. "This humble barn happens to be fraught with history. There's even a Texas Historical plaque outside on the wall. And rightly so, because in this tavern more Texas legislation has been written, or killed, than in all the mighty halls of the Capitol. And more UT students have learned more about life in Scholz's than in all the classrooms on the Forty Acres."

"It's a dump," says one.

"You people got no class," I snort. "Waitress, a pitcher of dark for us, and some Cokes for these wretched little Munchkins. Now, family, you must have full appreciation for this place for two reasons. First and foremost, this is where I courted your mother."

"You didn't!"

"I did," I say. My wife nods in reluctant agreement.

"Why?"

"Two reasons. Scholz's was cheap and I was broke."

"Some things never change," says one, wandering off to look at the jukebox.

"After Russian class we would come here, particularly on Saturdays. You'd be surprised how German beer can help Russian participles. I guess half the class would come. We'd drink and talk and have a marvelous time. We'd have the only table in the back garten that could tell dirty jokes in Russian."

"Big deal."

"Do not make light of my past," I say testily. "Without it, you'd have no present."

"That's very profound, Daddy. Let's go."

"Eat tacks, buster."

"Daddy, did you propose to Mommy here, in Russian?"

"I don't remember. You'd have to go outside and read the historical marker for the details."

"You said there were two reasons we should revere Scholz's. What's the other reason? Did you flunk out here, too?"

"Sharper than a serpent's tooth. No, I did not flunk out here. The other reason hangs in that back dining hall. Go look at it."

Sighing and moaning, the crowd dutifully files to the back room, only to reappear shortly.

"They've got a picture like we've got. The one hanging in the back bathroom."

"That's because we've only got one mantel," I say. "That picture is The University's football team of '07."

"What position did you play?"

"Don't get wise, I wasn't here in '07, but your great-grand-uncle was. Worth Jones. He's the one right in the center. Middle of the middle row. He's my grandmother's brother."

"Did your grandmother go to UT, too?"

"No, there were six children in the family. Their father, Enoch Oscar Jones, had a ranch in East Texas. The Circle Y. On a cattle drive to market in Kansas, as Enoch Oscar and his cowboys were going through the Indian Territory—which is Oklahoma today—the Indians stampeded the herd during a rainstorm, stole the cattle, and there went the family fortune. So the three oldest children couldn't go to college."

"Is that why you like to beat Oklahoma, Daddy?"

"You people have no feeling for history."

"Did grand-uncle Worth beat Oklahoma?"

"Yes, indeed. In '07 they whipped the Okies 29 to 10. They had a 6-1-1 record. Their only loss was to Missouri, 5-4."

"Did they play the Aggies?"

"Yes, they played A&M twice, beating them once and tying once."

"Did they play Baylor?"

"Yep, beat the Baptists 27-11."

"Those were the good old days, eh, Dad?"

"Don't get smart. If you look at the team picture, you'll see things were rather informal in those days. Their uniforms don't match. Their cleats were really spikes, like baseball. The most interesting part is that there were only 12 men on the entire team."

"Whatever happened to Uncle Worth?"

"After his football career, Uncle Worth went straight downhill. He became a lawyer and was the first mayor of Bellaire."

"Fantastic," says one of my brood. "Let's go."

Musings in a church cemetery

TRINITY LUTHERAN CEMETERY—"DA SIE ABER IHRE AUGEN AUFHUBEN SAHEN SIE NIEMAND ALS JESUM ALLEIN." Since they lifted their eyes, they saw no one else but Jesus.

It's carved here on this tombstone, one of about a hundred sprinkled about this 92-year-old cemetery, hidden away in the center of Houston. All around here is strictly twentieth century—a helicopter buzzes overhead, traffic rumbles along the freeway, and under a spreading oak tree, a policeman in a radio patrol car snoozes.

But here it is different. A rabbit is hiding in a thicket which has grown over one of the dearly beloved. A squirrel darts from tombstone to flower pot, and two workmen from La Grange are eating lunch. "This one doesn't have a death date," says one of them, setting his Thermos on a granite slab. "But you can tell by the way the ground has settled that she's down there. What happens is that people without children often buy their own tombstones, and they are told that any extra lettering will cost more, but they never leave any money in their wills to put in their date of death, so it never goes on."

He takes a final bite out of his sandwich.

"That one there, the tall one, is made of marble, but you can't get anyone in Texas to cut it like that anymore. Maybe in Georgia, but not in Texas. All those who could cut it like that have gone to their own reward. Sometimes there is a mistake in the date or the name is misspelled. We ask 'em, they see it all cut in, they sign the contract, then later on they come and tell us that it's wrong."

A nearby stone is an example of terminal typographic errors. It belongs to a staff sergeant from the 9th Infantry, 2nd Infantry Division, who was killed on Aug. 2, 1944, when he was 22 years old. The "Staff" originally read "Satff" but it's been corrected.

There are several other military men buried here. A corporal from the 129th Infantry, World War I. A private from Company F, 5th Regiment, Infantry, Spanish American War. Another corporal, this one from the 46th Infantry, Ninth Division. It doesn't say which war.

They all lie here in this acre and a half which the Trinity Lutheran Church bought for $300 in 1881. The seller was one Adam Clay, who had a grocery store. At the time of the sale, the church was on Louisiana Street between Texas and Prairie. It later moved to Riesner, then in 1961 moved on to Houston Street. But its little cemetery stayed right here, a mile and a half from the courthouse and north of the bayou.

When the land was bought, the church members moved their departed here, so the death dates go back before 1881. Among the first to be reburied here was Marie Hoop, a little girl who died of yellow fever two weeks after her family moved to Houston in October of 1867. Her parents, Johann and Friedericke Hoop, had immigrated from Germany, as had most of the church's members. (Services were held in German until 1917 when the pressures of World War I forced a change.)

Today, Johann and Friedericke Hoop are buried here, along with many members of their family. And their granddaughter, Mrs. Therese Mohnke, still remembers those days back then, when her grandfather was a wheelwright and her father had a blacksmith shop (Hoop Bros.) on Preston.

Roaming around, among the huge oaks and pines and magnolia trees, it is quickly evident that Maria Hoop is not the only child buried here. Little markers in the Saint Augustine are reminders of how perilous life was to small children in Houston not so long ago. The good old days were really not all that good.

Examples are everywhere. A small marble dove with both wings broken off sits on top of a tombstone for Margaret, who died a half century before her parents.

One family plot has small graves for three children aged one, seven, and simply "1874." Some tombstones say only BABY.

One row of stones raises an ominous question. Brother died at age 7, Sister at age 19 and Grand Pa at age 72. They all lie here together. They all died in 1891. What happened to the Leverkuhn family in 1891? Still, not everyone met an early end in nineteenth-century Houston. One immigrant, born in 1790, lived until 1871, which was pretty good, considering all the perils. There are two or three others who lived into their 90s.

Over there is Wilhelmina and Max, Rufhard, Frieda, Agusta. Buried in the promised land, in neat little plots, mowed and trimmed and cared for by descendents they never knew.

The helicopter has disappeared. So has the sleepy policeman. But the traffic still rumbles along, just over the way.

The workmen put their tools back in their truck and prepare to leave. "That fellow over there, the big stone," says one of the workmen. "He was one of our best men. The plot next to him is his son, an army chaplain. There's no marker on it at all. I don't know why, since the father was our best man. Our top tombstone salesman."

The one and only

AUSTIN—This is the Texas State Cemetery, and we are out here today looking for Section C, Row A-0, Site 1-C. There are no signposts, but eventually the right row is found. There are three identical pink granite tombstones. One belongs to Robert Oliver, a Texas Marine Corps captain. The next is that of Midshipman Fielding R. Culp also of the Texas Navy.

But we are interested today in the final slab:

Republic of Texas
Charles F. Fuller
Lieut Navy
Died
Feb. 11, 1812

Lt. Fuller was the one and only victim of the one and only Great Texas Navy Mutiny. It took place in the Mississippi River off New Orleans aboard the Texas Navy schooner San Antonio.

The San Antonio had rescued the crew and passengers from a sinking American ship, touched in at Galveston briefly and was ordered to go to New Orleans to let off the shipwreck survivors and pick up supplies.

So it did. Ah, New Orleans, every heart beat faster at the prospect of a night on Bourbon Street. The ship pulled in, and began loading supplies. Beef (a dime a pound), bread (a nickel a loaf) and potatoes (a dollar a bushel). That's all. The diet on Texas ships was inexpensive to the taxpayers, but not too varied for the crew.

So it is now night, the night of Feb. 11, and the ranking officers set off for the bright lights of the big city, leaving the crew aboard for the very good reason that, once ashore, most would never come back. A man can stomach only so much beef, bread and potatoes.

Some passing boatmen slip aboard a few bottles of booze, and the sailors – breaking with strict naval tradition – imbibe. Grumble, grumble, grumble, down in the hold. Topside, Marine Sgt. Seymour Oswald accosts Lt. M. B. Dearborn and demands shore leave for himself and some friends. No soap, Sergeant. They get into an argument and Lt. Fuller, the ranking officer still on board, pops up on deck to see what's happening.

Things are getting touchy, so Fuller resorts to the usual solution to shipboard problems: he calls out the Marine guard, Sgt. Seymour Oswald, commanding. It usually works, putting the cause of the problem in charge of the solution. Only somebody forgot to tell Sgt. Oswald. He begins passing out weapons, not only to the Marine guard, but to his fellow mutineers. He keeps a Colt pistol and a tomahawk (the Texas Navy was uniquely prepared for Indian attacks).

Under the guise of reporting that the guard is ready, Sgt. Oswald approaches Lt. Fuller. Oswald cracks the officer smartly on the head. Fuller grabs his own pistol, Oswald fires his. The Marines rush topside. So do the mutineers.

Bang. Slash. Stab. Shoot. Fuller falls dead and the crew attacks his body with cutlasses and muskets. Two midshipmen, Alden and Odell, rush to protect Fuller and are promptly wounded. Lt. Dearborn is "knocked down the cabin hatch and the companion drawn over him."

Oswald and his cronies lower a couple of boats and head for the fun, but the battle has attracted the notice of sailors aboard a nearby U.S. revenue cutter, the Jackson. Those Texians are always a rowdy bunch, but this is too much. The Americans investigate and find poor Lt. Dearborn down below, yelling for help. The U.S. sailors and the New Orleans police quickly round up the Texas mutineers and toss them in jail.

When the San Antonio finally leaves port it only has two of the mutineers aboard (not to mention a lot of beef, bread and potatoes). International extradition snags and keeps the others in jail.

The captain decides not to hold the court martial immediately since the sight of crewmen dangling from the yardarm might put a damper on his recruiting in New Orleans (there were some unexpected vacancies). Lt. Fuller is also left behind – buried in the Girod Street Cemetery.

President Sam Houston is upset when he gets the word ("this subject is the first in my recollection which has occurred in any port of a foreign nation") and finally gets most of the others back, although the ringleader, Sgt. Oswald, has escaped and is never heard from again.

The head of the Texas Navy, Commodore Edwin W. Moore, finally gathers all concerned and puts them aboard the good ship Austin, and heads for the high seas where legal frills aren't so frilly. The state's case is hampered by the fact that the San Antonio and its entire crew seems to have disappeared, just like Sgt. Oswald.

In any event, Moore convenes the case. Frederick Shepherd, after some questioning, announces he has seen the light and turns state's evidence. He gets off but is killed three weeks later in a battle. One Benjamin Pompilly, who died in prison, had already confessed he killed Lt. Fuller. So F. Williams is let off with 50 lashes while William Barrington and Edward Kenan get 100 each.

But Pvt. Antonio Landois and Cpl. William Simpson of the Marines and Seamen James Hudgins and Isaac Allen were sentenced to the yardarm. On April 26, 1843, at high noon, they were strung up. Prayers were said over each of the departed, who were then buried at sea.

As for Lt. Fuller, he stayed in New Orleans until 1936 when he was brought here to this beautiful, shady place in east Austin. New Orleans needed the Girod Street Cemetery. They had to widen Girod Street

Of large mind

"I categorically deny that the American ship of state is chartered in Liberia," said State Rep. Dave Allred of Wichita Falls.

That should give you some idea of what's going on in Austin these days. As a further indication, we have yet another quote from Allred, who — in turn — was quoting an anonymous Capitol source: "It is not true the Legislature spends money like a drunken sailor. A drunken sailor spends his own money."

"As a country boy," reports one Wesley Miculek Jr., of Angleton, "I had the opportunity to have numerous pets of many diverse types. One of my favorites, however, was a young Leghorn hen I had raised from a chick. Can you imagine sitting under a tree with your pet chicken on your lap and suddenly discovering you've been awarded the Pullet Surprise?"

Scott L. Weeden reports a sign on a restaurant wall: "If you wish to stub out your cigarettes on your plate, we will be happy to serve your food in an ashtray."

Weeden, as you can see, frequents some odd places. Such as the shop next door to the launderette which sports the sign: "Every third customer asking for change for the launderette will be shot. The first two have just left."

Finally (at last!), Weeden has the nerve to trot out this golden oldie: "An unhappy, diminutive banker knocked on the door of the U.S. Embassy in Prague and asked for political asylum in the West, saying: 'Can you cache a small Czech?' "

This brings us to puns, which some call the lowest form of humor. But David T. Mayschak of the Dominican Fathers in Galveston, a punster himself, finds a witness for the defense in Jacques Barzun's *The Energies of Art*, which says: "The lovers of puns have always been the great men of largest mind, who can afford to be silly. And puns are condemned by all the men of sharp intelligence who suppose, from their own need of constant exertion, that the great men fail to grasp the difference between the serious and the trivial. The point is that the great artist is by nature lordly. He cares less than smaller men about how his work will appear and about opinion generally. He trusts himself to be loved as he is."

Father Mayschak reports that Barzun, in this particular passage, was defending Shakespeare's fondness for puns. I knew there was something about the Bard I liked, but I could never put my finger on it.

Did you know that the incarcerated bank robbers out in Arizona discuss their methods so freely that it is said among lawmen that the pen is the heist forum of Yuma?

Moving on, and none too quickly, Howard L. Kusnetz writes that he has just received word from England that the leader of a female musical group, the Rocking Stones, is both promiscuous and a fetishist. She'll make love with anyone except someone who has recently utilized the services of an orthopedic surgeon. As she puts it, "Let him who is without a cast sin with the first Stone."

Fred Price, of McGraw-Hill World News, steps forward to tell us that when Ben Franklin was a boy, he built a footbridge over a stream in his neighborhood, and charged a penny toll to cross, ringing up the money on his cash register. As two men crossed the bridge and heard the register jingle, one said to the other, "These are the chimes that cry Ben's tolls."

Last, and indisputably least, John M. Ryan of Houston has stumbled upon a little-known fact: At one time the Doge of Venice was an Irishman, of all things, named O'Hara. During O'Hara's dogedom, a visiting Texan was arrested for public intoxication. O'Hara sentenced the Texan to 40 lashes and laid on the last 20 himself. He then sent the inebriated Texan out to sleep it off.

The next morning the Texan sought revenge, and marched to St. Mark's Square. He called for the Doge, but the Doge, not wanting to face the Texan, decided to send down his bartender, thus taking sly advantage of the Texan's weakness for booze.

"What do you want?" asked the bartender.

"I want," said the hungover Texan, "O'Hara, the Doge that beat me."

All right, so it's not Shakespeare. But remember what Barzun said. I trust myself to be loved only for what I am: your leader.